Pitt Latin American Series

IMAGES
AND
INTERVENTION

U.S. Policies in Latin America

Martha L. Cottam

UNIVERSITY OF PITTSBURGH PRESS

Pittsburgh and London

To my parents

Published by the University of Pittsburgh Press, Pittsburgh, Pa. 15260
Copyright © 1994, University of Pittsburgh Press
All rights reserved
Manufactured in the United States of America
Printed on acid-free paper

Library of Congress Cataloging-in-Publication Data

Cottam, Martha L.
     Images and intervention : U.S. policies in Latin America / Martha
L. Cottam.
          p.   cm. — (Pitt Latin American series)
     Includes bibliographical references and index.
     ISBN 0-8229-3797-2 (cl : alk. paper). — ISBN 0-8229-5526-1 (pb :
alk. paper)
     1. Latin American—Foreign relations—United States.   2. United
States—Foreign relations—Latin America.   3. United States—Foreign
relations—1945–   4. International relations—Decision making.
     5. Decision-making—United States.   6. Perception.   I. Title
II. Series.
     F1418.C845   1994
     327.7308—dc20   93-46841
                                                                   CIP

A CIP catalogue record for this book is available from the British Library.
Eurospan, London

Portions of chapter 4, "Cracks in the Cold War Worldview," previously appeared
in *Political Science Quarterly* (Spring 1992).

Contents

Acknowledgments

I BEGAN THIS STUDY WHILE TEACHING AT THE UNIVERSITY OF DENVER'S Graduate School of International Studies. A group of faculty members there was fortunate to receive grants from the Ford Foundation and the Pew Charitable Trust to study and compare interventions by the United States and the Soviet Union. The entire group owes a great debt to Karen Feste, whose leadership and determination helped secure the grants.

The project explored multiple factors in intervention. My portion of this project involved an examination of patterns in intervention decision making. The framework that emerged was then applied to cases of U.S. interventions in Latin America. Both the theoretical and case study phases of my study benefited greatly from interaction, discussion, and debate with Tom Rowe. Graduate research assistants provided important help in investigating the cases explored in this book, as they faced and surmounted serious obstacles to the research. I am grateful to Priscilla Falcon and Yiqun Pei for their hard work, their willingness to learn and to use a difficult analytical technique, their good humor, and their emotional and intellectual support.

The completed manuscript was read and given thorough critical evaluations by Ole Hosti and Otwin Marenin. Their comments and suggestions made me aware of numerous simplifications, oversights, and mistakes. Finally, the University of Pittsburgh Press picked the perfect anonymous reviewers for this manuscript. Their insights and questions certainly made the final product a better one.

IMAGES AND INTERVENTION

INTRODUCTION

As THE UNITED STATES ENTERS THE POST–COLD WAR ERA IN THE 1990s, Latin America is once again on the bottom of the heap in U.S. foreign policy. It is striking how quickly Latin America loses its place in U.S. concerns. During the 1980s, with revolutions in El Salvador, Guatemala, and Nicaragua, with Latin American debt a major worry for U.S. banks, and with the majority of countries in the hemisphere moving from military to civilian governments, Latin America was often in the headlines. In 1983 and 1989 the United States launched military invasions of Grenada and Panama. Yet within months, both were forgotten. The pattern of public attention to Latin America reflects the pattern of U.S. policy making toward Latin America, which lurches from the extremes of military intervention to outright neglect. As the twentieth century grinds to an end and the world is seemingly given a reprieve from the dangers of the cold war, U.S. policy toward Latin America only stays the same.

This is a study of how U.S. policies toward Latin America during and immediately after the cold war were decided. It is not a comprehensive overview of U.S. Latin American policies: indeed, some of the most important policies, such as the Alliance for Progress, are not included. Rather, it is a study of U.S. responses to conflicts between the United States and Latin American countries, examining cases in which U.S. officials decided to use diplomatic, economic, or military leverage to coerce Latin American governments and other political actors to abide by U.S. policy preferences. These were all cases of intervention, if intervention is broadly defined to include "involvement in the internal economic, social, or political processes of another society with the aim of determining the character of political institutions, personnel, or policies in the target country."[1]

The central focus is the psychological factors and the decision-making processes that prompted U.S. policy makers to use coercive

3

intervention in conflicts with Latin American countries. The central questions are, How did U.S. policy makers' cognitive images of Latin America influence the selection and the timing of their policies, tactics, and strategies to address conflicts with Latin American states? And can those images explain the patterns of U.S. policy in Latin America during and immediately following the cold war?

EXPLAINING U.S. ACTIONS IN LATIN AMERICA

Latin America has been treated as the U.S. backyard and sphere of influence since the Monroe Doctrine. And since the beginning of the cold war, the United States has intervened with direct military force in the Dominican Republic, Grenada, and Panama and with covert operations in Guatemala, Cuba, Chile, and virtually all of Central America. It has used economic aid programs such as the Alliance for Progress in the Kennedy administration and general foreign aid in every administration since then to achieve U.S. goals concerning narcotics (the Nixon and Bush administrations), human rights (the Carter administration), and internal revolution (virtually all administrations). Closely related to economic aid programs are the military aid and assistance programs that were employed throughout the cold war era to influence the internal and external affairs of Latin American states.

At the same time, Latin America was often ignored by U.S. policy makers unless a crisis or civil war was brewing. This pattern of extreme activity followed by neglect is symptomatic of U.S. perceptions of Latin Americans, perceptions dominated by a sense that the United States is a superior country with superior people and that Latin America should do as it is told since, by virtue of U.S. superiority, U.S. decisions are correct and fair. Academic recognition of this paternalistic perceptual orientation is reflected in the titles of many works on U.S.–Latin American relations, such as *The Hovering Giant, Condemned to Repetition, Trouble in Our Backyard,* and *The Ordeal of Hegemony.*[2]

U.S. policies in Latin America are ordinarily explained from one of three theoretical perspectives on international relations: the Realist, the dependency, and the pluralist. Latin America is a fruitful area of study for all three approaches, and the evidence that supports all three approaches, thus producing an endless debate about the true cause of U.S. policies. In addition, the theoretical dividing lines among these approaches tends to become fuzzy as studies of U.S.–Latin American relations focus on the substance of policy rather than the development of theoretical concepts. Thus, many studies are not theoretically "pure" or even very interested in theoretical issues.

REALISTS AND FELLOW TRAVELERS

The Realist approach, while seemingly easily supportable as an explanation of U.S. policies in Latin America, is actually the weakest. The Realist argument has been applied to both U.S. security policies and U.S. political economy policies in Latin America. Many security policy arguments focus on competition between the United States and the Soviet Union for influence in Latin America. The central argument holds that the Soviet Union saw any revolution in Latin America as an opportunity to gain a foothold in the hemisphere and, ultimately, to challenge U.S. national security.[3] Many advocates of the Realist perspective are not concerned with theoretical concepts, which leads to a central problem with this body of literature: it consists more of assertions and assumptions than of careful analysis. Most important, this approach assumed a U.S.-Soviet competition in Latin America, never asking whether that competition was real on the Soviet side.

If the Soviet interest and presence in Latin America were only or even primarily in the minds of U.S. policy makers, then U.S. perceptions—not an objective, identifiable, and measurable superpower competition—underlay U.S. policies. One cannot get to the root of the competition for power versus perceptions argument unless one develops and operationalizes the concepts of power and competition for power. The argument that would have to be made is that there were measurable forms of Soviet activity that threatened measurable elements of U.S. power and that consistently led to particular U.S. policy responses. Often this was not done. Instead, a typical study begins like this: "The victory of the Sandinista revolution in Nicaragua heightened Soviet hopes for increased influence in Latin America. The Kremlin sought to make this hope a reality through intensifying ties to the new Nicaraguan regime and by encouraging the emulation of the Nicaraguan experience elsewhere in the region."[4] In the argument that follows, the assumptions are (1) that the Soviets would seek influence anywhere as long as the cost was low and (2) that an increase in Soviet influence could be prevented only by U.S. counterintervention. With breathtaking assurance, the author makes statements about the intentions, power, interests, and actions of all players; neither concepts, causal arguments, nor facts are important.

This is not to say that Realist or power arguments are irrelevant or unusable in explaining U.S. relations with Latin America. Stephen Krasner presents an interesting and, more important, a testable argument about political economic policies from a Realist perspective and uses several U.S.–Latin American cases as illustration.[5] A number of analysts, including Abraham Lowenthal, Harold Molineu, and Guy Poitras, focus on the notion of hegemonic power as a central factor in explaining U.S. policy toward Latin America.[6] In general, the focus is again on the substance of policy rather than on the development and application of the theoretical perspective. Guy Poitras, for example, examines U.S. power vis-à-vis Latin America as it waxed and waned in the twentieth century. For Poitras, intervention is a manifestation of U.S. efforts to arrest its own hegemonic decilne, and the target is more complex than that presented by the Soviet-as-bogeyman school. Instead, most "targets have been regimes whose very existence challenged the credibility of its hegemony in the hemisphere"[7] Poitras's focus is upon the concepts of power and hegemony, and he elaborates those concepts before attempting to use them to explain U.S. policy.

Nevertheless, the explanatory chain is still uncertain, as Poitras declares, for example, that "the basic goals of the United States changed very little with its rise to hegemonic grandeur in the Americas. It had always embraced the nineteenth-century ideal of an isolated, stable hemisphere in which the United States would remain secure and preeminent, and the ascent to hegemony merely placed these objectives within reach" (p. 10). One must question the extent to which power was the driving force in U.S. policies. Even when done well, the realist argument has difficulty being precise in predictions about U.S. actions. Predicting a response to threats to U.S. power is easy; predicting the exact nature of that response is much more difficult.

THE QUASI-ECONOMIC DETERMINISTS

Another prominent school of thought that examines the details and causes of U.S. policies toward Latin America is the dependency or neodependency school. The latter is the preferable name, for there are differences within this school of thought, and *dependency* should refer to those closest to Marxist theory. The essential thrust of the argument, to put it broadly and crudely, is that U.S. intervention and aid programs all derived from manifestations of U.S. imperialism brought on by U.S. economic interests in Latin America and the need to maintain the global capitalist system. Studies focus on different aspects of the policy arena, ranging from interventions to bilateral policies and relations to political economy policies.[8] Robert Pastor summarizes this school thus:

> Adherents of the neodependency perspective assert that (1) the crisis originates in the poverty and injustice in the region, which is due to the U.S. fostering a system of dependence; gradual

reform is not possible; (2) the United States has played a central and malign role historically; (3) trade and investment in the region serve the interests of the U.S. and to a lesser extent, local business; (4) U.S. economic interests are central to U.S. policy (though some, like LaFeber, believe economic and security interests coincide); (5) the answer to the region's crisis is revolution; and (6) if revolutions are prevented, they will only erupt later in worse form.[9]

The theoretical and analytical problems in this perspective are similar to those faced by the Realist approach. First, the central explanatory concepts are extremely difficult to define and operationalize. Imperialism comes to mean everything from military intervention to the sale of Coca Cola and lipstick. Economic interests are often treated as though they are either obvious or monolithic. As with Realist analysis, unless concepts are defined, operationalized, and placed into a precise causal chain, there is little difference among assumption, assertion, and analysis.[10]

In the case of U.S. policies toward Latin America, for example, it is frequently maintained that the United States has intervened to prevent political-economic trends that threaten U.S. interests, either objective economic interests or subjective concerns about the stability of pro-U.S. political forces. The problems with the argument are, first, that this intervention has not always occurred and, second—and more important—that predicting U.S. opposition tells us very little about what U.S. policy is likely to be. If socialism in Latin America is such a threat to U.S. capitalism, why has the United States failed to remove Fidel Castro from power? If the United States opposes threats to its economic interests, *how* will it respond? U.S. reactions to nationalization, for example, have been quite varied. And the U.S. response to the Latin American debt crisis was piecemeal and uncertain.

THE ECLECTIC PLURALISTS

The third approach assumes internal sources for U.S. foreign policy, ranging from domestic pressure groups (which are often economic but can be ideological or moral), to public opinion, to bureaucratic competition, to U.S. political values.[11] This literature, even more than the approaches discussed above, focuses on the substance of policy rather than on the development of theoretical frameworks for the analysis of that policy.

Of greatest interest to this study is the subfield within this school that examines the interaction between U.S. domestic politics and U.S. political values and beliefs. In terms of U.S. policy toward Latin America, there has been little systematic evaluation of U.S. values and perceptions. Again, the concept of values is a daunting one to operationalize, let alone measure. Nevertheless, many nonsystematic assessments of U.S. perceptions of and beliefs about Latin America have been written. Martin Diskin argues that the U.S. view of Latin America is a "mythic image," which includes "the assertion that Central American countries are, at heart, city-states, not larger (and more complex) nations; that political life in them is intimate and even tribal; and that a guiding principle in politics is the fear of (and need for) order, discipline, and authority."[12]

Kenneth Coleman argues that the Monroe Doctrine embodied the beginning of a large set of myths about the U.S. role in the Western Hemisphere. According to Coleman, the Monroe Doctrine helped "reconcile the contradiction between the professed values of U.S. culture and the actual behavior of the U.S. government."[13] The Monroe Doctrine justified U.S. determination of political, economic, or social conditions in Latin America. Associated with this myth are other beliefs that influence U.S. policy, including the idea that the United States has the moral responsibility to "lead the world in efforts at moral renewal" and that the interests of the United States are synonymous with those of all humanity (p. 105).

A different assessment of the impact of U.S. values on policy toward Latin America is presented by John Martz, who argues that "diplomacy represents an effort to impose values on other societies, ones whose cultural outlooks and historical roots are often decidedly different."[14] U.S. democratic values, in their various manifestations over the decades, have thus influenced U.S. policy toward Latin America. As a result, "(1) U.S. diplomacy attempts seriously to encourage democracy only when geopolitical security interests are not presumably imperiled by so doing; (2) its constricted definition of democracy ignores, indeed insults the more basic components of the concept; (3) ethnocentric assumptions about Latin American society and politics produce paternalistically distorted expectations; and (4) Latin American perspectives on democracy are themselves injuriously twisted as a result of historical experience" (ibid.). Martz then traces various U.S. policies toward Latin America by examining the different techniques used to impose democratic values, U.S.-style, on Latin America.

Finally, there is the work of Lars Schoultz, who offers a more detailed and nuanced assessment of the dominant beliefs held by U.S. policy makers and substantiates his argument with interviews.[15] He finds U.S. policy makers fairly ignorant about specific Latin American countries and conditions, but despite this shallowness of information, their beliefs are often deeply held.

Schoultz proposes the existence of two belief groups in the United States. One group, found across the political spectrum and throughout branches of government, believes that political instability is caused by factors internal to Latin America, particularly poverty (pp. 71–73). It further recognizes that forces of modernization, such as integration into the global economy, transform societies and contribute to the mobilization of formerly passive sectors of the population. But these forces alone do not account for structural change in Latin America: "[A] substantial group of [these] policy makers believes that for several decades a number of forces, most of them foreign in origin, have been attacking the foundation of Latin America's traditional social structure. Modernization is occurring, and one aspect of this modernization is a new consciousness among many Latin Americans that their poverty need no longer be accepted with the fatalistic passivity of an earlier era" (p. 86). Increasingly, they recognize the Catholic church as an important political force that has helped organized the newly mobilized popular sectors in Latin America.

The second belief group, exemplified by the Reagan administration, although it also acknowledges the impact of poverty on Latin American politics, minimizes it as a cause of instability. This group also does not believe that structural change leads to mass mobilization. Instead, they attribute mobilization, popular demands, and instability to communist adventurism (p. 102). This set of beliefs includes subthemes: "Soviet communism is evil and expansionist," "the United States is vulnerable to attack from Latin America" (i.e., the USSR sought a foothold that would have been a dagger aimed at the U.S. heartland), "Latin America is vulnerable to Soviet subversion"; and "Latin American radicals threaten U. S. security" (ibid., pp. 109–36).

As interesting as Schoultz's study is, it, like the other works mentioned above, does not devote equal attention to theory and policy. This constitutes not a criticism of these works, but it does point to a hole in the literature. At a minimum, these works leave one wondering how U.S. Latin American policy differs, in terms of power, economics, and perceptions, from U.S. policy toward other Third World countries.

COGNITIVE IMAGES AND U.S. POLICY TOWARD LATIN AMERICA

The two belief systems that Schoultz describes are not unique to U.S. perceptions of Latin America. They are part of a general perceptual worldview that has guided and shaped U.S. policy making throughout the cold war and into the post–cold war era. In this study, I argue that those perceptions are not sets of beliefs so much as complicated bundles of cognition organized as images of types of states. The distinction is important. Images are perceptual filters that organize our environment and enable us to predict and respond to that environment. Often, images function like stereotypes: they contain "facts," which we hold as true, which enable us to interpret the behavior of others, and which tell us how we can and should respond to that behavior. They also contain an emotional response to the steroetyped group: racists hate people of certain skin pigmentation just because they do. If asked to think why, they will delve into the stereotype and present one with a variety of "facts," the validity of which is staunchly maintained.

So it is in international politics. Policy makers and citizens alike have images of types of states; some types are dangerous, some are benign, and some are sources of opportunity. The most familiar and intuitively obvious image of a type of state is the image of the enemy. The image of the enemy has been studied in individual cases, ranging from John Foster Dulles to the Reagan administration, and in societywide studies such as John Dower's horrific examination of U.S. and Japanese mutual perceptions during World War II.[16] When a state is perceived as an enemy it is attributed with evil intentions, harmful ambitions, and an insatiable desire to dominate and destroy. It and its people are seen as culturally strange and bad but sophisticated enough to be dangerous. The enemy is seen as powerful, as powerful as one's own state and, therefore, not easily defeated; its aggression therefore cannot be treated lightly. Enemy regimes are assumed to be run by a cabal of evil geniuses who plan elaborate strategies and who wait patiently for their opportunity to put those plans into effect.

For example, the U.S. policy of containment during the cold war, advocated by John Foster Dulles, was designed for such a prototypical enemy. As this image of the Soviet Union ebbed and flowed during the cold war, the tactics of containment changed also.[17] With this prototypical enemy, negotiation, compromise, and mutual accommodation are seen not only as doomed to failure (since this enemy cannot be trusted) but naive and dangerous (since the enemy does not want to coexist but to defeat). Moreover, since the enemy is equal in power to one's own state, war should be avoided. Thus the most sensible way to control the enemy's inherently harmful behavior is to contain it. It can be convinced to not do what it surely wants to do—attack—only by shows of strength in commitment, resolve, and power on the part of one's own country.

Another image in the political worldview is the dependent, or client, image. The dependent image is that of a childlike people, incapable of making and implementing decisions without guidance from one's own state. This image incorporates the beliefs Schoultz describes in the second belief group.

This book focuses on the impact of the dependent image on U.S. policies toward Latin America. Because the study covers many cold war years, it necessarily examines the psychological effect on policy makers of the double images: the dependent and the enemy, the latter hovering nearby, ready to strike. It also examines U.S. treatment of Latin American countries when the dependent image was the sole operative image. Of course, not all U.S. policy makers have perceived Latin America as dependent. Some of the cases reported below show differences in degree (wherein policy makers had strong or weak dependent images) and in kind (wherein policy makers did not see a particular Latin American country as dependent at all but rather as neutral or nonaligned). Differences in policy preferences are linked to the differences in perception. Evidence of policy makers' perceptions is provided for each case, drawing upon press interviews, personal interviews, written recollections, congressional hearings and reports, and secondary sources.

While the framework presented in chapter 1 does link perception to behavior, it also provides room for systemic characteristics, internal domestic considerations, and bureaucratic forces. Systemic characteristics set the policy context and determined important aspects of policy makers' leverage, domestic considerations limited their options, and bureaucratic battles influenced their tactics. Nevertheless, the starting point of these analyses is always policy makers' operative perceptual images.

THE CASES

The cases below were not selected randomly but for particular reasons. In all cases policy makers' perceptions, the policy debates and bureaucratic arguments, and the cold war or post–cold war context made for highly complex patterns of behavior, all ultimately associated with cognitive images.

Chapter 1 presents the general analytical framework. Specific behavioral patterns are shown to be associated with individual images and with images in particular combinations. The interaction between images on the one hand and systemic, domestic, and bureaucratic political factors on the other is examined and policy, tactical, and strategic preferences are proposed for certain of these interactions. The cases examined in the chapters that follow illustrate the patterns of policies, tactics, and strategies.

Chapter 2 explores the early cold war cases of intervention in Guatemala in 1954 and in Cuba from the revolution through the Bay of Pigs. These cases illustrate both the impact of the dependent image and the policy disputes caused by differences in perception. While the prevailing image of Guatemala was not questioned in the Eisenhower administration, the prevailing image of Cuba was, and there were serious policy disagreements between those who saw Cuba as an errant dependent hurrying into the arms of the Soviet Union and those who saw Cuba as a fledgling neutral. These cases are contrasted with a third case, Bolivia, in which the pattern of U.S. decision making was different. Finally, the Guatemalan and Cuban cases are looked at as important learning experiences for U.S. policy makers, since the lessons learned in these cases had a direct impact on the selection of tactics in later cases.

Chapter 3 covers another case of intervention, this time a distinctly covert case: Chile from 1970 through 1973. This case is contrasted with another case of coercive use of instruments but one that did not involve covert or military intervention: the Nixon administration's response to Peruvian nationalizations in the late 1960s and early 1970s. These cases provide us an opportunity to observe the differences between a case in which a dependent is seen as falling under the influence of the enemy and that in which the conflict involves only the dependent. The tactics were similarly coercive, but the timing and perception of threat was so different that the instruments selected varied significantly.

Chapter 4 presents U.S. responses to two Latin American crises: revolutions in Nicaragua and El Salvador. These cases, and the Carter administration as a whole, provide an excellent opportunity for us to examine image differences in strength and in kind. Three perceptual groups are identified, two of which share an image but differ in degree, the third having a different image. Policies are associated with the differences in perceptions.

Chapters 5 and 6 trace the reestablishment of the prototypical dependent image as the prevailing image of Latin America in the Reagan administration, after its brief hiatus under Carter. Chapter 5 explores that image in the Reagan administration and its profound association with the enemy image in the Central American context. It also reexamines some of the theoretical issues regarding images and decision making. It considers the implications of the end of the cold war for U.S. images of the enemy, the dependent, and the self and proposes important implications for U.S. policy toward Latin America deriving from the demise of the Soviet enemy and threats to the U.S. self-image. General U.S. policy toward Central America and the activities of the Bush administration in response to the peace process in El Salvador are examined.

Chapter 6 leads us out of the cold war, but it shows that, in deciding to intervene militarily in Panama and to run the drug war in Peru, the United States still based its policies on the dependent image and its associated tactical preferences.

The conclusion reviews the findings in the context of the post–cold war international arena. It reflects on the U.S. cold war policy-making pattern, and current problems. It asks if U.S. policy makers are taking advantage of the opportunity to improve U.S. policy toward Latin America offered by the end of the cold war.

1

IMAGES, STRATEGIES, AND TACTICS

POLITICAL PSYCHOLOGY AND THEORY BUILDING

This chapter uses a political psychological framework employing the concept of images to analyze policy makers' selection of strategies and tactics.[1] The framework takes the minimalist approach, using only a few concepts from psychology rather than the maximalist alternative of incorporating virtually every psychological finding, pattern, and model into political analysis. Studies that try to explain political decisions and events by examining the human mind are certain to run headlong into the dilemma of choosing richness or rigor. The human mind is enormously complex, and each individual is unique; human decisions are equally complex, and they can be examined in more detail or less. Should one therefore study decision making in terms of personality factors and the role of the individual leader in political decisions making? For some, the answer is obviously yes.[2] For others, personality studies are too reductionist. The writings of Alexander George demonstrate this, as his work moves from personality to cognitive studies.[3]

Political psychology has also developed its own internal levels-of-analysis problem. One can see its impact in the extent to which studies of political decision making talk past one another. Studies of public opinion in foreign policy rely upon the attitude concept and are compiled with vast amounts of information on elite and mass opinion. What is the relation between these patterns and the decision-making heuristics or image-based decisions explored in other studies? Are the data interchangeable (i.e., are attitudes, heuristics, and images the same thing)? The answer is no; yet opinion data can be useful to those studying heuristics or images. All three lie at different levels of analysis and involve concepts differing in scope and breadth.

Most important, theory building in political psychology raises the question, What do we lose when we select one set of psychological concepts rather than another? The question parallels that asked of political psychology by virtually every nonpsychological theoretical perspective in international relations. How can one ignore all of those obviously important variables? The answer depends upon whether we are dealing with mutually exclusive competitive independent variables, or multiple independent variables, or multiple independent variables plus intervening variables. This is implicitly recognized throughout the literature; study after study demands that frameworks account for multiple psychological and nonpsychological factors in political decision making.[4]

It is possible that the root of these challenges to political psychology is the use that social scientists have made of philosophy of science and the scientific method. For years natural scientists have considered and debated the idea that the fundamental approach taken to science is, if not wrong, misdirected. In natural science, and in more rudimentary theorizing in social science, many models are static and linear. The assumption has been that models only approximate reality because reality is plagued by random, and thus unpredictable, influences from outside the theoretical system. When these influences were revealed to be random, the pattern of cause and effect emerged. This result led to an ability to predict within certain approximations. All one had to do was to find the central (psychological) variable, and those other troublesome potential causal factors could be eliminated as random nuisances.

Challenges to the idea of randomness emerged in the natural sciences and are described in detail by James Gleick.[5] He recounts the efforts of Edward Lorenz to study and model weather patterns. When Lorenz was unable to achieve complete replication in computer runs of his weather model, he suspected that there was "more than randomness embedded in his weather model. He saw a fine geometrical structure, order *masquerading* as randomness," order that is, nevertheless, aperiodic and unpredictable. Thus Gleick argues that "in science, as in life . . . a chain of events can have a point of crisis that could magnify small changes" (pp. 22, 23). Those crisis points are everywhere in complex systems, can have enormous impact, yet are not at all random.

The theory—not really a theory but a twist on the philosophy of science—that emerged from the queries of people like Lorenz is called *chaos*. It argues that the search for linear relations causes us to be unable to see the complexity of systems and their pattern of order without periodicity. This is the nature of chaotic systems. If considered seriously, this view of science has something to say to international relations theorists, for if any systems are complex and chaotic, political systems are. First, this view immediately challenges the rationale of the levels-of-analysis frame, wherein theories at the international, national, and individual levels compete with each other, each arguing that the other is only a manifestation of relatively insignificant factors that disturb but do not greatly alter the pattern that their own preferred variable produces. This means that there are no uncaused causes and that, for example, the transition of the international system of the pre–World War I era to that of the pre–World War II era could not have been predicted solely by system-theoretic factors.

Unless domestic conditions, perceptual conditions, and personalities are accounted for, the explanation is not only incomplete, it is misleading. It is misleading to ignore the interaction among factors that change their form but repeat themselves constantly. While it is true that Adolf Hitler's personality was unusual, it cannot be cast off as a random piece of noise that unfortunately influenced the entire system at a certain point in time. If not this personality, some other might have had such an impact. The impact of Hitler's personality directed the system in a distinct direction and was a crucial part of change in the system. Similarly, we cannot argue that the changes in the worldview of policy makers after World War II was only accidentally influenced by the military capability changes caused by nuclear technology. These changes were not random; capability technology has long had an influence on perceptions. But its qualitative difference made its impact enormous and permanent. To ignore this in an effort to "prove" that perceptions alone caused events of the cold war is simply silly.

And finally, as will be seen in the cases included in this volume, people have always perceived enemies, but the enemy image during the cold war was conditioned by a number of systemic factors, including the existence of nuclear weapons and of two superpowers. Again, the specifics were accidental (e.g., two superpowers rather than three or four) but not random, in that the distribution of capabilities have always influenced perceptions. Moreover, the impact of these extraneous, nonpsychological factors was profound and influenced perceptual evolution in unrelated areas when one superpower disappeared. In short, we cannot have dynamic models of international politics if we remain wed to the idea that levels-of-analysis cannot be crossed and a devotion to linearity.

The problem is replicated in microscopic form in political psychology: stable models are constructed wherein scholars expect and hope that particular psychological factors will produce specific policy decisions and that this cause and effect can be replicated. When predictions do not pan out, they search for the random, unpredictable, and unlikely-to-reoccur phenomenon that threw the system into momentary instability. Yet perhaps political psychology is much like the weather.

General systemic conditions are set by the need for balance, yet the system's basic nature can be altered by smaller factors, such as attribution, or by larger factors, such as capability differentials or, even more problematically, the capacity of human beings to learn. This means that the psychological decision-making process is enormously complex and that it changes as it evolves, because the process of using it changes it. Analytical frameworks have to be open to such change to be dynamic, and this requires an analysis of self-generated change that is distinct from, and not to be confused with, tautology—or changing the framework to fit the data.

Chaos theory also has serious implications for predictions of cause and effect. Because of interaction and feedback, our ability to predict in chaotic systems is reduced in time, not in principle. Prediction can still be a goal, but interactive factors make it sensible to predict only for the short run, particularly in crises. As physicists know, if you kick a chaotic system there is no telling where it will go in the long run.

The main purpose of beginning this chapter with a discussion of the need for a dynamic political psychology is that, as we explore the psychological origins of the use of coercion in U.S. policies toward Latin America, we see order without periodicity. There are clear patterns, but they are never exactly repeated—because people learn, perceptions shift, and psychological and nonpsychological factors nudge the causal flow and shift its course. This is strikingly obvious with the end of the cold war. There is still continuity, order, and predictability in perceptions and the resulting policies, but there will never be a full-circle return to the policies of the pre–cold war era. The analytical framework presented below draws upon different psychological theories and searches for patterns of interaction among psychological processes, political worldviews, and environmental factors. It does not present testable and disprovable hypotheses. Instead, it takes a less confident approach to the relation between cause and effect. It proposes general patterns of perception and policy preference and attempts to anticipate and explain change in those patterns as the use of coercion in U.S. policy toward Latin America is examined.

THE ROLE OF IMAGES IN FORMING A WORLDVIEW

The use of the cognitive psychology and the concept of images in the study of international policy decision making has grown since the 1960s. Early pioneers include Alexander George and Ole Holsti, both of whom continue to advance the field's understanding of psychological processes in foreign policy behavior.[6] Cognitive processes have received attention in general studies and in a growing number of models.[7] This study uses a model based upon the assumption that policy makers organize and simplify their environment in a cognitively efficient manner to permit them to understand the meaning of the actions of other countries and to formulate a response without having to filter and interpret all the information available to them.

Cognitive images play a role in all stages of policy making, from influencing the choice of strategy to processing information as the strategy is implemented. An image can be defined as a set of objects, people, or countries we perceive as similar. It is a basic assumption in cognitive psychology that we are not capable of processing all the information we receive about our environment and that we use images (categories, schemas, perceptual patterns) to organize and simplify our environments. Images simplify the environment by accumulating information about that environment that we assume to be correct. Incoming information about the environment is filtered through those images, providing us with an automatic screen that helps us determine what information is correct and important and what is false or irrelevant.[8] Images contain information about another actor in our environment, and that information is used to evaluate new information, to predict future actions of that other, and to plan our response.

The international worldviews of policy makers and of citizens are composed of specific, identifiable images of types of states.[9] In U.S. policy toward Latin America in the post–World War II era, two conflicting images of Latin American countries influenced policy, the *dependent* and the *neutral* images. Of those, the dependent image has been dominant. In addition, the enemy image of the USSR had a tremendous impact on U.S. policy and on the tactics used in Latin America.

The use of images as filters does not lock us into a prismed prison. We prefer to assess information through an image-based filter, but this is not always possible, and we do adapt to change. Furthermore, images are not always suitable for the efficient management of changed environments. When an image is not available, we still search for cues, but we evaluate information in a piecemeal manner.[10] Piecemeal information processing involves the evaluation of specific pieces of information regarding particular attributes and actions of the other. Without a guiding image, we must attend much more closely to the incoming information, and we are not able to engage in the long-range predicting that an image permits.

The farther a country is from a prototypical image, the more complex the perceptions of that country become. However, even when a country does not fit a particular image, our perceptions do follow a particular pattern. The attributes that compose images when clustered in a specific combination are still the same attributes that we use to judge a country that does not fit an existing image. These attributes are politically relevant and help policy makers evaluate politically relevant information. It is assumed here that the most common judgment pattern involves placing countries into an image and using the image as a basis for evaluating that country's behavior. The assumption is based on arguments in psychology indicating that "people's preferred mode is to categorize others whenever possible."[11] Even when we cannot categorize and must rely on an attribute-by-attribute assessment of others, we continue to attempt to categorize, implementing several possible recategorization processes. Subcategorization that allows us "to use [our] schematic knowledge, with some modifications, to respond to an exceptional individual" is one such process, as is generating an entirely new category (p. 404).

Interestingly, policy making ought to be at its more refined and sophisticated when a country is seen as complex rather than when it perfectly fits an image. Under the former conditions, it will be seen as unique, and our attention will be directed more intensely to the specifics of the situation and the nuances of information. Americans have not yet experienced a general need to engage in piecemeal information processing regarding Latin American countries. The enemy image of the USSR may have disappeared, but the dependent image of Latin America remains alive and healthy in the U.S. worldview.

A number of specific country images are suggested in the literature.[12] Psychological studies indicate that we use seven (plus or minus two) images (or categories) to organize our environment.[13] Country images include at a minimum the enemy, the ally, the neutral, our dependent, and the enemy's dependent. Once a country is classified, information about that country is evaluated through that particular perceptual screen. Each image has associated with it certain attributes; the policy alternatives deemed appropriate for use with countries fitting the image and the "lessons of history" associated with that particular country image. By using this general model, we can construct hypotheses about superpower responses to other countries and test these hypotheses in specific situations. Thus, we are not confined to situation-specific analysis and can strive for predictive statements.

A fairly complete list of attributes associated with each image has been developed (see appendix). Each image contains information concerning a country's military and economic strength, its domestic polity, its goals relative to those of our own country, and its cultural sophistication. This information contributes to summary perceptions of the type of state's intentions toward our own country (threatening, benign, positive, and friendly), its power, its cultural sophistication, its expected behavior, and our own responses. Assumptions are made as to the motivations and intentions of each type, and these too are permanently ensconced in particular images.

The enemy, at its prototypical extreme, is a country approximately as powerful as our own country, different in domestic polity and culture, evil in motivation, inflexible, and completely incompatible with the goals of our own country. The perception of threat is most intense at the prototypical extreme. Once a country has been classified as an enemy, it is assumed to have all the characteristics of the image, and strategy is formulated on that basis. The closer a country is to the prototype, the more confident policy makers are of their evaluation of that country and of their choice of strategy.

The categorization of a country is a complicated psychological process and goes well beyond the simple act of matching attributes. Rather, we make inferences about the relation between perceived attributes, observed behavior, and the decision context. Conclusions about the character of the perceived state, and hence its category membership, are derived not simply from the presence or absence of a bundle of attributes but from conclusions about the meaning of those attributes in a particular context.[14]

In short, categorization is not merely a psychological act of summarizing the properties of the observed actor or object. It is affected by the context in which the judgment take place, and it must make sense to us by conforming with an ongoing explanation of the other's behavior. Listing attributes is useful for research purposes in that the list can guide our search for evidence of perceptions. However, these attributes are little more than indicators of our preconceptions about different types of international actors in our political worldview. Our perceptions of intention, power, and cultural sophistication are the core concepts in that worldview.

PERCEIVING INTENTION

Countries placed in the prototypical version of an image are seen as having simple intentions, either threatening (as in the case of the prototypical enemy and its dependent) or defensive (as in the case of the prototypical ally and our own dependent).[15] Perceptions of threat can be described as including potential harm or loss, "challenge," and "an opportunity for growth, mastery or gain."[16] Perceptions produce a number of primary judgment patterns. First, any of these three perceptions can give rise to stress, although the emotion differs: harm or loss are accompanied by negative feelings, challenge or opportunity by positive feelings. Second, context conditions interact with the image others' have, which can reinforce and intensify our perceptions of threat or opportunity, influencing the extremity of the image. Under very threatening conditions, for example, we are inclined to keep our image of an enemy at the extreme. Thus the strength of an image is in part context-dependent. Finally, self-image plays a role in that our beliefs about our ability to control events influence our appraisal of others' intentions (p. 841). This perception rests in part on assessments of our own power and efficacy relative to that of others in the situation.

It is logical to expect an enemy image to be associated with threat and an ally image to be associated with defensive intentions. But the intentions associated with a dependent of the enemy and those associated with our own dependent need further clarification. The enemy's dependent has threatening intentions toward our own country, but these intentions are conditioned by our relationship with the enemy. These intentions enable the enemy to widen its influence. The enemy's dependent is also assumed to be weak and thus unable to exercise those dangerous intentions without the help of the enemy. Conversely, our own dependent is seen as having simple defensive intentions: it intends no harm but merely seeks to protect itself and our own country, as well. However, this assumption of merely defensive intentions is attributed only to dependent elites loyal to our own country and to our country's superior position. Nationalistic, radical, or even merely critical elites in the dependent country are not perceived as defensive.[17] Instead, their perceived incompetence and ineptitude make them dangerous and susceptible to the evil machinations of the enemy.

PERCEIVING POWER

Our perception of a country's power heavily influences our selection of strategy, bargaining position, tactics, and negotiating style. In preliminary studies of tactics associated with countries classified as dependents, there appears to be a tendency to quickly resort to force in a conflict with a weaker country. Thus, there are significant behavioral predispositions associated with countries classified in particular images. The impact of the image will be both general, as the situation is evaluated, and specific, as the information is interpreted. In addition, due to stress and other factors, policy makers tend to move toward more simplified, more extreme images as the perceived threat intensifies. This, in turn, will elevate confidence in evaluations and strategy selection, to the neglect of reality testing.

The perception of power rather than actual power is an important analytical consideration for several reasons. First, actual power relations do not explain how policy makers define and evaluate a conflict with another country, since policy makers do not perceive intentions on the basis the other country's actual power. For example, Western Europeans' had differing perceptions of the United States and the USSR. Given the once similar power and similar military capability of these two countries, the Western European perception that one was not a threat and the other was could not have been a result of the Western European's simple assessments of the capabilities of each.[18] Second, attention to the differences in the perception of power is important because of the tendency for the more powerful country to use that power exploitively when the interaction with another country is assumed to be zero-sum.[19] This indicates that, in conflicts with Latin American countries, U.S. policy makers tend to use coercive means to achieve their goals.

How coercive those means are is dependent upon additional perceptual elements. Two situations are clearly possible in U.S. conflicts with Latin American countries. In one, the United States simply uses its superior power to achieve its aims. In the other, another country is also involved. When, as was the case during the cold war, the other country is a perceived enemy, its presence changes the intensity of the perception of threat as well as the perception of relative power. For superpowers such as the United States, this combination of images invokes its global strategic goals and a very different assessment of capabilities than does the single image alone. This brings us to the third reason that attention to perception is important: we must assess our own power, the other country's power, and the resulting leverage if we are to act, but there are identifiable patterns of divergence from an objective assessment of power.

PERCEIVING CULTURE

A perception of culture involves assessing a country's capacity to create policies, to carry them out, and to achieve its goals. This is a perception of the cultural sophistication and efficacy of that country's people. This perception is an absolute judgment, but it is also a relative judgment in that such cultural sophistication is judged relative to our own. As in the perception of power, the perception of culture is locked into the attributes of the image. The people of a dependent country are seen as unsophisticated and inferior, those of an imperialist or hegemonic country as sophisticated and dominating.[20]

The U.S. assessment of others as inferior has had a huge impact on

U.S. policy toward Latin America. The dominant U.S. perception of Latin American countries is as dependent, a childlike image of inept-ness, inefficiency, an inclination toward self-serving corruption, loyalty to the United States, and being constantly in need of guidance and counsel. This leads to bargaining patterns wherein the dependent gov-ernment is not permitted to bargain as an equal but is given an option and expected to accept it.[21] This expectation is based in part on the U.S. perception of power but also on the U.S. perception that it knows what is best for everyone concerned.

In threatening situations, such as situations where the enemy is perceived as seeking to influence the dependent, the latter's ineptitude becomes ominous. Inferior people cannot be expected to withstand the efforts of the enemy to dupe them and to thereby gain influence and power. It is seen as analogous to an adult observing a pervert attempting to entice a child into his car with an offer of candy. The adult's response is not to ask questions about the pervert's intentions or the accuracy of his interpretation of the situation; he simply grabs the child and calls the cops. One does not negotiate with a pervert or explain to a child that the pervert is bad and expect the child to avoid the temptation of candy. One must also act quickly, protect the child whether she wants protec-tion or not and use coercion (the police) to stop the pervert. So it is when the enemy tempts a dependent.

THE ROLE OF AFFECT

While the concept of images is cognitive, images are also closely associ-ated with affect. Positive and negative affect ("affective tags") are associated with each image and derive from image attributes.[22] The role of affect is complex, and the interaction between cognition and affect is rarely directly addressed in political psychology.[23] There is some debate in psychology as to whether emotion precedes or follows cognition.[24] While the framework discussed here begins with the cogni-tive organization of the political worldview, this organization does not exclude affective characteristics. "[E]motions are an important way in which information is organized in the mind. Emotions do not replace other organizational systems, but rather constitute another network of associations by which events are understood and, more important, linked to each other."[25] The emotional component thus plays a role in information processing—in conjunction with cognition, since policy makers are predisposed to experience stress in conflicts with countries they categorize in an image associated with threat.

Affect also plays a role in the categorization itself. Many psychological studies describe a categorization that is based upon attributes that signal an image in the perceiver's mind. Categorization also occurs on the basis of affect when an affective tag cues an image.[26] The affective component of a judgment is more image based when the other is easily categorized and more attribute based when categorization is difficult.[27] Thus, policy makers respond to countries they place in the prototypical extreme by using the affective tag for that category. But when countries are seen as complex, and thus less easily categorized, the affective response is based on specific characteristics, such as the nature of its domestic polity or the strength of its military force.

Positive and negative affective states influence information processing, as well. People tend to be more receptive to positive information when in a positive emotional state and to negative information when in a negative emotional state. People solve problems better and their memories are stronger when they are in positive emotional states.[28] There is also evidence that people have stronger affective responses to those whom they see as relatively less complex.[29] Thus countries categorized as dependent will arouse stronger affect, since the dependent by definition is simple and childlike and its people easily manipulated.

SELF-IMAGE, THE FINAL INGREDIENT

Others are assessed in contexts that include perceptions of self. Although there is some disagreement, psychological studies indicate that, at least initially, people judge themselves as they judge others. However, the self-image is more affect-laden than are images of others, and the collective self constitutes a national in-group. People tend to engage in "group-enhancing biases or distortions when faced with a threat to their collective identity" when that collective image is positive; when it is not positive, those biases are much less likely to occur.[30] When their self-image is positive, people often explain their own behavior as a product of situational circumstances, while internal characteristics are identified as causes the behavior of others.[31] This tendency is particularly strong when the evaluation of the behavior is negative.[32]

A country's perception of its own power is based on assumptions about its ability to mobilize resources and power instruments rather than on a careful analysis of the specific elements of national power, such as the economic base or the educational level of the populace.[33] Complementing perceptions of power are perceptions of control. This is a "perceived ability to significantly alter events" or a "likelihood that an event can be prevented or brought about or its consequences changed by the *natural agents* known to the individual."[34] To believe we are powerful requires an identification of power instruments; to believe we have control requires our believing that we are capable of using those instruments. When we believe we have control, we perform better, are more positive, and are more interested in creative problem solving. We tend to evaluate ambiguous information positively, although we are not blind to negative information. We are able to "directly tackle or confront adverse events that [we] anticipate, and this promotes a confrontative rather than a repressive response to stress."[35]

Finally, perceptions of self-efficacy influence behavior in that, if we see ourselves as weak and inefficacious, we may fail to identify the options and leverage available to us.[36] This can prevent us from resisting the demands of those we perceive as more powerful. We do tend to submit to those we see as more powerful, but a positive self-image can lead us to identify our own power instruments. Thus policy makers from seemingly weak countries may not see themselves as weak and may act as though they are not.[37]

IMAGES: THE DEPENDENT, THE ENEMY, AND THE NEUTRAL

During the cold war, the United States commonly viewed Latin American leaders and people as dependents. But the perceptual basis for U.S. cold war policies toward Latin America cannot be understood without understanding the enemy image. U.S. policy makers feared the incursion of enemies into the Western Hemisphere beginning with the British, then Mexico (which the United States in the early 1900s believed had imperialist and bolshevist inclinations), then the Nazis before World War II, then the Soviets during the cold war.

Latin American countries are the prototypical example of the U.S. dependent image: weak, childlike, inferior, inept, and led by a small and often corrupt elite. This type of country is viewed with contempt, and its society and polities are seen in very simple terms; they are not treated as equals because they are not seen as equals. When conflicts arise, the perceiving country knows who has more power, it does, and there is no hesitation in using that power. In some cases the United States has perceived South American leaders as nationalists, radicals, or populists. If they rejected the traditional relation with the United States, they were seen as loose cannons and likely to fall under the influence of the enemy. Their rejection of the traditional relation was not seen as a sign of independence. Instead, the U.S. concern was that they would become dependents of the enemy. Perceptions of their character did not change; only their allegiance was in danger of changing.

The image of the neutral or nonaligned country is different.[38] Although this type of country is not given an attribute of high power, it is seen as culturally sophisticated and as politically complicated by the presence of nationalism. It may be poor and have a low literacy rate, but that does not speak to the nature of the people and their cultural sophistication. Different but equal has a real meaning in this image. U.S. responses to this type of country are also quite different: although the United States may have superior power in terms of instruments, it bargains with the neutral country as though with an equal and does not force its decisions on it. Moreover, the United States does not associate a neutral country with opportunity. Instead, it is assumed that such a country has its own goals and will pursue those goals, which may or may not be beneficial to the United States.

Nevertheless, simplification still occurs in this, as in every, image. The role of nationalism in decision making by the leaders of neutral countries follows a recipe: decisions are predicted in terms of the truisms of nationalism. Nationalism is acknowledged as a decision making factor, but simplified. The perceived drive to follow self-interest also leads to simplification, in that it is assumed that the neutral country will attempt to play off the United States against other powerful countries to achieve its own goals. This image was not usual in the U.S. worldview until the late 1960s. Since images arise in response to an environment that can be categorized, until nonaligned countries emerged as an international force with distinct characteristics, such an image was neither useful nor necessary.[39]

The enemy is a familiar image. In its stereotypical extreme it is the evil empire. It is led by a cabal of evil geniuses and is as strong as one's own country. Culturally, it is one's equal. Although its moral characteristics may be foul and its values rotten, it is smart, it has the ability to carry out its plans, it knows science, and it is extremely dangerous. The image is associated with threat, since the enemy will use any means to carry out its intention to harm one's own country.

When a policy maker does not use an image to categorize a country, the perception of that country is termed *complex*.[40]

IMAGES AND POLICY SELECTION

To put some movement into the psychological framework described above, to explain how images influence U.S. policy decision making, it is necessary to digress to another analytical level and to describe the environmental context in which decisions are made—to place the mind of the policy maker into that environment, permitting it to have its impact on policy making. When these factors combine in particular patterns, policy makers are predisposed toward particular strategic choices. The analytical task is to explore the interaction of these variables and to identify patterns in strategy decisions and in the selection of instruments to achieve the goals of that strategy.

A strategy can be thought of as a set of policy plans designed to achieve specific goals.[41] Policy makers formulate strategies through an identifiable decision sequence, and strategies vary in scope. First, they will identify a problem and define it: this is the beginning of the analysis, and at this stage evaluations of the situation, of the other country, and of one's own interests and goals are general and impressionistic. During this time, little feedback is available to test speculations concerning the other country and the situation. Capability differences affect assessments of possible interests and available leverage, while psychological images of the self, the other country, and third parties are crucial in defining the problem. Images contribute to both background evaluation (that is, a general impression of the threat and the opportunity extant in the current situation) and interpretation of immediately available information.

After the problem has been identified, policy makers consider their objectives (which will also fit logically into past policies or general international strategy—for example, an application of containment on the global level to the specific tactical problem). At this point, self-image and the images of the other country and of third parties play a role in setting objectives. In addition, audience effects come into play, including the bureaucratic audiences that lobby for other strategies and tactics, the domestic audiences, and the international audiences. Further, perceptions of national power, although they may be distorted, are crucial in affecting goal setting, for policy makers will tackle problems in accordance with their perception of their own power and its resultant leverage. This is the stage in which the decision-making group forms, the definition of the situation is debated, goals and policy options are discussed, a policy position is selected, and messages are sent to other countries conveying official positions. Commitment to a policy stance is conveyed to other countries through signals and indices.[42]

Both power and images play a role in this process. Images of countries affect perceptions about their power, their intentions, their flexibility, and their threat or the opportunity they afford. They may or may not be weaker in fact, but perceptions and expectations dominate the interpretation of information, which is more likely to be accepted when it conforms with beliefs.

Strategies designed to meet one foreign policy problem do not occur in isolation from other foreign policy problems. Foreign policy strategies range from a global strategy, designed to affect or control the shape of the entire system in which a country exists, to general strategies incorporating policies designed to pursue goals of a narrower scope (perhaps regional; perhaps a broad set of policy problems, such as national defense policy), to a strategy applied to a specific country or situation—the narrowest scope. Strategies, or sets of policies, can be organized in an inverted pyramid, with different levels representing different "levels of conflict."[43]

The depiction of policies at different levels is a device to illustrate the differences in scope and parameter of a country's repertoire of foreign policies. The coherence of policy at these levels can vary, and policy makers do not necessarily always move from broad concerns to specific tactics. The chronology of policy formulation may begin at any of these levels, and the important situational details will be better understood and more explicitly examined by policy makers as they move from general to tactical policy levels. In fact, policies at each level will differ because of the extent to which policy makers examine their assumptions and debate the characteristics and utility of each policy.[44] For example, U.S. foreign strategy at the global level during the cold war was containment, and this strategy was rarely debated in the U.S. political arena. It took a crisis of the magnitude of the war in Vietnam to produce a debate, and even then the debate focused more on the question of the true nature and significance of the conflict in Vietnam rather than containment as a whole. Moreover, the debate faded quickly after the United States pulled out of Vietnam. U.S. defense policy, a policy that lay at the general policy level, was strenuously debated, often with a fairly detailed discussion of the expected behavior of allies and opponents and the impact of specific weapons systems. But rarely was U.S. defense policy debated in the context of a reconsideration of containment or of an alternative global strategy.

Nevertheless, global strategy does set the acceptable policy parameters for policy at the tactical level. To continue the defense policy example, all variations of U.S. nuclear policy options, ranging from assured destruction to flexible response, were designed to contain the Soviet Union. There was very little discussion in elite policy-making circles of a defense policy that did not serve the containment strategy. The end of the cold war destroyed the rationale for containment and left the United States without a global strategy. The lack of a global strategy has an effect on regional policies; those formulated within the containment strategy no longer fit strategic guidelines and have the appearance of being ad hoc responses to one crisis after another. Intervention in a specific country, for example, cannot be analyzed in isolation from other foreign policy considerations. Policy objectives in a specific situation are influenced by general, even global, strategic objectives. In addition, an identification of broad objectives provides more information concerning trends, which are of concern to policy makers and which they want to affect.

Several additional points concerning goals are important here. U.S. policy makers have multiple (and not necessarily consistent) goals in their global, regional, and country-specific policies. The goals vary in importance among policy makers. Threats and opportunities caused by political events may shift the importance given to one or more goals relative to others. The importance of goals may shift as other countries become involved: a strategic interaction is not always strictly bilateral. During the cold war, all bilateral conflicts between the United States and another noncommunist countries involved limited situation-specific, objectives. If the Soviet Union was perceived to be a participant, then U.S. goals reflected those goals incorporated in its global containment strategy, and those objectives took priority over goals that derived from the bilateral conflict. Thus an analysis of strategies must include the situational characteristics, the situational goals, and the goals of the policy makers.

THE DECISION CONTEXT

Not all situational characteristics are about power or capability, but they nevertheless affect perceptions of other countries and the self and, hence, affect decisions. A number of context effects can be found in political and psychological studies. Time pressure is often a potential source of poor decision making in that it amplifies threat perceptions and makes for hasty and often cavalier treatment of information. Ambiguous information is also a common situational characteristic, increasing policy makers' tendencies to rely upon their perceptions for their information. The presence of third parties, whether friendly, hostile, or neutral, may affect perceptions of threat and opportunity. Finally, one's goals, the salience of those goals determined in part by one's commitment to them, and one's interpretation of the goals of others can be important context effects. A country with few salient goals may be more sensitive to an opportunity to achieve some gain, whereas a country with highly salient goals may be more sensitive to threats to these goals.

It is difficult to state precisely the impact of situational characteristics on perception, but there is clearly an interaction between them and psychological images. "The person and the environment are in a dynamic relationship that is constantly changing and . . . this relationship is bidirectional, with the person and the environment each acting on the other."[45] Situational characteristics are related to, but are not synonymous with, capabilities. The term *capabilities* refers to elements of national power. They include a country's resource base (natural resources, industrial and technological capacity, human resources, and economic strength); a country's mobilization capabilities, or the extent to which it can uses its resources (characteristics include nationalism, government legitimacy, leadership, and the administrative system); and the power instruments into which the resources and mobilization capacities translate (the military, the diplomatic corps, the intelligence community, and the ability to grant economic or technical assistance).[46] A measure of a country's potential leverage can be derived from an assessment of its capabilities in a conflict situation. However, how that leverage will be used depends on the country's images.

Bureaucratic and domestic factors (competing policy recommendations from competing bureaucratic agencies and domestic factors such as public opinion, interest groups, and elite nongovernmental think tanks and policy advocacy groups) are additional elements in the decision context. Their role is less one of creating the policy choice than one of influencing the selection of particular instruments for implementing policy and acting as constraints on government actions.

Bureaucratic factors contribute to the impact of images in several ways. They tend to share—or at least have an intuitive understanding of—their country's prevailing image (that is, the top-level policy makers' image) of the other country, the situation, and third parties. This is particularly true of the most important bureaucratic players, top-level cabinet officers, who are politically appointed. Those who do not share the prevailing view (the view held by top-level policy makers) may argue against policies emanating from it, but due to role requirements and career interests, they will not prevent a policy choice unless a number of them act in concert. In most cases, the prevailing image will be shared, and therefore the definition of the situation and the acceptance of a particular policy will be agreed upon. The bureaucratic argument, therefore, should be specific and should concern the instruments and situational strategies most likely to achieve the desired goals. Bureaucrats may attempt to prevent tactics from being implemented when they dispute the prevailing image. In these cases, the policy disputes are likely to spread to the public arena. Unless audience effects are strong, the policy preference of the top-level decision makers will dominate, but the bureaucrats will affect the selection of tactics.

The impact of domestic factors is more difficult to determine and evaluate. In general, the public will accept the top-level policy makers' worldview. They will see the enemies, the threats, and the opportunities the leadership sees. But the public can also act as a restraint on these policy makers, influencing tactics (for example, restraining assassination attempts), insisting that an image of another country is wrong (for example, that North Vietnam was not merely a puppet of the USSR), or preventing top-level policy makers from implementing a new approach to the other country when the prevailing image has changed but the public's has not.

POLICY PATTERNS

Some images have a threatening affective component (the enemy or a dependent of the enemy). Others either are mixtures of threat and opportunity (the neutral country or the ally—because the image is often evoked during crises, when one needs an ally) or are primarily opportunity (the dependent). These affective components of images affect the situational characteristics. At the same time, situational characteristics influence perceptions. Characteristics viewed as strengthening or weakening the enemy or as strengthening or weakening one's own country are seen as inherently important and therefore as requiring a response. By placing hypothetical images in hypothetical decision contexts, it is possible to anticipate policy preference patterns.

These hypothetical situations are focused on U.S. policy makers' approach to Latin America. One pattern is U.S. involvement in a strictly bilateral conflict with a country it perceives as dependent. In this situation, psychological and environmental conditions converge to form a strong U.S. predisposition to use coercion. The self-image of the United States during the cold war was positive, and in U.S. perceptions of its power, control, and ability to determine the future of Latin America, this self-image was overwhelmingly positive. The dependent image itself led to a U.S. propensity to ignore the subtle political realities of Latin American countries that might have indicated that powerful instruments alone would not be sufficient to determine the course of events. The asymmetry of power between the United States and a Latin American country has favored the United States. Third parties were not perceived to be involved; thus the power assessment was bilateral (or regional) and situation-specific. Goals were also bilateral and situation-specific. The degree of threat in this situation was minimal, because a dependent is not associated with threat. In fact, U.S. policy makers may have seen opportunities to achieve certain aims but little more than an annoying threat to those aims and no threat at all to its larger international concerns.

Since U.S. policy makers perceived the dependent country as weak and inferior, they also perceived a variety of options available to them in implementing their strategy. They assumed they could determine the best course of action for all concerned and were inclined to force the dependent to accept their decision rather than to negotiate alternatives with the dependent. Because time pressures and threats were minimal, policy makers selected instruments that were slow acting, such as economic sanctions, diplomatic pressure, and covert infiltration of the dependent's political system. Military intervention and the use of covert or paramilitary techniques to overthrow the dependent's government were unlikely. However, the important point remains that U.S. perception of its own superiority and its contempt for its dependent produced a willingness to use force.[47]

The second pattern occurred when the United States perceived the enemy as actively interested in a situation involving a U.S. dependent. The image of the enemy is that of a country as strong as oneself. The interaction between the image of the dependent and the image of the enemy creates a cognitive soup with two distinct temperatures, one hot and one cold. A distinction must be made between cases in which the leadership of the dependent country is perceived as loyal and those in which the leadership is perceived as radical and dangerous.

In bilateral conflicts with the enemy, containment was the preferred strategy of U.S. policy makers during the cold war. The perceptual logic of containment was difficult to challenge: an enemy, being as strong as oneself, highly aggressive, with harmful intentions, and untrustworthy as well, could be defeated or changed. Thus containment was a sensible approach. Enemy tactics perceived as aimed at enhancing its power were matched by competing tactics to counter or prevent that increase in power. However, given the equality of power and the dangers of escalation, a direct and coercive assault on the enemy was usually considered too risky.

If the United States perceived its enemy as interested in or involved in developments in a U.S. dependent, many elements of the decision process changed. First, the power differential changed, as the power of the enemy altered the power equation and the range of options and leverage available to the United States. Second, U.S. goals changed dramatically, with goals and threats associated with the enemy suddenly being identified in the current situation. If the United States felt intensely threatened, it selected tactics to achieve quick results without escalating the conflict. Coercion was the preferred tactic, since negotiation with the enemy in this context was seen as suicidal: the enemy would simply have taken advantage of the opportunity. (Descriptions of the strategies, goals, and tactics used in response to the dependent and enemy images are given in table 1.)

The distinction between the "good" dependent and the "bad" de-

TABLE 1.
Images and Policies

Policy Characteristics	Dependent Image	Enemy Image	Dependent Plus Enemy Images
Strategy	Situationally derived	Containment	Containment
Goal	Bilateral	Global	Global
Tactic	Coercive, non-compromising negotiating, very low threat, implementation beginning with slow-acting instruments instruments	Competitive, matching, non-compromising, negotiating, high threat, demonstrating resolve, credibility, urgent implementation	Coercive, non-compromising, negotiating, high threat, fast implementation with quick-acting instruments

pendent with a hovering enemy is crucial. In the case of the good dependent, the U.S. task was to order the situation so that the enemy could not gain a presence. The solution was intervention to create and enforce the dependent's political stability, to shore up the dependent's coercive forces, and to repress political dissent. If the dependent seemed about to succumb to the enemy, actual physical intervention was called for. A hot soup developed when the dependent's leadership was perceived as having fallen under enemy influence. U.S. policy makers then searched for vulnerabilities to exploit. The capabilities of the dependent were still assumed to be low, but the shadow of the enemy influenced the perceived degree of threat. Because threat was high, capabilities were seen to favor the United States; and as time was short, more active forms of intervention were used, including military intervention and covert operations designed to overthrow the dependent government. Other factors were important in these determinations as well; for example, domestic pressure to act may have contributed to the decision to intervene.

Here, the United States used swift, localized military or covert (particularly paramilitary) operations. U.S. actions were inflexible because of the high degree of threat. Also important was the assumption that the people in the dependent country were childlike and easily led, duped, or controlled by the enemy. When the stereotype of a people is childlike and they act in unexpected, particularly rebellious, ways, the assumption is that the cause of that behavior is some third party.

In U.S. conflicts with countries perceived as nonaligned, a third policy pattern emerged. Nationalism was not perceived to be a link with the enemy but an independent drive that produced resistance to being ordered about and a sensitivity to any appearance that the United States was dictating policy. The response to nationalism therefore was to be "sensitive," to avoid situations wherein a nonaligned government could be accused by its domestic opponents of following the U.S. lead, and to avoid any suggestion of an unequal relation. Nevertheless, since a non-aligned country played games with the enemy (whoever that may be), it was important to win over its leadership. Thus, carrots were used liber-ally and sticks rarely, and both were used discreetly. Underlying the strategy was a perception that the goals and concerns of the nonaligned country were shallow, that the country was simply not as powerful as the United States or the enemy, and that it was only bilaterally or regionally important. For U.S. policy makers, the enemy always set the parameters of global concern. And although the nonaligned country might not fall into the hands of the enemy and was capable of resisting the enemy to some degree, it was still not to be trusted.

There was a difference between countries seen as nonaligned and those seen as complex. In the latter, the various political groups were recognized not simply in formulaic terms but in terms of platforms, potential alliances with other groups, the personalities of their leaders, and internal conflicts. The complex country was considered unique, and in a conflict situation great attention was paid to the details of the country and the conflict. Solutions were bilateral and were derived from the situation itself.

CONCLUSION

All stages of U.S. policy making vis-à-vis Latin American countries—from forming policy through carrying it out—have been influenced by U.S. images and perceptions. Once policy considerations began, any return to an earlier stage was difficult. Incoming information was man-aged to confirm these earlier interpretations and decisions and to allow consideration only of alternatives in the current stage. Policy disputes derived from differing images of the dependent or the self. Once the prevailing view was set, however, disputes over goals and strategy dimin-ished as the search for workable tactics proceeded. The prevailing view extended through the bureaucracy and into the public. When there was significant disagreement over the image of the dependent, which mani-fested as debate about appropriate strategy and, possibly, debate over the intentions and motives of the dependent. Top-level policy makers strove for a unanimous view or tried to restrict the size of the audience by operating in secrecy.

There were numerous important audience effects on U.S. policy makers' formation of strategy and its ultimate implementation. An audience could push policy makers toward conservatism and inflexibility: once a commitment to a particular strategy was made, a change in position might demonstrate lack of resolve (thus sending a dangerous message to the dependent as well as to salient supporting audiences). Audiences also influenced policy makers' ability to empathize with opponents: group identification made it difficult if not impossible for policy makers to comprehend the position of the other side in a conflict. Thus audiences influenced the selection of strategy and goals and limited U.S. flexibility in adjusting to events as the strategy was implemented. Goals were thus not selected through a careful examination of alternatives; indeed, as the U.S. perception of threat increased, the quality of goal and strategy selection diminished.

Most of the U.S. policy-making cases examined in this volume took place during the cold war, which had a profound effect on the worldview of U.S. policy makers. This worldview influenced the U.S. perception of threat from the USSR and the selection and timing of the responses to conflicts assumed to involve the USSR. In this way, this worldview strongly affected U.S. policy toward Latin America.

However, the cases explored in the following chapters demonstrate that the dependent image existed independent of the cold war and the enemy image and that it had an identifiable and consistent impact on U.S. decision making. By looking at U.S. worldview images as elements of a chaotic political system, which includes the international environment, we can grasp how much or how little U.S. policy making toward Latin America will change with the end of the cold war. Images organized that environment; part of that environment changed with the demise of the Soviet Union. Other parts of that environment did not change. Thus the dependent image is left as the dominant image guiding U.S. policy making toward Latin America. But the United States still operates in a chaotic political system, and change in one part—the cold war between the United States and the USSR—will inevitably change other parts of the system. In Latin America, that change is occurring slowly, and it cannot be adequately responded to through the old dependent image.

2

THE COLD WAR COMES TO
LATIN AMERICA: INTERVENTION IN
GUATEMALA AND CUBA

IN THE FIRST THREE DECADES OF THE TWENTIETH CENTURY, THE UNITED
States used coercion in conflicts with Latin America quite regularly.
Multiple military interventions took place in Central America and the
Caribbean, and some resulted in a military presence for years at a time.
After Franklin Roosevelt introduced the Good Neighbor Policy, military
intervention was no longer acceptable, although the coercive use of
other policy instruments, both economic and diplomatic, continued.
With the cold war, U.S. policy makers once again accepted military
intervention, along with the use of covert and paramilitary operations to
achieve U.S. goals in Latin America. Not all of these efforts were successful, and as the cold war wore on, U.S. administrations learned from
the mistakes of their predecessors. The use of coercive diplomacy in
Latin American became more sophisticated, at least until the Reagan
administration and its return to the practices of the 1950s.

This chapter begins with the early adventures of the cold war. It
explores two cases of U.S. policy making, each of which ended in
intervention. The U.S. selection of policies and instruments was linked
to the prevailing images of the Latin American countries in question.
The lessons that the successes and failures of this era provided for
future attempts to achieve U.S. goals in the hemisphere are also examined. A brief review of each case is followed by an examination of the
images the United States held of these countries and the impact of those
images on U.S. strategy.

The cases considered in this chapter are the interventions in Guatemala in 1954 and in Cuba in the early 1960s, up to the Bay of Pigs fiasco. Both cases include the use of diplomatic, economic, and—ultimately— paramilitary coercion. In both cases, coercion was eagerly applied when the leaders of Guatemala or Cuba were seen in dangerous association or collaboration with the Soviet Union. Conflicts within the U.S. decision- making hierarchy concerning the appropriate actions in each case can be attributed to clashing perceptions of these leaders.

GUATEMALA, 1954

The first cold war U.S. intervention in the Western Hemisphere oc- curred in Guatemala in 1954 and involved a covert plan to overthrow the government of President Jacobo Arbenz. The central U.S. officials in- volved in decision making in this case were President Dwight Eisen- hower, Secretary of State John Foster Dulles, Central Intelligence Agency Director Allen Dulles, several top-level CIA officers, including Frank Wisner and J. C. King, and several CIA agents.

Traditionally, the U.S. government and U.S. businesses had a great deal of influence in Guatemala. The United States was the major market for Guatemalan products. In many ways, Guatemala was the stereotypical banana republic: its economy was dependent upon ag- riculture, its polity had been ruled by various military dictators, and its distribution of income was exceptionally unequal. Further, U.S. am- bassadors held tremendous power in Guatemala, and U.S. leverage in Guatemala was extraordinary. When revolution took place in Guate- mala in 1944, U.S. influence and leverage diminished because a re- formist, nationalistic government came to power. Nevertheless, U.S. businesses continued to dominate Guatemala's economy and the United States continued to have extraordinary economic and political influence.

The Guatemalan government and people were perceived by both the Truman and Eisenhower administrations through the dependent image. State Department officials were surprised when revolution oc- curred in 1944, unable to understand why the dictator's "children" would oust him.[1] Similarly, there was no recognition of the importance of Guatemalan nationalism, typical of one holding the dependent im- age. U.S. opinion about the nature of the 1944 revolutionary govern- ment turned from optimism at the prospect of a moderately liberal government to fears of communist infiltration as reforms were enacted. Embassy officials worried about communist penetration of the country via labor unions. They bemoaned the reformers in the administration of Juan José Arévalo, the first president after the revolution. One official remarked, "No one of the former governing class of old 'good families' was or has since been a member of this government."[2]

Evidence of U.S. policy makers' simplification of the Guatemalan political arena is readily available. Virtually anyone who called for reform, whether from the left, center, or right, was branded a communist. Piero Gleijeses examined Truman administration evaluations of numerous Guatemalan political actors and found that those who were "at most mild leftists or even right of center" were branded as communists or communist sympathizers:

> The prominent PAR [Partido Acción Revolucionaria] leader [Augusto] Charnaud was not considered "a *proven* communist in the card carrying sense," yet his strong procommunist orientation was flagrant, "since 1944 at least." In fact, Charnaud, who hardly knew who Marx was in 1944, was, by the end of Arévalo's term, an eloquent populist with slight leftist proclivities. The same virulent Red virus allegedly contaminated Foreign Minister Muños Meany, another moderate leftist whose major sins were strong hostility to dictatorship and sincere nationalism. . . . Even Clemente Marroquín Rojas, a prominent right-wing intellectual, roused the suspicions of U.S. officals. His nationalism, which was tinged with criticism of the United States, confused them, for they were accustomed to Guatemalan conservatives who loudly sang the praise of all things American. (Pp. 101–02)

Of particular importance is the combination of a simplification of Guatemalan politics and an inability to recognize nationalism as a political force that can accompany a variety of ideological outlooks.

The Truman administration looked at Jacobo Arbenz, who succeeded Arévalo in the presidency in 1950, in a similarly simplified and stereotyped manner, regarding him as just another opportunist. One State Department official described Arbenz as lacking "any deep-seated intellectual alliance to the leftist cause, and, as such, no real sympathy for the lower classes or for the many outside communists who have infiltrated Guatemala" (ibid., p. 125). Another U.S. official said that, "if Arbenz continues to ally himself with the leftists, this will probably only be a temporary move in the interests of expediency. . . . (My long run guess is that Arbenz no longer has anything to gain by alliance with leftists, that a clash will occur from his pressure to contain them, and that he will, sooner or later, use this as a pretext for overt action in his own interests)" (p. 126).

It was not long before these beliefs were replaced by deepening suspicion among U.S. officials and businessmen. Once Arbenz became president of Guatemala, U.S.-based companies, particularly United Fruit, launched a very tough and effective propaganda campaign against him designed to influence official and public opinion in the United States. Thus there was no significant disagreement in the U.S. political arena on the nature of the Arbenz government. Eisenhower's memoirs indicate that he considered Arbenz to be a communist or a communist puppet.[3] He also believed that Arbenz ran a campaign of terror throughout Guatemala and that he had no popular support (p. 425). Allen Dulles indicated his agreement with Eisenhower, as did U.S. Ambassador to Guatemala, John Peurifoy. John Foster Dulles described Guatemala as the victim of an "alien intervention" motivated by an "evil design" that would ultimately imperil the hemisphere if not stopped.[4]

The perception of Arbenz as a communist puppet or stooge is particularly important in that it reflects the underlying assumption that Guatemalans, being childlike, would easily fall prey to manipulation by the USSR. The simplification of perceptions of political change in Guatemala is reflected in the famous statement by Ambassador Richard Patterson when he revealed to Congress his method of identifying a communist via the duck test. "Many times it is impossible to prove legally that a certain individual is a communist; but for cases of this sort I recommend a practical method of detection—the 'duck test.' The duck test works this way: suppose you see a bird walking in a farm yard. This bird wears no label that says 'duck.' But the bird certainly looks like a duck. Also, he goes to the pond and you notice that he swims like a duck. Then he opens his beak and quacks like a duck. Well, by this time you have probably reached the conclusion that the bird is a duck."[5]

In a State Department report on these developments in Guatemala, communist efforts to infiltrate and subvert are described in detail. Communists, it said, took advantage of unethical, power hungry, corrupt local politicians and gradually moved into positions of importance. They did this through clever manipulation, control of labor, and by putting themselves forth as "the most fervent and intense advocates of national values and symbols. . . . Communists are fully aware that ambitious and unscrupulous politicians are interested only in votes. . . . At crucial moments artificial 'popular' demonstrations can prove of great value to scheming politicians. In Guatemala, Communists knew that to control some segments of the population was an indispensable condition for placing the Communist-Arbenz alliance on a durable basis."[6]

The extreme simplification of Guatemala at the top levels of the U.S. government was also noted by Guatemala's ambassador to the

United States, who was surprised at how little Eisenhower actually knew about Guatemala.[7] U.S. policy makers were certainly not cognizant of the tremendous complexity of Guatemalan nationalism or of the nature of the left in Guatemala. Nationalism was not the sole property of the left in Guatemala. Moreover, the left coalition that supported Arbenz was volatile, composed of the Communist party, revolutionary parties (of which there were four, then five, then one, then four again during the Arbenz presidency), and two labor unions. The revolutionary parties were in constant conflict, but that conflict was not related to ideological differences since "no faction had a coherent ideology or strategy."[8]

The extreme view of Guatemala as a dependent with a government falling under the influence of the enemy was widely shared in the Eisenhower administration. A slightly more complex picture of Guatemala was evident in the U.S. national intelligence estimates for Guatemala in 1952 and 1953. There it was argued that Guatemala's revolution was a result of a history of military dictatorship and economic "colonialism." These estimates also acknowledged that the Guatemalan army was anticommunist, a finding they used against Arbenz when the covert operation went into effect.[9] Despite the CIA's recognition of the popular desire for an end to the old order, the CIA still maintained that Arbenz was an opportunist allied with communists even though not controlled by them.[10] He was seen as able to dupe the people, again a reflection of the dependent image—the people being too ignorant to understand reality. Neither the CIA nor Eisenhower and his closest advisers acknowledged that Arbenz came out of that noncommunist military and that his policies were reformist (union legalization, education programs, agrarian reform). Moreover, the earlier assessment of Arbenz-the-opportunist was ignored or forgotten in the face of the new, threat-filled evaluation.

Because of its dependent image, the Eisenhower administration analyzed Arbenz's decisions and actions based on this stereotype, while rejecting arguments and evidence that the stereotype was incorrect. For example, Arbenz's decision not to sign the Rio Pact, the presence of a legal Communist party in Guatemala, Guatemala's agreement with the accusation that the United States had used biological warfare in Korea, and Guatemala's observation of the minute of silence in the United Nations when Stalin died were all taken as evidence of communist leanings. Guatemala's protestations that it had abstained from the Rio Pact due to a territorial dispute, that Guatemalan communists were politically insignificant, and that Josef Stalin was a wartime ally were ignored.

Additional "evidence" consisted of the nationalization of United Fruit Company holdings in Guatemala, the assumption that Guatemala had covertly sponsored a strike in Honduras (which was incorrect), and the fact that Guatemala had purchased arms from Czechoslovakia. Information was distorted to conform to image-based expectations. The United Fruit Company was nationalized as a result of reform efforts by the Guatemalan government and years of exploitive behavior. The Honduran strikes were attributed to Guatemalan influence merely because three representatives of the Guatemalan government had visited Honduras shortly before the strikes. Arms were purchased from Czechoslovakia because the United States had initiated a boycott of arms sales to Guatemala, and Arbenz had to pacify his noncommunist army.

As conflict between the United States and Guatemala intensified during 1953 and 1954, discussions of Guatemala by U.S. officials became increasingly simplified. Arbenz was more frequently referred to as a communist, and concerns grew that Guatemala would attack its neighbors. By 1953, threat became the dominant affective characteristic of these policy makers. The use of coercion to change the direction of Guatemalan reform began during the Truman administration, which banned the sale of arms and planes to the Guatemalan military, initiated (but then abandoned) a plot to overthrow Arbenz, and funneled aid to right-wing military officers hoping they would stage a coup.

The Eisenhower administration made some tentative efforts to resolve the growing tension between Guatemala and the United States through diplomatic channels, but these efforts amounted to ordering Guatemala to change its internal policies. Assistant Secretary of State for Inter-American Affairs John Moors Cabot, who was sent to Guatemala to demand compensation for expropriated fruit company holdings, complained about the presence and influence of communists and demanded that the Guatemalan press stop criticizing the United States. Cabot was told that many of the suspected communists were not communists or had left their positions and that Guatemala's free press was not controlled by the government.[11] Unconvinced, Cabot returned to the United States and told the State Department that Guatemala was being overrun by communism and that "the Foreign Minister was a complete jackass who talked endlessly without making sense. President Arbenz had the pale, cold-lipped look of the ideologue and showed no interest in my suggestions for change in his government's direction. He had obviously sold out to the Communists and that was that."[12] These diplomatic efforts reflect the typical diplomatic approach to a dependent-image country. It is not bargaining—it is commanding, the usual pattern when one side perceives the other as both weaker and inferior and thus unable to make correct choices. The diplomatic efforts failed to get the desired change, although it is difficult to see how those aims could have been achieved when U.S. officials refused to believe Guatemalan assurances that communists were an insignificant political force in Guatemala.

The Eisenhower administration inevitably came to the conclusion that it should pursue covert intervention to overthrow Arbenz. The form of this intervention reflects both the administration's extreme dependent image of Guatemala and some important context characteristics. In August 1953, Eisenhower approved a covert operation to overthrow Arbenz, an extraordinarily risky plot suitable for a James Bond film. An important context was clearly the recent success of the plot to overthrow Iranian Premier Mossadeq.[13]

The plot hatched for the termination of the Arbenz government involved the following scenario: the United States would create and support an anti-Arbenz army of liberation that would "invade" Guatemala; meanwhile, through radio broadcasts and propaganda, the CIA would promote the myth that this army was inspiring a massive popular uprising. This, in combination with a bombing campaign—allegedly by the army of liberation but actually by U.S. planes with CIA operatives at the controls—would frighten the Guatemalan people and the military. The latter would then depose Arbenz, and the CIA-picked head of the army of liberation would take the reins of government. The entire operation sounds incredible, considering that so few exiles could be found willing to form an army of liberation that the CIA had to hire mercenaries—and at that, had a force of only about 150 men. Those "soldiers" were not to do much in the way of fighting, anyway. After performing poorly in early contacts with the Guatemalan army, they were ordered to sit in a village waiting for the Arbenz government to self-destruct. Success largely rested on the CIA's ability to dismantle the tiny Guatemalan air force. This was done by convincing one pilot to defect with his plane. Arbenz fell right into the CIA plot by grounding the rest of his air force, thus making aerial confirmation of the size and strength of the army of liberation impossible.

This entire plot reflects many characteristics of the dependent image with the addition of concern about the enemy's influence. First, there was no consideration of Guatemalan politics. Arbenz certainly did have domestic opposition, but it was not well organized, lacked strong leadership, and represented essentially the upper class and the Catholic church. Arbenz had strong backing from important sectors in the Guatemalan polity, and the military in 1953 clearly did not want to overthrow him. Nevertheless, Arbenz's popularity and the condition of the opposition did not faze the CIA. The CIA picked an opposition "leader," Carlos Castillo Armas, chosen in part because he had the physical features of a Guatemalan Indian (and presumably could therefore pass as a "man of the people"). Castillo Armas also had a long record of hostility toward Arbenz and had support from the church hierarchy.

Kermit Roosevelt, master spy in the Iran operation, claims that the selection of Castillo Armas frightened him off from participation in the Guatemalan operation, although he did try to convince John Foster Dulles that the opposition ought to "want what we want."[14] Further, although the top-level U.S. decision makers recognized the need to keep the operation secret, they were relatively unconcerned about the impact exposure would have on U.S. relations with the rest of Latin America. Instead, they saw the operation as containing the USSR, which was the larger and more important struggle. They were aware that the chances of success were low: Allen Dulles estimated them to be "better than 40 percent but less than even" (p. 108). Nevertheless, they proceeded with the plot.[15] It is likely that they believed that Guatemalans such an inferior foe that they could easily beat the odds. And the plot did work.

The operative who planned this plot, Colonel Albert Haney, had been the CIA's station chief in South Korea before assignment to this case and was chosen for his successful record in South Korea rather than any expertise on Guatemala. His view of Guatemala was a bit more complex than that of Eisenhower and the Dulles brothers. Although he masterminded this plot, he recognized that there was not enough opposition to Arbenz for an army of liberation to arouse a popular revolt. When the overthrow began, the State Department reported that "anti-Communist uprisings were underway" in various Guatemalan cities and that "Guatemala has been invaded by land, and probably by sea in a drive to unseat the Communist-infiltrated Government of President Jacobo Arbenz."[16] The State Department claimed that there were no indications that Guatemala had been invaded by a foreign force but rather that it was experiencing an internal revolt.

In 1957, the State Department produced an analysis of communist penetration of Guatemala during the Arbenz administration, describing Castillo Armas as "an anti-Communist Guatemalan patriot" who "had become a popular and colorful figure among the patriotic element of his country."[17] The document explains that Castillo Armas built an army of liberation and that Guatemalan soldiers would not fight against his forces: "Communism was alien to Guatemalan soldiers, and they had no heart to fight for the Communist cause; putting patriotism first, they soon decided to come to terms with the forces of liberation" (p. 56).

When the next chance came along to rid the hemisphere of a similar menace, the Guatemalan myth was used as a guide—which leads us directly to Cuba.

CUBA, 1960

The history of the U.S. presence in Cuba, as in Guatemala, gave the United States extraordinary leverage. Cuba had been a U.S. protectorate in the early twentieth century, and until the Cuban revolution the U.S. ambassador was considered one of the most important individuals in the country. U.S. economic interests and policy influence in Cuba were exceptional. U.S. businesses had around a billion dollars in investments in Cuba, and the United States was the major market for Cuba's exports. Like Guatemala, Cuba depended upon agricultural exports.

When the Cuban revolution took place, the international context had changed somewhat from that during the Guatemalan episode. The Suez Canal crisis had occurred, Third World nationalism was a growing problem for the United States, and most important, Latin America was becoming increasingly hostile toward the United States. Vice President Richard Nixon was stoned during his 1958 trip to Latin America. The Eisenhower administration was reexamining its Latin America policy when Fidel Castro and the July 26 Movement forces marched into Havana in January 1959.

Local situational factors were also important. Castro was an enigma to U.S. officials. Little was known about him during his revolutionary years in Cuba's Sierra Maestra partly due to an information blockade imposed by Cuban dictator Fulgencio Batista. A nationalistic revolution would clearly deprive the United States of some leverage in Cuba, but the extent to which leverage would be diminished depended largely upon the nature of the Fidelistas—and that was a mystery: hence, there was greater uncertainty about U.S. leverage than in the case of Guatemala. But the images U.S. policy makers had of Guatemala in 1954 and Cuba in 1959 were similar in many ways. In fact, Guatemala taught the Eisenhower administration a number of lessons about Third World "communism" and how to dispose of it. Unfortunately, perceptual distortions and misinterpretations were the basis for those lessons.

Two images of Castro's Cuba were held by the U.S. government. One was of a dependent country under a hostile influence. Radical right-wing members of Congress, for example, believed Castro had been a communist from the beginning, and many important members of the Eisenhower administration branded Castro a communist or a communist dupe. The second image, held primarily by career State Department officers, was more complex. It does not conform to the neutral image (indeed, such an image probably did not exist in 1958), but it demonstrated a far greater understanding of Cuban political trends, factions, and nationalism and saw the need for a sophisticated strategy in dealing with Cuba.

Americans initially believed that the Cuban revolution would end with the ouster of Batista, interpreting the revolution as a change of government rather than the complete social, economic, and political revolution that it was.[18] This interpretation reflected a real lack of understanding of Cuban politics and socioeconomic conditions. Further, Americans were perplexed by Castro's nationalistic, angry condemnations of U.S. interference in Cuba. President Eisenhower, for example, said, "The record of close relations between Cuba and the United States made it a puzzling matter to figure out just exactly why the Cubans would now be so unhappy" (p. 86). The administration was unable to understand the nationalistic basis for revolutionary Cuba's hostility toward the United States. Other indicators of the simplicity of the image of Cuba and Cubans are evident in the Eisenhower administration's ambassadorial appointments to Cuba. The two ambassadors in residence before the revolution were absolute amateurs: they did not speak Spanish, knew nothing of Cuba's politics or economics, and spent all their time with Batista and Cuba's elite. "Indeed, senior levels of U.S. government had given little attention to Cuba, or to the rest of Latin America. If Secretary Dulles thought about them at all, it seemed to be simply to assure himself that their governments were anti-Communist, no matter what else they might be."[19]

As the revolution proceeded, the CIA determined that Castro was a danger to the United States. The CIA was hesitant to brand Castro a communist, but the suspicion existed within the CIA before the revolution, and it increased after the revolution. Allen Dulles warned that "Communists and other extreme radicals appear to have penetrated the Castro movement. . . . If Castro takes over, they will probably participate in the government."[20] In March 1959, Allen Dulles warned that "the Castro regime is moving toward a complete dictatorship. Communists are now operating openly and legally in Cuba. And though Castro's government is not Communist-dominated, Communists have worked their way into the labor unions, the armed forces, and other organizations" (p. 523). Eisenhower was "highly suspicious" that Castro himself was a communist. He was also "disgusted at his murderous persecution of his former opponents" (ibid.).

In April 1959, Castro came to the United States at the invitation of the American Society of Newspaper Editors. He aroused a good deal of popular enthusiasm; he also told the editors that he was not a communist. Eisenhower and others remained suspicious. Vice President Nixon met with Castro and announced that he was "either incredibly naive about Communism or under Communist discipline."[21] Eisenhower told Allen Dulles that Raul Castro, Fidel's brother, "must certainly be a Communist," and Allen Dulles responded that "if he's not, he's awfully close to being one."[22]

It took several months for the image of the dependent to become associated in Cuba with the image of the enemy. Castro's moderate reforms during the first six months of his revolutionary government partly accounts for the delay. In November 1959, CIA Deputy Director C. P. Cabell testified before a Senate subcommittee that "Castro is not a Communist. . . . the Cuban Communists do not consider him a Communist party member or even a pro-Communist."[23] In his memoirs, Eisenhower remarked that, even though the possibility of Cuba becoming a Soviet satellite was alarming, this possibility was still discounted by many of his advisers in late 1959 and early 1960.[24] (Nevertheless, the ambivalence was not uniform and many members of the CIA were convinced that Castro was coming under Soviet influence by this time.)

Another reason the image association took so long may have been that Nixon's stormy visit to Latin American in 1958 shifted the perceptions of Latin America held by some of Eisenhower's advisers, most notably his brother Milton.[25] However, the Eisenhower administration maintained that the attacks on Vice President Nixon were communist inspired and directed and that, where discontent did exist for economic reasons, communists took advantage of it.[26] Thus, one should not imagine that the Eisenhower administration recognized the new social and political forces in Latin America: it failed to grasp the connection between U.S. imperialism and nationalistic revolution. (At the same time, the United States was more accepting of Castro's reforms than Castro claimed.)

In any case, U.S. confusion turned into hostility, as the administration increasingly saw Castro's rhetoric as a threat to U.S. prestige and an indicator of Castro's communist leanings. This, too, is typical of the shift from perception of a dependent to the perception of a dependent falling under hostile influence. When people perceived as inferior act in an incomprehensible manner, it is taken as evidence that they are controlled from without. Other indicators of the contemptuous U.S. view of Cubans include the administration's assumption that Castro would not find other markets for Cuban sugar (hence a cut in the U.S. quota would be an effective instrument) and that Cubans were not capable of running the oil refineries they expropriated from U.S. companies.[27]

After the U.S. dependent-plus-enemy image of Cuba was formed (toward the end of 1959), whatever complexity there was in the U.S. assessment of Castro disappeared. Several perceptual changes are notable. Before the shift in perception was complete, U.S. policy makers and diplomats concentrated on individual, bilateral conflicts with Cuba, including expropriation and compensation issues, political repression and press censorship in Cuba, and the participation of the Communist party in the Castro government. After the shift, which was completed with the announcement of a trade agreement between Cuba and the USSR in February 1960, U.S. concerns became global rather than bilateral. Now U.S. policy makers worried about the international threat Castro posed to the hemisphere (ibid., p. 98). This is exactly the shift in goals and threats one would expect when a government shifts from a dependent to a dependent-plus-enemy image.

U.S. policy was to overthrow Castro "in one way or another."[28] The CIA developed a plan to invade Cuba at the Bay of Pigs. The CIA assumed that a popular uprising in Cuba, in conjunction with the invasion, would get rid of Castro, completely ignoring the popularity of the charismatic Castro. But although this popular uprising was an important component of this poorly developed policy (actually, more a wish than a policy), it was contemptuously noted that "80 percent of the Cubans will never join an insurrection until they are sure that it is winning" (p. 158).

Additional examples of the simplification of perception are found in congressional debates concerning the sugar quota. The Eisenhower administration moved to cut the Cuban sugar quota in June 1960 (after the CIA had been given permission to formulate covert operations plans). By this time, various congressmen clearly saw Castro as a communist:

> Congressman Rivers said, "Think of what is happening—Castro and Communism—both must be destroyed. . . . God Save America." Congressman Haley said, "The time has come to deal with Castro where it hurts: in the pocketbook." Congressman McDowell said, "It is high time that the bluff of the Cuban Prime Minister and his colleagues was called." Congressman Conte said, "I am a patient man, but I am also an American. I cannot allow my country to continue to suffer the constant humiliations and opprobrium heaped upon her in an irresponsible manner. . . . We are, in fact, supporting the rapid growth of international communism at our very door step."[29]

Congress's analysis of how a cut in the U.S. sugar quota would affect Cuba reflected a simplified image of Cuban politics in several ways.

There is no evidence that it considered that such a cut would drive Cuba closer to the USSR. Instead, it appeared to assume that Castro's domestic support was based upon repression and that a deterioration in economic conditions caused by a cut in the sugar quota would cause his ouster. As Congressman Harris McDowell put it, "If Cuba's splendid people understand that they must sell their sugar or their economy will be destroyed, they will themselves find a way to deal with the present misleaders and fomenters of hatred" (ibid., p. 194). Since Cuba was at this time purchasing arms from the USSR, why would these congressmen presume that sanctions would not push Castro closer to the USSR? Perhaps the USSR perceived Cuba as the same "speck of an island" that they did—that is, not worth the effort to support and easily crushed.

President John Kennedy shared this image of Cuba and Castro, and it was Kennedy who implemented the Bay of Pigs plan. Kennedy was openly hostile to Castro's government. During the presidential campaign, he argued that stronger actions were necessary for dealing with Castro, "such as arming opposition forces both within Cuba and in exile."[30] Like Eisenhower, he did not want the United States to be associated with a coup, but he refused to renounce the use of intervention. Kennedy told Nikita Khrushchev that "there are unmistakable signs that Cubans find intolerable the denial of democratic liberties and the subversion of the 26th of July Movement by an alien-dominated regime."[31] The global nature of the perceived threat from Cuba is evident in Kennedy's statement: "A nation of Cuba's size is less a threat to our survival than it is a base for subverting the survival of other free nations throughout the hemisphere" (p. 304).

As the revolution began, Earl Smith, the U.S. ambassador to Cuba, thought Batista should appoint his own successor, a "Batista stooge," to run Cuba. But the State Department at this time believed that no one associated with Batista could govern the country.[32] Career officers at the embassy in Havana did understand that Batista was hated but they did little in-depth analysis of Cuban political factions and trends and had no strategy for dealing with the developing revolution. This may have been due to the repressive rule of Ambassador Smith, who was himself a Batistiano. By this time, the State Department did not want Castro to assume power and approved two CIA efforts to prevent that from occurring. However, these efforts were poorly thought-out and developed. The State Department, for example, did not pursue the option of a national unity government (which could have deprived Castro of power) until it was too late. Yet, as late as December 29, 1958, the State Department had argued that Castro would be "compatible" with the U.S. interests in the hemisphere.

After the revolution, and after the arrival of the new ambassador, Phillip Bonsal, the State Department rather than opposing Castro, advocated a cautious approach and was even willing to discuss U.S. aid to Castro. This was not a uniformly accepted view, however. Undersecretary of State Robert Murphy, for example, disagreed with the benign assessment of Castro, as did top career officers in the embassy in Cuba. This image did not influence U.S. policy after 1959, but State Department perceptions remained complex even as the Bay of Pigs approached. By 1959, State Department officials concluded that Castro would have to go and reviewed policy options in mid-1960 (ibid., p. 62).

Ambassador Bonsal's memoirs reveal his image of Cuba and Castro.[33] He understood full well the reasons for Cuban anti-Americanism, being cognizant of Cuban resentment of U.S. domination of Cuba since the turn of the century as well as the association between the United States and the Batista regime. Further, he was very concerned that Cuban officials not see him as acting paternalistically. Bonsal argues that U.S. officials who were suspicious of Castro from the outset were right but for the wrong reasons: there was no evidence that Castro was a communist even at the end of 1959 (when the CIA started to recruit Cuban exiles for the Bay of Pigs invasion). But there was evidence that Castro made Fidelistas out of communists (p. 116). Bonsal's analysis of the revolution hinged on Castro's personality: his drive for power, his charisma, and his ability to outmaneuver any opposition. By December 1959, Bonsal determined that the United States could never have a satisfactory relationship with Castro based on regular diplomacy (p. 111). He believed the best U.S. policy was to support internal opposition to Castro. This opposition, although a minority, was liberal democratic in ideology. Bonsal also understood that the Cuban exiles were generally Batistianos and would never be able to remove or replace Castro.

This voice ultimately lost what little influence it had. In early 1960, the Eisenhower administration began to use oil and sugar boycotts to bring Castro down. Bonsal opposed these boycotts. He understood that if Castro could withstand U.S. economic pressure with Soviet aid, his regime would be even more popular for having withstood the Colossus of the North. He also understood that these economic sanctions would make Cuba more dependent upon the USSR (ibid., chap. 16). The State Department reportedly had no knowledge of the Bay of Pigs plan and thus did nothing to moderate it.[34]

In the case of Cuba, there was limited attention to information and an acceptance of information that conformed to existing beliefs. Castro, in his early political and revolutionary life in Cuba, produced a variety of speeches and writings about Cuba's problems and future, material that the CIA could have analyzed. But early on, the CIA decided that Castro was a communist. Those with the alternate image of Castro and Cuba, however, were not convinced that Castro was a communist or a communist stooge. The policy preferences of the two groups were also different. The latter favored a policy of moderation, even as Castro moved leftward and became more and more hostile toward the United States. The CIA and some members of Congress preferred stronger action to destabilize Castro. Eisenhower apparently shifted to this view sometime after the first six months of 1959. Those who saw Castro as a communist attended to supporting information, such as his growing ties with the USSR. The moderate period of Castro's revolution was not considered significant, nor was the fact that the United States itself may have pushed Castro toward the USSR as it increased pressure on Cuba's economy and supported exiles.

One could argue that Castro *was* a communist and that Eisenhower recognized this, but that argument is irrelevant here. We are concerned with perceptions and their relation to information processing and strategy selection. Those who saw Cuba under Castro as a dependent under a hostile influence interpreted information to conform to that view.[35] Their image rested on not only perceptions of Castro but contempt for Cuba and Cubans—assumptions that they were childlike, nonnationalistic, inferior, and malleable. This image of Cuba affected their choice of strategy.

With hindsight, it appears that only policy makers with a complex view of Cuba could have chosen a different strategy. U.S. policy makers had not yet experienced such hostility from formerly docile people; they could not understand its origins, nor could they devise a policy that would accept and moderate Castro's independent course, since that course included ties with the Soviet Union and its allies. Even State Department personnel who had a complex image of Cuba preferred an interventionist policy. Their prescription for changing Cuba also included getting rid of Castro—but by manipulating domestic Cuban opinion.

No faction seems to have seen Castro as a strongly nationalistic, antiimperialist, anti-Yankee leader who could have chosen a nonaligned foreign policy rather than an alliance with the USSR. This is not surprising given the era in which these events took place. The image of nonaligned neutrals was not yet part of the worldview of U.S. policy makers. That perceptual change was on its way, produced by such events as the Suez Canal and Nixon's trip to Latin America, but this change occurred at the lower levels of officialdom. Top-level policy makers in the Eisenhower administration, those who set the prevailing worldview were slow to change.

CONCLUSION: WHY NOT BOLIVIA?

The Guatemalan and Cuban cases illustrate the relation between perception and the use of coercive policies. For example, there was little hesitation in using diplomatic or economic coercion when the countries were perceived as dependents. In neither case was there intense diplomatic negotiation between equals—or, failing that, slowly increasing pressure. The crucial shift from coercion to efforts to overthrow the governments came when these governments became associated with the enemy image. At that point, policy goals shifted from bilateral to global.

It could be argued that these cases show nothing more than U.S. pursuit of its economic or power interests and that its perceptions were irrelevant. But Soviet influence was not clear in either case, as the interpretation of the "evidence" shows. Furthermore, there were differences within the Eisenhower administration concerning Castro's political predisposition and the appropriate policy response. Certainly, in both cases U.S. economic interests were threatened. But ideology was not a constant in either case: although both the Castro and Arbenz governments espoused home-grown, nationalistic policies that advocated some rearrangement of class privileges, there was no clear economic thrust to either government's reform program.

The case for perceptual factors is strengthened by examining one more case, one in which the economic and ideological elements were present but in which U.S. opposition was not. In April 1952, a revolution occurred in Bolivia. It was led by the Movimiento Nacionalista Revolucionario, or MNR. The MNR was a political party with a very complicated history and a poor reputation in U.S. policy-making circles. During the World War II it was accused of being sympathetic to nazism. After the war it was supported by socialists. The MNR leaders were also allegedly associated with Juan Perón while they were in exile in Argentina during the late 1940s, and Perón was considered a rabid anti-American.

After taking power, the MNR government of President Victor Paz Estenssoro embarked on a series of radical reform programs. The tin mines were nationalized, a state monopoly was formed to control the export of minerals, new restrictions were placed on the ownership of Bolivian petroleum, increasing the environment's share, and an agrarian reform law was developed. The new government did not make immediate arrangements to compensate the owners of the expropriated mines, although compensation was promised.

Despite the reputation and actions of the MNR, the Eisenhower administration not only did not oppose the government, it actually tried to help it. The United States recognized the new government seven weeks after it took power, although it was conditional upon compensation for expropriated mining enterprises. In July 1953, the Eisenhower administration finalized an agreement to buy Bolivian tin despite the fact that the United States had more than enough tin stockpiled, because the Bolivian economy was in desperate need of a market. The tin was purchased at the world market price. The United States also initiated an economic assistance program for Bolivia.

Why did the Eisenhower administration aid, rather than oppose, this government? First, the Bolivian leadership understood full well that it had to neutralize the United States and did so purposefully immediately upon taking office. It announced that the government was not communist and that "international communism had no true interest in stating and solving the problems of the country in which it operates."[36] Second, the MNR government had one crucial champion, Dr. Milton Eisenhower, the president's brother. Milton Eisenhower went to Bolivia and became convinced that the revolutionary government was well-intentioned.

> He used the Bolivian example to show how politicians, the mass media, and business leaders sometimes tag governments or political parties as Communist, "in good faith but without essential knowledge." He added: "Sometimes men with selfish interests knowingly make false statements which poison the American mind and enrage Latin Americans. . . . It is harmful in our own country and devastatingly hurtful throughout Latin America for us to carelessly or maliciously label as 'Communist' any internal efforts to achieve changes for the benefit of the masses of the people. . . . We should not confuse each move in Latin America toward socialization with Marxism, land reform with Communists, or even anti-Yankee with pro-Sovietism." (Ibid., p. 133)

Where was Milton Eisenhower when Arbenz needed him? U.S. support for the Bolivian government shows the profound impact that perceptions have. The Bolivian government fit the characteristics of those the United States opposed elsewhere, but its leaders had the single advantage of knowing that U.S. hostility would be the kiss of death for their revolution. They therefore set about manipulating the Eisenhower administration's image of the Bolivian revolution and had the added advantage of direct contact with the president's brother. This ensured that the image the Bolivians wanted to project was received in Washington, D.C.

The cases discussed in this chapter demonstrate the power of the dependent image. It produced a U.S. predisposition to act in a coercive manner no matter what policy instrument was chosen. When policy makers decided that the dependent country was playing a dangerous game with the enemy, the predisposition became even more volatile and the selection of instruments more coercive. They did not ask questions about the potential failure of these policies; they had no doubt, for example, that the United States had the power capabilities to be successful in Guatemala and Cuba. Moreover, because nationalism was not a part of the dependent image, the long-term impact of U.S. coercion on the internal politics of the dependent country and the long-term relation between that country and the United States were not considered.

The cases also demonstrate the extent to which an image can be divorced from political ideology. Images are not political formulas: they are organizing devices, shells without ideological content. The Bolivian case demonstrates that the mere presence of leftist, socialist ideas and the expropriation of businesses were not sufficient to provoke coercive behavior by the United States. Bolivians separated the U.S. image of themselves from the U.S. image of its enemy, ensuring that the Eisenhower administration did not think the enemy was present in Bolivia. This prevented the United States from using the most coercive and dangerous tactic—intervention through covert or overt military force.

But how did the Bolivians get the United States to help their revolution? Two major issues threatened to divide the United States and Bolivia, the dangers of communism and the expropriation of U.S. companies. Bolivia attended to both issues by giving in to the United States. The United States got reassurance that the revolution was not a communist revolution and it got compensation for U.S. companies. Moreover, Bolivia had its own U.S. representative, Milton Eisenhower, who was favorable toward reform in Bolivia. In short, when the United States demanded, Bolivia complied. The conclusion, therefore, is that U.S. coercion was conditioned by the presence of the enemy image in conjunction with the dependent.

3

WHAT DIFFERENCE DOES AN ENEMY MAKE? OVERTHROW VERSUS SANCTIONS IN CHILE AND PERU

THE BAY OF PIGS FIASCO TAUGHT U.S. POLICY MAKERS SOME LESSONS about plotting to overthrow other governments. In addition, the failure in Vietnam and the success in negotiating arms agreements with the Soviet Union contributed to a greater range of perceptions within the administrations that followed the Kennedy era. The factions differed in the extremity of the dependent image of Third World countries and the enemy image of the USSR. As some policy advocacy groups began to see Latin American countries as less than prototypical dependents, their tactical preferences changed. The same was true of those who saw diminished threat from the USSR. This did not mean that the cold war was over nor that the interaction of the dependent and enemy images changed. The fundamental policy remained the same: the two images together signaled the necessity for quick, coercive action in the form of intervention. The dependent image alone called for coercive uses of other policy instruments. However, variations in the strength of these images did produce conflicts concerning the preferred tactics.

Those who moved away from the prototypical dependent image of Latin American countries did so in a consistent pattern rather than randomly or uniquely. They acknowledged nationalism as a potent political force, and this in turn reflected an assessment of Latin Americans as independent minded and able to make decisions for themselves. Although simplification of the political groupings within the dependent country continued, it too was modified by an increase in knowledge and understanding of political competitors in these countries.

When the enemy image of the Soviets became less extreme, the United States perceived Soviet capabilities as diminished and its threat reduced. This is distinctly different from changing U.S. perceptions of Soviet intentions. Those who saw the USSR as less than the prototypical enemy did not therefore conclude that the USSR was simply defensively motivated; instead, they saw the USSR as opportunistic rather than rabidly aggressive and diminished in capability, particularly the ability to override its economic weaknesses through authoritarian control of its population. There was also some awareness that the Soviet leadership was not monolithic and that there were competing policy factions within the USSR.

The two cases presented below illustrate the use of coercion in two different perceptual situations. The first, intervention through covert means in Chile from 1970 to 1973, demonstrates the impact on U.S. tactical debates of varying degrees of the dependent image. The second case involved U.S. economic coercion in response to Peruvian actions between 1968 and 1971. This case demonstrates that there was a distinct difference in tactics when a dependent "misbehaved" but was not associated with the enemy. Moreover, the case indicates that the country's dependent image, rather than its ideology, was the determining factor in U.S. policy and tactics.

CHILE, 1970–1973

There are important similarities and differences among the U.S. interventions in Chile, Guatemala, and Cuba. Like the others, Chile's economy was heavily dependent upon the U.S. market. Its copper exports were Chile's most important source of income, and its copper industry was dominated by U.S.-based multinational corporations. The United States saw Chile in a very favorable but patronizing light as an example of the success of the Alliance for Progress goals of gradual economic reform and political democracy, U.S.-style. The United States in fact interfered in Chile's 1964 presidential election, funneling money into Eduardo Frei's campaign. The United States also supplied aid to Chile under Frei. In general, U.S. aid, the CIA's intimate knowledge of the political system, close ties between the United States and Chilean political figures such as Frei, and the importance of the U.S. market for Chilean copper gave the United States leverage in Chile.

The Chilean political system was different from those in Cuba and Guatemala. Chile had had a constitutional, parliamentary, democracy since the 1930s, with many competing parties forming shifting alliances. Although Chileans were poor and the country was in desperate need of economic reforms (particularly in the agrarian sector) and a more equal distribution of income, it was not a country emerging from years of dictatorship, as Guatemala and Cuba were.

A perceptual pattern similar to that toward Guatemala and Cuba can be seen in U.S. policy makers' view of Chilean President Salvador Allende Gossens (1970–1973). Allende was a Marxist who had had a long career as a parliamentarian in Chilean politics before being elected to the presidency in 1969. Allende's program included the continuation of initiated by Frei, but in some areas his policies promised to go farther. He promised to follow the *vía Chilena* (the Chilean path) to socialism. He was determined to take control of the copper industry (a process begun during Frei's Chileanization program for copper) as well as to undertake major agrarian reform programs, the nationalization of the banking industry, and social welfare programs.

The Nixon administration never saw Allende as a devotee of constitutional or electoral politics. There were actually two views of Allende within the Nixon administration, one of which ultimately became the prevailing one. The first image, held by top-level policy makers, including Richard Nixon and Henry Kissinger, saw the Chilean political system as only slightly more complex than those in Guatemala and Cuba in earlier cases. Chile was not exactly the stereotypical banana republic, but it was seen as unimportant and inferior. The contempt for and simplification of Chile is reflected in the Chilean ambassador's account of Kissinger's remarks to him: "Mr. Minister, you made a strange speech. You come here speaking of Latin America, but this is not important. Nothing important can come from the South. History has never been produced in the South. The axis of history starts in Moscow, goes to Bonn, crosses over to Washington, and then goes to Tokyo. What happens in the South is of no importance."[1] The Nixon administration viewed Chile as a "child" (p. 263), and Allende as a communist and an agent of the USSR. Kissinger spoke to the press in September 1970:

> The election in Chile brought about a result in which the man backed by the Communists and probably a Communist himself, had the largest number of votes.
>
> The two non-Communist parties between them had, of course, 64 percent of the votes, so there is a non-Communist majority, but a Communist plurality. I say that just to get the picture straight.
>
> According to the Chilean election law, when nobody gets a majority, the two highest candidates go to the Congress. Congress then votes in a secret ballot and elects the President. . . .

In Chilean history there is nothing to prevent it, and it would not be at all illogical for the Congress there to say, "Sixty-four per cent of the people did not want a Communist government. A Communist government tends to be irreversible. Therefore, we are going to vote for the no. 2 man."[2]

Kissinger was convinced that, after Allende's election, Chile would never have another election (the irony here is overwhelming). Allende's career as a parliamentarian, his hostile relations with the Chilean Communist party, and his actual policies were not carefully evaluated. Instead, the U.S. analysis of U.S.-Chilean relations was undertaken on the basis of the image of Allende, as the head of a dependent country, leading that country to the USSR.

A second group of U.S. officials appear to have had a more complex view of the political system and the people of Chile but shared Kissinger's assessment of Allende. This group, including Ambassador Edward Korry and the CIA, categorized Chile in the dependent image but not at the prototypical extreme. The key difference in perception, in contrast to Kissinger's perception, was that they saw the Chilean people as somewhat sophisticated. There was less cultural contempt and more recognition of the sophistication of the political system. Korry reflected this image in a talk with William Buckley: "[Chile was] the freest democracy in South America, a democracy which was of a totally different profile than any other country in Latin America. Ninety percent of all Chileans are literate, were literate. Eighty five percent of those eligible voted in elections, which is better than in this country. Seventy percent of them were urban, very few landholders. There were practically no great fortunes in the sense that you had them in Peru or Colombia. . . . You had a huge middle class in Chile. You had social democracy."[3]

In other words, Chileans were like Americans. The complexity of the political system in Chile, with its many parties and its tradition of shifting alliances among those parties, was understood by the CIA. That agency had had years of experience with that system, beginning with its involvement in Frei's election in 1964. It had maintained contacts and influence in Chile throughout the 1960s. The CIA was interested in using that knowledge to try to prevent Allende from attaining office in 1969. That knowledge also led them to suspect that a coup—which Nixon and Kissinger hoped for to keep Allende out of office in 1970—would fail. However, this group tended to have the same simplified view of Allende that Nixon and Kissinger had.

Only one sector of the government, primarily officials in the State Department, had a very different view of Allende and Chile. They argued that the Chilean political system would not be subverted by Allende and that any interference in his election should be opposed.[4] This position was put forth during 1969 and 1970 but lost the policy debate in March 1970, after which the prevailing view was that of Nixon and Kissinger, the most simplified and dependent-under-hostile-influence image.

Allende was seen as very threatening by both Kissinger and Nixon. They feared that his election would result in communism in Chile that would then spread throughout the rest of Latin America. Peru, Argentina, and Bolivia were seen as likely targets.[5] Kissinger and Nixon were determined to prevent the USSR from increasing its influence and its number of allies in the Western Hemisphere. The Senate report on U.S. intervention in Chile notes, for example, that the "40 Committee decisions regarding Chile reflected greater concern about the internal and international consequences of an Allende government that was reflected in the intelligence estimates. At the same time as the Chile NIEs were becoming less shrill, the 40 Committee authorized greater amounts of money."[6]

U.S. intervention in Chile took place in three phases. The complexity of the plans varied with the complexity of their creators' images of Chile. The first intervention took place between March and September 1970 and was designed to prevent Allende from attaining the presidency. It was promoted by Ambassador Korry and the CIA in March 1969 and approved by the 40 Committee. Since the CIA understood that Chileans would have to be subtly influenced through a program of opinion manipulation, it cautioned that, rather than support of an alternative to Allende, an anti-Allende spoiling campaign would be the best bet. This project failed, and Allende received a plurality of the vote in September 1970.

Because no presidential candidate received a majority of the vote, the Chilean Congress was obligated to choose one of the top two candidates for president. These candidates were Allende, who had the most votes, and Jorge Alessandri, the most conservative candidate, who had come in second. Traditionally, in these cases the Congress would select the candidate with the largest vote, which meant that Allende was likely to be the next president. Long hours of negotiation took place as the Chilean Congress sought guarantees from Allende that he would uphold Chile's constitution.

The constitutional requirement that Congress select the president gave the United States another opportunity to keep Allende out of the presidency. The next phase of U.S. intervention took place during September and October 1970, as the Chilean Congress made its decision. Threat perception in the Nixon administration appears to have been high, and the intervention reflects both a determination to prevent Allende from taking office and an urgency in doing so. Two tracks were devised: Track 1 was under the direction of the CIA, which understood the system well enough to know how to manipulate it. They knew who to see and had access to the Chilean media to help spread the sense of threat. Propaganda was used to convince the Chilean Congress that Allende would destroy the country.[7] The CIA supported Alessandri, hoping to persuade Congress to elect him instead of Allende. The CIA also tried to convince former president Frei to agree to a plan wherein Alessandri would be selected by Congress and then would resign, allowing Frei to run again for office (Chilean presidents could not succeed themselves). Frei refused to go along with the plot. The simplified nature of the U.S. view had led U.S. policy makers to conclude that the Chilean elite could be convinced that Allende threatened Chile and that they should violate their constitution by participating in a plot to put Frei back in office. Not surprisingly, this plan did not appeal to those who had competed with Allende and other radicals for decades through electoral politics, since it was based on a sense of threat that was not shared by these Chileans.

Track 2 of the anti-Allende policy was much simpler and reflected the pure dependent image of its authors, Richard Nixon and Henry Kissinger. On September 15, 1970, Nixon ordered the CIA to make contact with the Chilean military in search of officers willing to participate in a coup to prevent Allende from taking office. This was to be top secret—neither the 40 Committee nor Ambassador Korry were to be informed of the plot. The CIA was ordered to "make the [Chilean] economy scream."[8] Nixon and Kissinger were unconcerned about CIA warnings that a coup was both unlikely and posed risks. According to Henry Hecksher, CIA chief in Chile, Nixon and Kissinger were "not too interested in continuously being told by me that certain proposals which had been made could not be executed or would be counterproductive" (p. 282).

It is important to emphasize the difference between those cognizant of the complexities of the Chilean political system and those who were not. CIA operatives may have been affected by time pressures and a sense of threat, but they knew whom to try to influence and how to do it. Nixon and Kissinger, on the other hand, had the simplified notion that a coup would occur. The fact that Chile had a long history of devotion to constitutional practices and that the Chilean military had not overthrown a government in forty years was not important. It is likely that the Latin American context had an effect here, as well: if one already has a simplified image of Latin American countries, one may well adhere to the stereotypical notion that coups occur regularly in cases of political conflict in Latin America. The refusal to listen to discrepant information can also be seen as a result of both an extreme image and mounting threat perceptions.

Track 2 was a bad plan and had bad results. The CIA did find a couple of generals willing to stage a coup, one of whom was retired. The coup plot collapsed after a constitutionalist general, Rene Schneider, was murdered. The result was not only the end of Track 2 but also of all CIA "assets" in the Chilean military. It took the agency nearly a year to rebuild contacts.

Once Allende was in office, the Nixon administration did its utmost to get rid of him, using multiple coercive instruments. Overt economic pressures in the form of aid cuts (except to the Chilean military) were very damaging to Chile's economy. The covert portion of the intervention continued as the CIA supported opposition parties, undermined Allende's political coalition, spread propaganda through the opposition media (which it also supported financially), and restored its contacts with the Chilean military, waiting for some officers interested in overthrowing Allende to emerge.

This case illustrates the propensity to use exceptionally coercive instruments in intervening in a country perceived as a dependent under (or about to go under) the influence of an enemy. There was no interest in dealing with Allende diplomatically; he was regarded as very threatening, and the need to dispose of him was not questioned. Further, the sense of threat appears to have influenced the quality of the CIA's decision making, the illustration being Track 1. Threat in conjunction with the more extreme image held by Nixon and Kissinger produced Track 2. Track 2 also illustrates the perception of U.S. power and leverage as overwhelming, an overestimation at best. A coup was impossible in 1970. It took three years before the Nixon administration finally got its wish.

PERU, 1968–1971

The Peruvian case was more subtle than Chile's. The dependent image dictated the choice of tactics; disagreements between individuals holding differing degrees of the dependent image centered on the choice of intervention instruments.

On October 4, 1968, a left-leaning, intensely nationalistic group of Peruvian military officers led by General Juan Velasco Alvarado overthrew the elected government of President Fernando Belaúnde Terry. Although the coup had been planned for some time, the precipitating events—and a major cause of the planned coup in the long run—concerned an agreement between the Belaúnde administration and the International Petroleum Company (IPC). The new regime was determined to take Peru down a revolutionary path that would develop the country economically, eradicate the power of the traditional oligarchy and multinational corporations, and institute a system of socioeconomic justice for the average poverty-stricken Peruvian. The military governors accepted some socialist ideas and frequently accused the United States of imperialist exploitation of Peru, but they declared that they were neither communist nor capitalist and would pursue a "third path" to Peru's future.

One of the first acts of the revolutionary government was the nationalization of the properties of the IPC, which had been in Peru since 1913 and had historically acted as the stereotypical exploiting multinational corporation. It had been accused of bribing and corrupting Peruvian officials, promoting coups, breaking laws, committing fraud, and depriving the country of millions of dollars through exploitive and illegal acts. The IPC's power in Peruvian politics and economics was in fact substantial and resembled the kind of influence that the classic exploiting multinational is reputed to have. The company was a wholly owned subsidiary of Standard Oil of New Jersey (now Exxon). It dominated the Peruvian oil industry for many years and even owned subsoil rights to a field called La Brea y Pariñas, which gave the firm control of the oil under the ground. This type of agreement hearkens back to the era of big stick imperialism and of corporations so powerful that they controlled entire governments. It was difficult for Peruvians to accept, and conflict between the IPC and the Belaúnde administration had been ongoing since the first days of that administration in 1963.

Belaúnde's approach to the IPC had been to refuse to discuss any issues with the firm until it gave up its rights to La Brea, but the IPC refused to give up these rights until other areas of disagreement were considered. This dispute put Belaúnde under great pressure, since he had made a campaign promise to resolve the controversy within three months of assuming the presidency. Five years later the dispute remained unresolved, and in 1967 the Peruvian Congress simply took nominal control of the La Brea fields. In 1968 an agreement, the Act of Talara, was reached with the company whereby Peru was granted the subsoil rights in exchange for the cancelation of IPC's tax bill of $144 million. However, shortly after the agreement was reached, scandal broke out. Loret de Mola, the Peruvian negotiator and signatory, announced that the agreement he had signed had eleven pages, while the IPC claimed the agreement had only ten pages. On that infamous missing page 11 de Mola had written a guaranteed price the state would be paid for oil. The crisis that erupted produced the coup of October 4, which brought Velasco to power.

The first act of the new military government was to nullify the Act of Talara and occupy La Brea and IPC's refinery in the nearby town of Talara. The Peruvian government then had to decide whether to compensate the IPC for the expropriated properties. The expropriation of IPC's property set off a six-month countdown to the invocation of the Hickenlooper Amendment, which had given Peru six months to compensate the IPC adequately or face the loss of aid from the United States and sales of Peru's sugar to the United States. In all, Peru faced an annual loss of around $25 million in aid and profits from sugar sales that were $59 million in 1968. The Hickenlooper Amendment would also cost Peru access to funds from the Export-Import Bank and the International Bank for Reconstruction and Development. The total dollar cost to Peru would be around $180 million.[9] Technically, the president of the United States was obligated to invoke the Hickenlooper Amendment by April 9, 1969, unless steps were taken to ensure adequate compensation. The U.S. response to these and other acts by the revolutionary military government of Peru is the focus of this case study. (I could easily begin the examination of U.S. intervention in Peru during the conflict between the Belaúnde administration and the IPC, since the United States followed similar policies throughout these years. But the perceptual aspects of the U.S. approach to the Velasco military regime are particularly interesting.)

The prevailing U.S. image of Peru was the dependent image. Traditionally, U.S. embassy officials used their position to influence Peruvian governments to treat U.S. business interests favorably. This is not to say that U.S.-Peruvian relations were dominated by a cabal of embassy and multinational corporation power brokers. In fact, by the 1960s many U.S.-based investors in Peru had little interest in using the U.S. government as a source of protection and preferred to deal with the Peruvian government on a bilateral basis. They frequently recognized the need to contribute something to the Peruvian economy and to keep their hands clean in legal matters. Others, notably the IPC, maintained the traditional view, and there is evidence that many officials in the U.S. embassy shared the dependent image of Peru during the 1960s. Peruvians certainly perceived a close bond between the embassy and the IPC, at one time even referring to the U.S. ambassador as "Mr. IPC."

Verbal evidence of the operative image is not easy to come by for this case. High-level U.S. policy makers did not discuss Peru often for the public record either before or after the 1968 coup. But the U.S.

pattern before the 1968 coup reflected the standard dependent image. For example, the United States cut Alliance for Progress aid to Peru in 1964 and 1965 in an effort to push Belaúnde to settle his conflict with the IPC, despite the fact that neither law nor foreign policy required the United States to do so.[10] Further, the IPC had not asked the United States for this assistance, and the United States did not attempt to get the IPC to make concessions in the interest of promoting a settlement. The United States also used economic coercion rather than negotiation when the Peruvian government tried in 1967 to purchase supersonic jet fighters. The United States refused to sell Peru the jets, explaining that it "just didn't think the Latins were ready for supersonics."[11] When Peru went to France for the jets, the United States punished Peru by reversing approval for loans for 1967 and 1968.

While these examples demonstrate the pattern of behavior associated with the dependent image—ordering rather than negotiating, using coercive instruments when none are called for, and expressing contempt for the dependent's people—other examples come from the interaction between the U.S. embassy and the IPC. As mentioned, IPC officials appeared to have held a dependent image of Peru: the company refused to give up its subsoil rights despite the fact that these rights were hated throughout Latin America and that the IPC was one of the last companies on the continent to retain such privileges. The corporation's behavior was said to be high-handed and arrogant. According to one lawyer who approached the company for his client, the company refused to negotiate, saying "This is the way it is" (ibid., p. 56).

> Even many officers of other substantial American businesses grumble privately about I.P.C. and claim that its conduct has endangered all foreign investment in Peru. "They got what was coming to them," one American businessman, while another, with a genius for understatement, said, "They had bad public relations" (ibid.).

More interesting is the evidence that at least some important members of the U.S. embassy accepted IPC's view of the conflict with Peru—and probably of Peru as well. The embassy relied solely upon the IPC for information about economic interactions between the company and Peru. One official called IPC's 1968 offer, the one that preceded the coup, "incredibly generous" and could not see what the IPC got out of it. In fact, the IPC had agreed only to provisions that would have dragged its relation with the government into the modern era, and it in turn would have received major concessions on taxes. More important, the embassy completely backed IPC's position on the infamous missing page 11. U.S. officials argued that Loret de Mola lied about the existence of page 11. U.S. officials did not launch an independent inquiry into the matter. Richard Goodwin's "Letter from Peru" contains the following conversation with an embassy official:

> When asked what happened to the original [agreement document], an Embassy official first responded that "there was no original." When it was pointed out that even Xerox's marvelous technology had not developed to this extent, he said that the original was too messy. But making a page neater while copying it is another feat that Xerox has not yet accomplished. If there were only ten pages, why didn't Loret de Mola sign at the bottom of the tenth page? "There was no room," it was explained. Yet one only had to glance at the page to see that there was plenty of room for an additional signature. None of this proves anything about "page 11," but perhaps it does illustrate some of the attitudes that have led many Peruvians to believe that the American Embassy is a faithful representative of Standard Oil (ibid., p. 84).

After the coup there was a gradual change in the image of Peru in the State Department and possibly the embassy, but that change was one of degree rather than category. The initial evaluation of the new regime was that it was another self-serving military government. Rather than understanding the power of growing Peruvian anger with the IPC and the genuinely different nature of the officers who took over, U.S. officials described the officers' motives "as 'political' . . . and their methods . . . as lying or demagogic" (ibid., p. 101). The official U.S. reaction to the coup was to suspend diplomatic relations and place aid programs under review, pending Peru's decision concerning compensating the IPC.

The coup and the expropriation took place during the last October of the Johnson administration. U.S. officials made few decisions concerning Peru while awaiting the transition to the Nixon administration. The outgoing administration officially "deplored" the coup, announced that aid would be terminated unless the IPC was compensated, and waited to recognize the new government until other members of the OAS had done so. Newspaper reports from those months indicate that there was a new U.S. assessment of the military government: rather than military strongmen, this government was seen as more technocratic and nationalistic. Latin American nationalism was still regarded with cynicism by U.S. officials. Some argued that the military was using the IPC as a tool for whipping up anti-U.S. sentiments in Peru.[12]

The U.S. image of the new government was essentially as a military government, a familiar creature in the Latin American context. U.S. policy makers announced they would make their decision on recognition "under the provisions of the Rio de Janeiro Declaration of 1965 covering a military takeover."[13] Although some officials (not all, as will be seen) were increasingly sensitive to Peruvian nationalism, the "American imperialism" rhetoric apparently was not seen as threatening. The Peruvian government was compared to that in Argentina and was called "Nasserist" (ibid.). Most important, Peru's independent foreign policy caused no concern to U.S. policy makers at this time. Peru recognized the Soviet Union, and within three weeks settled a trade agreement with the USSR. This did not disturb U.S. policy makers, who repeated that what really worried them was the IPC case.[14] This is an important perceptual characteristic and demonstrates the power of categorization. Here was a government that was explicitly antiimperialist and that accused the United States of being the world's biggest imperialist, announced it would socialize some sectors of the economy, nationalized a U.S. corporation without compensation, and opened relations with the Soviet Union. It eventually created committees to defend the revolution, modeled on similar organizations in Cuba, an action noted by U.S. officials but one that raised no particular concern.

Apparently the military attribute was so overwhelmingly important to U.S. policy makers that it prevented them from shifting to a dependent-under-hostile-influence image. The Latin American context may have been highly important in facilitating this perceptual process. U.S. policy makers were certainly familiar with Latin American military regimes and had experienced them as corrupt, right-wing, and antidemocratic, not nationalistic or left-leaning. This in no way reflected a U.S. shift in policy or in its perception of the Soviet Union's motives or those of its dependents. Cuba was still a bête noire. And within six months plans were in place to prevent Allende from attaining the presidency of Chile. Further, after Allende was elected, the White House expressed a fear that Chile would "go communist" and that this would spill into Peru.[15]

This continuation and modification of the dependent image of Peru was doubtless facilitated by the Peruvian leadership's insistence that they had no intention of making Peru a communist country. In addition, forty U.S. military advisers were stationed in Peru, and the CIA helped the Peruvian military eradicate a guerrilla movement in 1965. Had the perceptual readiness existed, there would have been plenty of "evidence" for U.S. officials to conclude that Peru was a dependent moving into the Soviet camp. They did not make that perceptual shift.

On October 9, 1968, the new military government of Peru expropriated IPC's property and began a conflict with the corporation that escalated into hostility. Within weeks, the government announced that the IPC owed it $690.5 million in payment for its life-long illegal profits. The IPC claimed that the Peruvian government owed it $120 million for the expropriated properties. The United States followed a consistent policy of trying to force Peru to compensate the IPC. There was debate only about how much leverage the United States had and how that it should be used. Johnson administration officials chose not to react strongly to the expropriation. It informed Peru's new government that the Hickenlooper Amendment would go into effect in six months. The U.S. terminated all preferential treatment for Peru (long before such actions were required by law) and cut off Peru's access to international financial institutions.[16] The State Department did not object to these reprisals, but it also did not announce that Peru would suffer such economic reprisals if compensation was not forthcoming.

The Nixon administration was uninterested in Peru. Months passed before Nixon nominated an assistant secretary for Latin America. A Nixon administration ambassador to Peru was not in office until August 1969, despite worsening U.S.-Peruvian relations caused by the compensation issue and by a new conflict, Peruvian seizures of U.S. tuna fishing vessels off the Peruvian coast. The initial policy debate took place among a number of individuals from the State Department and the National Security Council, who were often in transit from one post or position to another; these included Acting Assistant Secretary of State Vyron Vaky, who became Kissinger's adviser on Latin America, William Stedman, country director for Ecuador and Peru, and Arnold Nachmanoff, Vaky's assistant in the NSC (ibid., pp. 30–31). In addition, Congress was periodically interested in Peru, and the Treasury Department occasionally got involved in U.S.-Peruvian relations, as well.

Initially, the Nixon administration took a hard-line position on the IPC controversy, announcing that sanctions would be imposed unless compensation was forthcoming. Peru's reaction was equally strong, accusing the United States of economic aggression. By March 1969, however, concern about the impact of the invocation of the Hickenlooper Amendment on U.S.–Latin American relations in general had increased. Although on March 4 Nixon threatened to reduce Peru's sugar quota coming into the United States and invoked the Hickenlooper Amendment, he also appointed a special emissary, John Irwin, to go to Peru to negotiate a solution to the IPC problem.[17] Irwin actually accomplished very little in his negotiations with Peru, but he did provide the administration with a vehicle for deferring invocation of the Hickenlooper provisions. In late March, Peru placed $71 million in a frozen bank account for payment to the IPC once the company had paid its debt to Peru (which the IPC denied it owed). When the deadline approached, Irwin conferred with Nixon, who then announced that the IPC still had the recourse of an "administrative appeal" in Peru, which released the United States from the immediate obligation of invoking Hickenlooper. Not surprisingly, the fact that the IPC would undoubtedly lose that appeal was not mentioned.

Although a number of conflicts erupted between the United States and Peru during the next three years, the activities of the Nixon administration between January and April 1969 typify the approach to a dependent. From the appointment of the special emissary onward, the United States followed a two-pronged strategy of economic pressure and (essentially symbolic) diplomatic maneuvers to deal with Peru's expropriation. The problems that the administration sought to resolve with that approach were threefold. First, it wanted to change Peru's policy; second, it wanted to prevent Congress from forcing the invocation of the Hickenlooper Amendment (hence the tough talk and the acceptance of symbolic but empty diplomatic achievements); and third, it wanted to prevent the conflict with Peru from inflaming Latin American hostility toward the United States.[18]

The issue for the administration was not whether to apply sanctions but how to apply them. By not invoking the Hickenlooper Amendment, the administration had more flexibility in applying sanctions. As it was, the United States followed "the spirit if not the letter of the Hickenlooper Amendment."[19] New bilateral assistance was terminated by the Agency for International Development, although aid already approved was not halted. The World Bank provided nothing for Peru, and Inter-American Development Bank resources came only from funds in which the United States did not hold a veto. The sugar quota was not cut. Military sales to Peru were terminated in February 1969, under the auspices of the Pelly Amendment, which stipulates that no military sales may be made to countries that seize U.S. fishing vessels. The administration appeared to believe that the sanctions would be sufficient to force concessions.[20] In other words, it sought to use U.S. economic power rather than diplomacy to force a solution. Peru continued to refuse to compensate the IPC until its taxes were paid. Moreover, when in May 1969 it was publicly revealed that the United States had terminated military sales to Peru the previous February, Peru disinvited New York Governor Nelson Rockefeller, who was scheduled to stop in

Peru during his Latin American fact-finding trip for Nixon. They also expelled the U.S. military mission from Peru.

Two questions arise from this case. First, was there a perceptual difference between those who favored strong overt sanctions as opposed to soft, nonovert sanctions (the policy that was followed)? Second, why did Nixon go along with this policy of subtle intervention? In cases with a dependent and no enemy, one would expect intervention, but one that involved undramatic instruments, such as economic sanctions, without a strong sense of threat or a concern about a quick solution. This is what happened in Peru. However, my theoretical argument leads us to expect that disputes about instruments and their implementation may be attributable to bureaucratic as well as perceptual origins. That argument also seems to hold in this particular case.

For one thing, those who favored strong sanctions appear to have had a more prototypical dependent image of Peru. These individuals, such as Stedman, Secretary of State William Rogers, and members of the embassy staff, focused on the military nature of the Peruvian government. They were committed to the Alliance for Progress dream of promoting democratic governments in Latin America and were hostile to and condescending toward Peru's military government (ibid., p. 60). They were insensitive to Peruvian nationalism and to the nationalistic nature of its government. But this position was tempered by bureaucratic roles: Stedman, for example, refrained from advocating the formal invocation of the Hickenlooper Amendment, although he continued to promote strong economic sanctions even though his bureaucratic superiors preferred the softer approach. [21]

The faction favoring soft sanctions had a slightly more complex image of the Peruvian government. Rather than seeing this as another bunch of strongmen, Vaky and Nachmanoff of the NSC were sensitive to the regime's nationalism and "were persuaded that the Peruvian military experiment might, in fact, be devoted to reform and not just another opportunistic Latin American coup" (ibid., p. 61). They were also inclined to view Peru in a larger policy arena, in that they were concerned about the impact of U.S. policy toward Peru on U.S. relations with other Latin American countries. This can be attributed in part to their role as advisers from the NSC, where a more panoramic view is required.

There is some evidence that these variations in the dependent image of Peru produced different evaluations of U.S. strength in dealing with Peru. State Department officials in the Inter-American Affairs Bureau usually had the more complex, or modified, dependent image. They argued that reacting to expropriation by threatening sanctions needlessly restricted U.S. maneuverability and, in any case, assumed that the United States had leverage it did not have. Others, including incoming Secretary of Treasury John Connally and President Nixon, believed that the threat of sanctions should be a long-term, ongoing policy position (ibid., p. 93).

The evidence indicates that there was a correlation between degree of dependent image and instrument preference. An important related question is why Richard Nixon and Henry Kissinger, whose image of Latin America appears to have been the extreme dependent, went along with the policy group that advocated the soft option. Several points answer the question. First, given their image of Latin America, neither were likely to pay any attention to Peru when more important countries and issues were on the agenda. Peru was a problem inherited from the Johnson administration, and the Nixon group came into office with their attention directed to the war in Vietnam, to the Soviet Union, and to arms control. Second, Peru did not involve a Soviet threat, making U.S. goals in this case bilateral and regional but not global. This made it possible for the soft options group to sell their position by "talking tough." Third, no one advocated taking *no* action against Peru; hence, the question of instrument usage was more easily resolved by bureaucratic jockeying. And in 1969, the NSC, which favored the soft option, held the dominant bureaucratic position; its officials formulated policy options and presented them to their superiors, Nixon and Kissinger.

After January 1971, the bureaucratic momentum shifted to the Treasury Department, when John Connally took over as secretary. Connally had close ties with Nixon, and they agreed on the need to take a strong stand against uncompensated expropriation and to deny aid funds to countries that did not provide a good climate for private foreign investment. The United States then became more hard-line on loan issues, refusing to approve loans by international lending institutions "unless there was some clear signal that progress toward a solution on IPC was being made" (ibid., p. 82).

Peru illustrates the impact of the dependent image in a benign, relatively nonthreatening context. As expected, the U.S. propensity was to intervene without the perceived need for a quick solution. Instruments were slow acting, and the major debate concerned how to intervene, not whether to.

CONCLUSION

A comparison of the interventions in Chile and Peru provides an opportunity to address a central question: What difference did the presence of an enemy make? The answer is, with an enemy, instruments were selected that promised a quick solution; without an enemy, slow-acting instruments were preferred. These cases also demonstrate that, with an enemy, global goals were paramount; without an enemy, regional and bilateral goals got attention. The absence of an enemy also opened the door for bureaucratic infighting and competition and tougher debate on specific tactics.

One of the most striking patterns in the Chilean and Peruvian cases concerns the impact of images on the use of information. In Chile, the combined images of a dependent and an enemy blinded the United States to the complexities of the Chilean political system and the ample evidence that Salvador Allende was not, and would not become, an agent of the Soviet Union. In the Peruvian case, the leftist characteristics of the regime caused no alarm. Moreover, Peru's opening relations with the Soviet Union was not taken as an indicator that the Peruvian regime would provide the Soviets with another opportunity in the hemisphere. This difference between the two cases is even more important when one considers that they both took place during the Nixon presidency. One can ask not only what difference an enemy made but when an enemy was likely to be perceived.

Two cases provide only an opportunity to speculate about this final question. The prevailing image of both countries was the dependent, but a crucial difference in perception occurred because of a military government in one case and a democratic government in the other. It is possible that the military government fit the prototypical dependent image better—meaning that Peru fit the category best. Still, that would not explain why one leftist government was seen as pro-Soviet while the other was not. Perhaps the assumption of incompetence was so powerful in the dependent image that any country categorized as dependent that adopted democratic political procedures was seen as inherently unstable and susceptible to the evil machinations of the enemy.

It is also possible that the dependent image had regional variations. Military governments were so commonly associated with Latin America and with U.S. allies in the region that any military Latin American government was assumed to be securely pro-United States. If so, then the pattern of information processing may be different in other Third World regions, where the prototype of a dependent government does not have the military characteristic.

4

CRACKS IN THE COLD WAR
WORLDVIEW

THE EARLY 1970s WAS THOUGHT OF AS THE ERA OF DÉTENTE, AN ERA THAT ended, more or less, with the Soviet invasion of Afghanistan. Perceptually, détent resembled the earlier days of the cold war, in that the Soviets were still perceived as the enemy, albeit not necessarily the prototypical enemy. For a small group of U.S. policy makers, the Soviet Union was no longer even eligible for the enemy image. And although the Third World was still classified as dependent by many, some people saw Third World countries differently. The neutral image was largely a perceptual outcome of the political rise of the South.

The Carter administration's approach to two policy problems in Latin America illustrates the impact of these images as well as that of the minority worldview that slowly emerged, wherein the USSR and Latin American countries were increasingly perceived as complex. This chapter explores the perceptual groupings within the Carter administration and the effect of those perceptions on Carter's approach to the Nicaraguan revolution and the civil war in El Salvador.

THE CARTER ADMINISTRATION:
THREE WORLDVIEWS

It is commonly argued that the Carter administration was beset by conflict between human rights advocates, who called for a global policy of support for human rights before all other concerns (including national security), and national security advocates, who preferred the traditional policy of containment. Perceptually, however, the Carter administration is better understood as torn by disagreements among three perceptual groups rather than two: traditional cold warriors, modified cold warriors, and, for lack of a better name, the human rights group. The perceptions of these groups explain their policy and tactical preferences.

TRADITIONAL COLD WARRIORS

By the mid-1970s the language the United States used to describe Latin American countries had changed considerably. One rarely finds public statements describing Latin American countries as banana republics, and most people gave at least a polite nod to the role of social and economic inequities as a source of instability in Latin America. Nevertheless, many individuals still placed Latin America in the dependent category and perceived the Soviet Union as the classic enemy. They were present in the political arena during the Carter years, and some Carter officials shared their worldview. Its articulation in the context of U.S.–Latin American relations rose in decibels during the Panama canal treaty debates and continued throughout the Nicaraguan and Salvadoran crises. The group included members of Congress (Representatives John Murphy, Larry McDonald, Charles Wilson, and Kiki de la Garza, and Senator Jesse Helms, among others) as well as officials in the administration (for example, Zbigniew Brzezinski, Harold Brown, Frank Devine, and Walter Stoessel, Jr.).

The group can be distinguished in terms of several perceptual characteristics. First, they believed that the causes of regional instability included both internal inequalities and external subversion, but the emphasis was on the latter. Second, human rights advocates were seen as either naive dupes of the left or suspicious individuals using the cause of human rights as a screen to pursue their own, possibly traitorous, purposes. Third, Central American rightists were considered to be U.S. friends and leftists to be agents of the USSR or Cuba—as well as the perpetrators of most of the violence. The polities of Central America were vastly simplified, with divisions seen between left and right. A political center was seen as the force that the United States should promote; if it did not exist, the United States should create it. The center would then hold elections, producing democratic forms of government similar to that in the United States. Fourth, the USSR and Cuba were taking advantage of the chaos in Central America, aided by advocates of human rights. Fifth, Central America bore no similarities to Vietnam. Sixth, the United States had the capability and responsibility to defeat the left in Central America through economic and military aid and the proper guidance of Central American regimes who looked to the United States for aid and leadership. Nationalism was not recognized as

a potent force, nor was it a factor that U.S. policy needed to accommo-
date. Anti-Americanism was attributed to leftist subversive propaganda.

Examples of these particular perceptual characteristics are evident
among critics of the Carter administration as well as among members of
that administration.[1] The memoirs of Carter's first ambassador to El
Salvador, Frank Devine, provide an illustration. He describes three left-
wing guerrilla groups in El Salvador—the Popular Liberation Forces
(FPL), the Peoples Revolutionary Army (ERP), and the Armed Forces
of National Resistance (FARN)—as terrorist organizations. They dominated several popular organizations that acted as fronts. Members of the
popular organizations were in many cases duped by these devious terror-
ists. "At least some, perhaps many, of the members of the popular
organizations were relatively innocent demonstrators engaged merely in
legitimate public protest or demands for a better way of life. . . . [This]
tended to impart to them something of the character of cannon fodder at
the disposition of the three Marxist Leninist terrorist groups" (p. 24).
The Marxist guerrillas were thus able to control the peasants and workers belonging to popular organizations.

Devine describe the left as a small conspiratorial group directly or
indirectly responsible for the horrendous violence of the right: "Numerous factors pushed the nation toward violent resolution of its problems
and relatively few forces worked for restraint." But when it came to
specifying who did what, the left was the force opposed to peaceful
dialogue and negotiation: "In this situation, our Embassy regularly tried
to function as something of an honest broker. We urged reconciliation,
but had little success. The political Right was a willing audience, and
upon occasion we were able to persuade its leaders toward a construc-
tive course of action or head off some of their more violent instincts.
The moderate Left was also always open to dialogue with us. But with
the extreme Left and their popular organizations we found next to no
receptivity" (ibid., p. 193). There is no evidence that Devine considered nationalism, antiimperialism, or poverty as explanations for the
left's activity. Instead revolution was simply attributed to Marxist-
Leninist ideology.

If Devine saw the left as agents of the USSR, his view of the right
wing, the traditional oligarchy, was highly patronizing. The wealthy
elite were "a class of people who had always been good friends of the
United States" (ibid., p. 24). Devine clearly sympathized with them as
their luxurious life-styles were threatened. Peasants were described as
miserably poor but as having a "surprisingly high level of tolerance for
an impressively low level of standard of living." He notes, however, that

the peasants were becoming restless due to human rights advocates, the Catholic church and liberation theology, and "communist agitators and other subversive groups [who] sensed that this might in fact be the soft underbelly of the system, which they wished to overturn" (p. 25). He sees violence as endemic in El Salvador, the result of cultural characteristics more than of the efforts of the traditional elite to prevent change, in spite of the fact that information was easily available that the violence was primarily perpetrated by security forces, not the left. Devine describes the government's role in El Salvador's violence as either an understandable response to threat or as something that Salvadorans simply did. "Looking back, I suspect that prospects for meaningful political dialogue were probably never very good during this period. Political passions ran too deeply, polarization had progressed too far, the level of political sophistication was not sufficiently advanced, and the undercurrent of violence ran dangerously close to the surface in all strata of society" (p. 110).

Finally, he describes human rights advocates as arrogant, very powerful, insensitive to the political traditions and needs of El Salvador, and rude and undiplomatic. They were directly responsible for instability in El Salvador: "The overall system in El Salvador was too imbedded in a way of violence to permit any easy change. The inequities built into the system were too deep and long-standing to be altered in any immediate time frame—but this was what the country's extremist reformers demanded, and in this they found powerful support from the human rights lobby in the United States" (p. 48).

The assumptions were that leftist subversion was more important than internal causes of instability, that the USSR could easily manipulate that instability and weakness to its own advantage, and that Latin American countries are plagued with "a 'banana republic' political culture, in particular a tendency to resolve disputes with violence, that facilitated instability."[2] "I went to school in the 1960's," said the State Department's desk officer for Grenada in mid-1984, "and so I've been through all the imperialism and dependency crap. This isn't what screws up Latin America. What screws up Latin America is the Latin Americans. And they'll *always* screw it up, because *they're* screwed up" (p. 127). Perceptions of the vulnerability of these countries to external subversion were also important aspects the political simplification. In 1981, Walter Stoessel, Jr., under secretary of state during the Carter administration, said:

> Our actions with regard to El Salvador are being undertaken against the background of communist-inspired interference in

the Caribbean Central American region. Our economic assistance addresses inequities which have made El Salvador vulnerable to exploitation by our adversaries.

The United States cannot stand idly by while a reformist government comes under attack by externally advised and armed guerrilla groups that lack popular support. If we fail to make clear that the external encouragement of violence and instability in El Salvador will have serious costs, we ensure that other countries seeking domestic solutions to domestic problems will find their efforts thwarted by guerrilla groups advised and armed from abroad. In turn, our failure to respond adequately to externally supported attempts to overthrow governments committed to reform and to electoral solutions would cause other friendly countries to doubt our ability to help them resist assaults on their sovereignty.[3]

Additional simplified descriptions of Central America emerge in explanations of who the United States supported and who the contending parties were. In the case of El Salvador, Stoessel described them as a left, a right, and a center. He claimed that the left and right had no popular support, whereas the center was elevated to a unified front under the leadership of José Napoleon Duarte (ibid., p. 4). This was in early 1981, when Duarte joined the military junta, his Christian Democratic party had fragmented, and the military ran the country.

The simplification of the left in Central America was profound and familiar. One hundred and twenty-five U.S. congressmen with this particular worldview called the Nicaraguan revolutionaries "Soviet surrogates" who would assist the USSR in controlling "an area bordering on two oceans stretching from Panama to the vast oil reserves of Mexico," while other senators referred to them as Marxist-Leninists who sought to impose a "Cuban-style regime in Nicaragua."[4] The political divisions within the Sandinista movement, including the vast range of differences in adherence to various aspects of Marxist thought, were ignored. Similarly, the Salvadoran opposition was thought of as dominated by pro-Soviet Marxists, while the noncommunist revolutionaries were regarded either as nonexistent or "as little more than patsies, weak leaders who could not withstand the onslaughts from disciplined Leninist cadres."[5]

When this image of a Latin American country is accompanied by an enemy image of the USSR, a particular policy prescription results. Many people in the Carter administration did have this classic enemy image of the Soviet Union—National Security Adviser Brzezinski, State Department career officers Myles Frechette, John Bushnell, and Walter

Stoessel, Jr., and many officials at the Pentagon.[6] In 1977, Carter's Secretary of Defense Harold Brown painted a classic cold war picture of the USSR:

> Perhaps we have been too much of an international busybody in the recent past. But no one can doubt that there remains much to busy us in this dynamic world.
>
> Our principle long-term problem continues to be the Soviet Union. Whether we like it or not, the Soviet leadership seems intent on challenging us to-a major military competition. . . . While many of the issues [in world politics] may be specialized or regional in nature—and may not even involve the Soviet Union to begin with—they can escalate rapidly to the super-power level unless they are contained, defused, and eventually resolved. We must . . . be concerned about them on national security grounds.[7]

For Brzezinski, also, the Soviet Union came close to the prototypical enemy extreme. He continued to believe that the Soviet Union "would like to be number one."[8] Moreover, while acknowledging the inevitability of a redistribution of global power and political change given the emergence of many new states, Brzezinski expressed fears of Soviet efforts to use military power to take advantage of instability:

> While the central military balance of the world has remained remarkably stable, its context has been complicated by the shift away from conventional conflict, usually across national borders, to unconventional conflict, usually within national borders. As a result of this development, these internal conflicts pose opportunities and temptations for external intervention. And this process, too, is far from over. . . . Military weakness on the part of the United States can create openings and temptations for our ideological opponents to exploit turbulence for their own selfish ends. . . . This is a continuing challenge.[9]

He concludes that, while the United States will consult with its regional allies, "we remain the leader and must bear the burdens of that role" (p. 48).

This image was widely shared in Congress, although its articulation tended to be less sophisticated and more conspiratorial. In 1977, Congressman Elton Rudd complained that the Carter administration was bent upon destroying U.S. friends in Latin America in the name of human rights, which he saw as a cloak for a devious effort to advance communist influence throughout the hemisphere:

> Certain State Department officials are conducting a calculated campaign of deceit and propaganda against our allied anti-Communist friends throughout Latin America.
>
> Under the banner of human rights, Assistant Secretary Derian and other Carter appointees in the State Department have mounted a concerted assault on Latin American military governments that, because of the ever-present Communist guerrilla revolutionary activity in these countries, must maintain stability and freedom by implementing certain restrictions that are not acceptable in our own country.
>
> Either the administration's officials in the State Department are hopelessly naive and misinformed about the true situation in Latin America, or they are ideologically aligned with the revolutionary elements that seek to overthrow the legitimate governments of our allies. This is a situation that cannot be tolerated, and such officials should be dismissed.[10]

Rudd also argued that the Sandinistas were conducting a "carefully orchestrated plot, instigated and supported by outsiders" to overthrow Somoza (ibid., p. 30246). Similar complaints were registered by Congressmen McDonald, Wilson, and Murphy.

Other important perceptual characteristics of this group included self-image and the impact of context on images of Central America, the USSR, and the United States. These individuals were concerned about others' image of the United States but had few doubts about the U.S. ability to control the direction of change in Latin America. They were concerned that the United States might be viewed as a "paper tiger." A group of 125 congressmen complained to Carter in 1979 that failure to support Somoza in Nicaragua "has been interpreted by the Soviet Union and Cuba as American indifference."[11] The U.S. failure to act was only a result of lack of resolve, however. The power was there; all the United States had to do was use it. The perception was of an overwhelming asymmetry between U.S. power and Latin American power, to the U.S. advantage. There were two historical analogies of importance to this group of policy advocates: Cuba, a repeat of which they desperately wanted to avoid, and Vietnam, which they insisted was not at all relevant.

In the late 1970s, this worldview confronted Central America's crises in a very complex international context. Revolution had occurred in Iran, the shah was going and then was gone, to be replaced by a fundamentalist religious government that was incomprehensible to many Americans. The United States voluntarily negotiated an end to its control of the Panama canal and dealt with repeated strains in relations with Mexico. Revolution seemed to be brewing throughout Latin America. The enemy image of the USSR and the dependent image of Latin American countries combined to produce a U.S. preference for containment or rollback. The preference should have been for policies similar to the ones used in Guatemala in 1954 and Cuba in 1960: quick-acting coercive efforts to remove the threat and to establish control over the direction of change such that change was either in the U.S. image or did not occur.

Modified Cold Warriors

While the traditional cold warrior worldview plagued the Carter administration with criticism, the prevailing worldview was that of the modified cold warriors. The difference between the two groups is one of degree rather than kind. The USSR was still seen as an enemy, and Latin American countries were still seen as dependent. The images of this worldview departed from the prototypical image. I will connect those differences with assessments of the effectiveness and the acceptability of particular policies.

Many officials who formulated and implemented Carter administration U.S. policy toward Central America were modified cold warriors. The group included Secretary of State Cyrus Vance and Deputy Secretary Warren Christopher; State Department officials such as Terence Todman, Viron Vaky, and William Bowdler; the first and second ambassadors to Nicaragua, Mauricio Solaun and Lawrence Pezzullo; as well as the second ambassador to El Salvador, Robert White. Jimmy Carter was the most important member of this group, although he was not deeply involved in daily events or in U.S. efforts in Nicaragua or El Salvador. Members of Congress with this view included Representatives Edward Koch and Clarence Long and Senator Paul Sarbanes.

Since the modified cold warrior perception of the Soviet Union was not the prototypical enemy stereotype, their perception of threat was less. But—and this is very important—they did not reject containment as a global strategy. Instead, they saw containment as appropriate in fewer situations.

This description of Carter's worldview is supported in Jerel Rosati's analysis of numerous speeches by Carter and his top aides.[12] Rosati argues that Carter had an "optimistic" view of the Soviet Union and saw it as having "limited capability to affect the environment, constrained by the complexity of the international system, and, although occasionally opportunistic, overall peaceful in its intentions" (p. 166). In May 1977, Carter explained that the international role and concerns of the United States had changed since the early post–World War II years. "Our policy during this period was guided by two principles: a belief that Soviet expansion was almost inevitable but that it must be contained, and the corresponding belief in the importance of an almost exclusive alliance among non-Communist nations on both sides of the Atlantic. That system could not last forever unchanged. Historical trends have weakened its foundations. The unifying threat of conflict with the Soviet Union has become less intensive, even though the competition has become more extensive."[13] What is important in this statement is that Carter says that the foundations of containment had been "weakened," not that they were gone, and that competition was "less intensive," not that they were over. This does not reflect a benign, nonenemy image of the USSR. Instead, the Soviets were perceived as principled opportunists, "ready to take advantage of instability to increase their influence, but certainly not the basic cause of instability in the Third World"[14]

In the same speech, Carter stated: "We hope to persuade the Soviet Union that one country cannot impose its system of society upon another, either through direct military intervention or through the use of a client state's military force, as was the case with Cuba in Angola."[15] In March 1978, Carter repeated his perception of Soviet aggressiveness: "There also has been an ominous inclination on the part of the Soviet Union to use its military power—to intervene in local conflicts, with advisers, with equipment, and with full logistical support and encouragement for mercenaries from other Communist countries, as we can observe in Africa today" (p. 21). Secretary of State Vance expressed the same dilemma when he described the USSR as a serious competitor with "objectives in the world that are very different from ours." But at the same time he argued against a return to the "dangerous cold war spirit" of the past (p. 17).

Regarding the administration's image of Latin America, simplification continued, as illustrated by the continuing assumption that the United States could help Latin American countries create systems of democracy similar to its own and could find or create a political center that would permit state planning, particularly economic reform, but that would limit the potential for Soviet influence. And Soviet allies such as Cuba were still seen as dangerous surrogates that would take advantage of and mislead Latin American political leaders. But a review of Carter's speeches as well as the comments of others and the actions of the administration in its North-South policy reveals movement away from the stereotypical extreme. The administration recognized Latin American nationalism and multiple political contenders, and its suspicion of change diminished. In May 1977, Carter said of the Third World:

> In less than a generation, we've seen the world change dramatically. The daily lives and aspirations of most human beings have been transformed. Colonialism is nearly gone. A new sense of national identity now exists in almost 100 new countries. . . . It is a new world, but America should not fear it. It is a new world, and we should help to shape it. It is a new world that calls for a new American foreign policy—a policy based on constant decency in its values. . . . We can no longer expect that the other 150 nations will follow the dictates of the powerful, but we must continue—confidently—our efforts to inspire, to persuade, and to lead (ibid., p. 7).

This statement illustrates the extent to which Carter's image of the Third World departed from the dependent extreme but was still of the dependent. While the new countries of the world were recognized as wanting to determine their own destiny, the United States was still perceived as the natural leader. The Panama canal treaty was seen as a model of the new way in which the Third World should be dealt with.

One of the most important elements of this modified dependent image in its recognition of Third World hostility toward U.S. imperial domination, particularly when it was implemented through military force or when it manifested racial and cultural superiority. But by correcting Third World impressions of U.S. racism and militaristic imperialism, Carter expected the United States to be looked up to as a new moral leader. He still believed that the United States could "use [its] great strength and influence to settle international conflicts in other parts of the world before they erupt[ed] and spread" (ibid., p. 24). Its strength would not be military, but its influence would derive from moral and political leadership. There is a subtle but important difference between perceptions of others as not inferior and perceptions of others as equal. Carter's view of Third World people was the former. They were not ethnically or racially inferior, but the United States still had superior values and a political system that others would emulate if given a chance.

Cyrus Vance produced an example of this in a May 1979 speech, in which he argued that change in Third World countries should not be feared because it could and should be in the interests of the United

States. He understood that Third World countries would "fiercely defend their independence [and] reject efforts by outsiders to impose their institutions." Like Carter, he believed that they would want to become like the United States. "America can flourish best in a world where freedom flourishes," he said. "Should we not gain confidence from this expansion of democracy, which is taking place not because we force it but because of its inherent appeal? . . . And what is that inherent appeal? Surely it lies in the enhanced opportunity that democracy provides for the realization of fundamental human rights—the rights to political and religious expression, to political participation, and to economic justice" (ibid., p. 44). The modified cold warriors did not intend to sit around waiting for others to adopt U.S. values. Although they forswore military intervention, they would use any other form of leverage to control the direction of inevitable change. Again Vance:

> In seeking to help others meet the legitimate demands of their peoples, what are the best instruments at hand? Let me state first that the use of military force is not, and should not be, a desirable American policy response to the internal politics of other nations. We believe we have the right to shape our destiny; we must respect that right in others. We must clearly understand the distinction between our readiness to act forcefully when the vital interests of our nation, our allies, and our friends are threatened and our recognition that our military forces cannot provide a satisfactory answer to the purely *internal* problems of other nations. . . . In helping other nations cope with such internal change, our challenge is to help them develop their own institutions, strengthen their own economies, and foster the ties between government and people. . . . To do so, we must continue to provide them with increasing levels of development assistance. We must maintain human rights policies which work in practical ways to advance freedom (ibid.).

Thus military force was renounced as an acceptable means of forcing internal change, but it was not renounced in principle. The intention was to push for change that would produce polities with values like those of the United States, even though it was recognized that this may not come about.

These policy makers seem to have understood the Third World as desirous of independence, but whether or not they actually believed that the Third World could withstand Soviet machinations is another matter entirely—and it is a crucial element in the dependent image.

Regarding Central America, for example, Carter stated: "Central America and the Caribbean region are undergoing a period of rapid social and political change. There is a threat that the intervention by Cuba may thwart the desire of the people of the region for progress within a democratic framework and we have been working closely with the governments in the region to try to aid in the developmental process of the region and are prepared to assist those threatened by outside intervention."[16] Thus by February 1980, the President was assuming that Cuban subversion existed and worrying that it could not be handled by the Central Americans themselves.

This ambivalence about Latin American equality appears over and over in the public pronouncements by members of this perceptual group. An interesting example came in a December 1978 speech by Assistant Secretary of State for Inter-American Affairs Viron Vaky in which Vaky was particularly attentive to the Latin American perception that the United States was a hegemonic practitioner of intervention, that the United States bore some moral responsibility for human conditions in Latin America, and "that only the United States ultimately [had] the power to control events."[17] This perception disturbed Vaky in two opposite ways. On the other hand, he agreed that the United States should not have intervened in Latin America, particularly with military force. On the other hand, he thought that Latin Americans not only unfairly blamed the United States for everything that went wrong but also expected the United States to manage all events. Here is the ambivalence: Latin Americans are right in criticizing the United States for acting like a big brother, but they keep expecting, even wanting, the United States to be a big brother. Vaky was not prepared for the United States to abandon the big brother role completely. To some extent, he blamed the Latin Americans for this, and to some extent he attributed the necessity of continuing the role to the inevitable obligations of those with superior power:

> Thus our relations are conflictive but also civilized. Differences, once understood, can be accommodated. Indeed, now that Latin America's growth and changes in U.S. values make the presumption of U.S. domination less credible than in the past, the nature of our policy problem is somewhat easier. Instead of asking ourselves to resolve all problems throughout the hemisphere, our dilemmas center fundamentally on how to handle a series of intimate and often conflictive relationships in ways that can accommodate divergent interests.
>
> The dilemmas, however, are still acute. The new problems

we face require new kinds of leadership. And despite the many changes that have taken place, our relative power and wealth still impose major obligations on the United States (ibid., p. 1289).

These remarks indicate an image removed from the extreme dependent stereotype but not entirely out of the dependent category.

It is in this context that the full meaning of the human rights policy for modified cold warriors should be discussed. The human rights policy, far from reflecting a different image of Latin America, was instead a fairly good indicator of the modified dependent image. Like the Kennedy administration's Alliance for Progress, the human rights policy, for these people, meant yet another way for the United States to promote U.S.-style democracy and combat communism. It's value was not only in saving lives but also, and importantly, in promoting containment objectives by teaching others how to treat their citizens. As Vance explained in early 1977: "If terrorism and violence in the name of difference cannot be condoned, neither can violence that is officially sanctioned. Such action perverts the legal system that alone assures the survival of our traditions. The surest way to defeat terrorism is to promote justice in our societies—legal, economic, and social justice. Justice that is summary undermines the future it seeks to promote. It produces only more violence, more victims, and more terrorism. Respect for the rule of law will promote justice and remove the seeds of subversion" (ibid., p. 1276).

Vance insisted that the United States did not expect or demand that others emulate its political system, but he followed this with a repetition of the point that the United States supported "the right of all people to freely participate in their government" (ibid., p. 1277). But even though the United States did not insist that others adopt its political principles and form of democracy, that did not mean that it could accept just any form of government. By definition, the only forms of government that permitted human rights freedoms, as specified by Carter and others who shared this worldview, were governments much like that in the United States, with values similar to U.S. political values. Thus both human rights and containment had a goal of producing democracies, and the human rights policy therefore became yet another set of tactics for achieving containment. From this perspective, it is easy to understand why the administration pursued human rights in some countries but containment in others. The human rights policy could lead to the larger containment goal and was therefore interchangeable with policies designed to reach this goal, such as supporting traditional anti-communist allies like the shah of Iran. Since the ultimate goal was to spread democracy, uncomfortable psychological imbalance and difficult value trade-offs could be avoided.

Given this particular worldview, this group was more likely than the first group to see instability and even rebellion in Latin America as a manifestation of simple conflict with a dependent, where no enemy was involved. They saw the USSR as less threatening and less capable than the first group did and Latin America as producing its own politics. One could therefore expect this group to condone intervention in Latin American crises but with slow-acting instruments, such as economic and diplomatic pressure, since they would see more coercive measures as inappropriate. On the other hand, once the context changed and this group perceived any indication of Soviet activity in a Latin American country, they shifted to traditional containment goals and accepted more coercive instruments.

These individuals accepted the enemy-dependent scenario as a possibility. Their image of the USSR was as the enemy, and their image of Latin American countries was as dependents, meaning that the Soviets could and would dupe and overwhelm them. In short, the prevailing worldview of the Carter administration had not moved far enough from the typical post–World War II cold war images to produce a change in strategy. Although tactical preferences changed with a reassessment of the effectiveness of U.S. leverage, Latin America was still seen as dependent and the Soviet Union as the enemy.

THE HUMAN RIGHTS GROUP

There was a third worldview in the Carter administration. It is difficult to document for two reasons. First, its advocates had to articulate their views in the context of standard U.S. foreign policy concerns and so were often forced to discuss their policy preferences in language acceptable and convincing to those who did not share their worldview. Second, since they did not develop an alternative to the global containment strategy, they left behind no clear alternative policy format. The group included important policy advocates such as Senators Edward Kennedy and Christopher Dodd and Representatives Lee Hamilton and Tom Harkin. In the State Department, the most important members were Patricia Derian and her aid Mark Schneider, from the Bureau of Human Rights and Humanitarian Affairs.

This group did not recognize a real Soviet threat and did not describe the USSR in the enemy stereotype. They saw Latin America in terms of the nonaligned image. The exception to the nonaligned image were countries with right-wing dictators. The societies and politics of these countries were seen as complex but the puppet rulers as dependent. Thus the policies recommended for dealing with them reflected the dependent image's sense of asymmetrical power and the ability of the United States to determine events.

This group was "relatively small. Its members went into exile or into deep cover during the Reagan years. But even during the Carter era, unabashed members of this group—officials like Mark Schneider, Patricia Derian, and Andrew Young—were few; most of those who tended in this direction found it inappropriate to tend too distinctly. In Congress, members of this group are more evident—Senators Harkin, Kennedy, Dodd and Representatives Barnes, Gejdenson, Moakley and Studds are examples."[18] This group did not fear instability and change. While modified cold warriors such as Carter and Vance argued that Americans should try not to fear change, this third group really did not worry at all about change. This reflects two image characteristics: first, they did not expect the USSR to threaten the United States by taking advantage of Latin American instability; second, they believed that Latin Americans could work things through themselves without being duped by the Soviets and their alleged agents. Instability was perceived as not only inevitable but desirable, since it created the opportunity for change (p. 22).

This group's worldview influenced its human rights policy preference. They rarely expressed a recognition of any trade-off between human-rights-motivated pressures on right-wing governments and security threats to the United States, should instability result from these pressures. The ultimate goal of a human rights policy is not the creation of democratic governments but human rights, particularly safety from repression, from disappearance, from torture and murder by governments.

Two speeches by Patricia Derian, assistant secretary of state for Human Rights and Humanitarian Affairs, illustrate this fine perceptual line. In a speech at Florida International University in May 1979, Derian described human rights as an end in itself:

> In light of these principles [of human rights], we try to shape policies which will help to create a more favorable atmosphere for the practical observance of human rights and for improvements where these rights are not respected. This is a difficult and complex process, and we have to take into account the wide diversity in regional and national situations. This diversity, as well as the varying complexity of U.S. interests throughout the

world, means that our specific actions to promote human rights improvements will vary to some extent. We assess the situation in each country, try to ascertain whether there is a positive or negative trend, and then look at our available policy instruments to determine how we can and should proceed.[19]

Derian described the limits upon U.S. pursuit of human rights concerns in terms of usable leverage and the political complexities of specific situations. In a later speech, Derian did address the issue of the national security–human rights trade-off, but she did so brusquely: "Is it compatible with national security interests? Of course. It has always been understood that a human rights policy operates in tandem with our pursuit of other interests" (p. 1308).

Further indicators of a nonenemy image of the USSR and a complex view of Latin American political actors can be seen in this group's discussion of the causes and consequences of revolution in Central America and elsewhere. For example, in May 1979, Edward Kennedy discussed the crisis in Nicaragua without referring to the possibility that a radical government would emerge or that the situation would get out of control. Instead, Kennedy argued that the United States should not support a regime that murdered its own people and that it had a responsibility to terminate all aid to that regime, since the United States had helped create and maintain it in the first place. Nicaraguans were seen as capable of finding their own political destiny, and no concern about Soviet or Cuban machinations was presented: "The people of Nicaragua must ultimately resolve their own differences. But it is crucial that we no longer offer material or symbolic support to a government that sees its citizens as a threat, that victimizes them rather than protecting their interests."[20] Kennedy was also sensitive to Nicaraguan perceptions of past U.S. imperialism. In contrast to the modified cold warriors, this perception was translated into an absolute prohibition on military force (p. 16345).

Representative Hamilton also advised the administration to accept the direction of change taken by Nicaragua without requiring a U.S.-style democratic system: "It seems to me that we ought to put one of the primary goals of our policy toward Nicaragua, the cultivation of democracy there, in proper perceptive. We want democracy to flourish and we should work ceaselessly to see that it does, but our desires and actions must be tempered by the realities we know ourselves to confront. If we become impatient with their progress in the time ahead, perhaps our impatience will be eased by the realization that for us, too, the idea of democracy in Nicaragua is new."[21] Because this policy group had significantly different perceptions of the USSR and Latin American countries, one can expect their policy preferences to be different as well. They advocated policies with goals that were not containment based. Their sensitivity to Latin American nationalism made them particularly hesitant to exercise U.S. power in an imperialistic way. This does not mean that they were antiinterventionalist but that they saw intervention as unnecessary and, when it conflicted with nationalism, self-defeating. However, where the dependent image still held, as in their perceptions of Latin American dictators, they advocated intervention if it appeared to be appropriate. An illustration of this last tendency can be found in remarks by Representative Harkin:

> We have to start being more adamant and more forceful in our relationships with those countries [that violate human rights]. We always hear it said: "Well, we don't want to interfere in those countries. We don't want to go in there and mess in their internal affairs." I don't see why not. We have been doing it for over a hundred years anyway. . . . We are going to influence Latin America. We will influence every country there. The question is, how. Are we going to keep supporting these dictators down there who violate human rights with some kind of sense of security? Or will we forcefully, once and for all, say "No, we won't put up with it"?[22]

Despite their rejection of continued U.S. hegemonic behavior in Latin America, when they perceived a regime through the dependent image, the human rights group advocated intervention.

NICARAGUA

The U.S. government was an active participant in Nicaraguan affairs since the mid-1800s. It created the Nicaraguan National Guard, which was commanded by Anastasio Somoza García, who then took control of the government in 1936.

The first Somoza ruled Nicaragua until his assassination in 1956. He was succeeded by his sons, first Luis and then Anastasio Somoza Debayle. The Somoza dynasty thus lasted from 1936 until 1979. The family used Nicaragua as its private reserve and governed through heavy repression of dissent. Nicaragua's economy was based upon the export of coffee, cotton, sugar, and beef. During the 1960s and 1970s, Nicaragua's gross national product grew as the agroexport industry expanded, but the poor did not benefit. Discontent with these conditions was repressed by the National Guard, controlled by Somoza. Somoza also had a political party, the Liberal party, through which he co-opted the upper class and manipulated the political system.

Somoza strongly supported the United States, and the favor was returned. The United States trained recruits in Nicaragua for its Bay of Pigs invasion and Somoza was a firm opponent of Castro and all radical leftist forces in the hemisphere. Somoza had been educated at West Point and had close personal ties with some public officials in the United States, such as Representatives Charles Wilson and John Murphy and with conservative Florida businessmen and Roman Catholic church officials. Although his understanding of U.S. politics was locked in a 1940s time warp, he did understand the U.S. fear of communism well and was shrewd in manipulating that fear. U.S. ambassadors associated socially with the Somoza clan and the Nicaraguan elite. The seeds of the Nicaraguan revolution lay in the political and economic structure of the country and was manifested in efforts to overthrow the regime during the 1960s. The Sandinistas, (the Frente Sandinista de Liberación Nacional, or FSLN), organized in 1961. They had few successes and were quiet for long periods during the 1960s. The moderate opposition attempted to depose the Somozas through coups and elections, but these were never successful and were met with brutal repression.

An earthquake in 1972 provided Somoza with the opportunity to enrich himself with stolen relief aid, which helped mobilize opposition to Somoza. The Sandinistas became active again, and in 1974 the moderate opposition—business, labor, and political associations—organized the Democratic Union of Liberation (UDEL). The most prominent member of the UDEL until 1978 was Pedro Joaquín Chamorro, editor of the newspaper *La Prensa*. Labor unions became more vociferous, and the Catholic church began to criticize Somoza's brutality and the condition of the poor. In 1974 the Sandinistas gave a forewarning of things to come when they took over a farewell party for the departing U.S. ambassador to Nicaragua. Somoza gave in to their demands but followed up his concession with two years of exceptionally harsh repression as he tried to destroy the guerrilla movement.

Opposition to Somoza spanned the political spectrum. The Sandinistas, whose membership expanded after the 1974 spectacle, were quite diverse ideologically. They were strong nationalists and saw the United States simply as an external actor that had supported and maintained the Somoza regime. When they joined the movement, many Sandinistas were students who had been influenced by Marxist thought and by the legacy of their hero, Augusto Sandino. Sandinismo, not a clearly defined ideology, was imbued with nationalism and attention to national ills. It called for social and economic justice, democracy, agrarian reform, and a mixed public-private economy. The FSLN had three factions, or "tendencies."

The organizations comprising the UDEL were the Christian Social Party, the Independent Liberal Party, the Socialist Party of Nicaragua, Conservative National Action, the Constitutional Movement, National Mobilization, National Salvation, the General Confederation of Labor, and the National Workers Federation. The rise of the UDEL reflects the extent to which Somoza had lost support even from those who had benefited from the pre-1972 status quo. In January 1978, UDEL leader Chamorro was assassinated, sparking street demonstrations and augmenting the revolutionary momentum. In 1978, the UDEL was replaced by the Broad Opposition Front (Frente Amplio de Oposición, or FAO), an even broader coalition of sixteen opposition organizations, including one of the three Sandinista factions. By 1979 only the Somoza family, the Liberal Party hierarchy, and the National Guard continued to support Somoza.

However, the opposition did not form a coherent political center. It was a coalition of convenience, necessitated in part by the brutality with which Somoza met any dissent. It contained members who could not agree on a common platform and who would under other circumstances be natural political and programatic competitors.

PHASE 1: JANUARY 1977–SEPTEMBER 1978

The first phase of U.S. policy toward Nicaragua lasted throughout 1977 and into the summer of 1978. During this period, there were real policy disagreements among all three perceptual groups. Traditional cold warriors and modified cold warriors shared a basic containment goal but disagreed on the utility of a human rights policy in achieving that goal. The human rights group disagreed with the modified cold warriors about core goals, but that disagreement was not aired, since they agreed on a general approach through a human rights policy. Instead, they disagreed about the implementation of the human rights policy. Intervention took the form of diplomatic pressure and military aid sanctions. The direction of change the United States pushed upon the Somoza regime was toward political reform, democratization, and the elimination of repression.

In 1977 the Carter administration suspended military aid to Nicaragua due to reports of National Guard abuses of human rights. The suspension of aid was not the result of the single-minded application of policy; instead, Congress implemented the president's policy against the wishes of the State Department, which appears to have been unable to resolve an internal debate about the extent to which the policy should be applied.

Hearings were held in Congress in April 1977 concerning human rights and economic aid. Those calling for an examination of human rights problems in Nicaragua were led by Congressman Edward Koch. The House Appropriations Committee accepted the amendment, sponsored by Koch, to suspend military aid to Somoza. Cuts in military assistance were made by the House Foreign Operations Subcommittee in late May 1977. In the following month the State Department and members of Congress such as Murphy and Wilson who were supportive of Somoza lobbied heavily to reverse the decision when the full vote was taken. They were successful in June 1977. However, the Carter administration assured the House that the aid would not be delivered to Nicaragua unless there was a demonstrated improvement in human rights there.

Debate continued along bureaucratic lines within the Carter administration concerning the disposition of aid to Nicaragua. When Somoza lifted a nearly four-year state of siege in September 1977, the Bureau of Human Rights and the Bureau of Inter-American Affairs at the State Department argued about the meaning of Somoza's act and the appropriate U.S. response. The Human Rights Bureau insisted that the lifting of the state of siege was not enough to warrant releasing aid, while the Inter-American Affairs Bureau argued the opposite.[23] The decision ended technically in Somoza's favor, in that the administration signed a military aid agreement with Nicaragua, but the funds were not released immediately nor were they approved with that intention in mind. The decision was due in part to the dictates of the fiscal calendar. But there was more to it: Douglas Bennet, Jr., assistant secretary of state for congressional relations, wrote that the State Department wanted to "preserve [its] options" but also that there had been a "diminution of charges of serious human rights abuses by the Nicaraguan National Guard" along with the termination of the state of siege.[24]

During the next six months, Nicaragua underwent greater and greater turmoil and instability. Sandinista activity picked up, and the rest of the opposition began to believe that success in deposing Somoza required forging a united front with the FSLN. Moreover, Chamorro met with some Sandinistas in search of a common position between the UDEL and the FSLN. Meanwhile, the Sandinistas began to get important diplomatic and material support from Costa Rica.[25] In January 1978, Chamorro was assassinated, and the lid blew off Nicaraguan politics. Massive demonstrations broke out, and a general strike was called, led by the business community's major organizations. Demands for Somoza's resignation grew.

The human rights policy was seen by two of the worldview groups as a way to pursue their different goals. For the human rights group, the goal was to get the Somoza repressive regime to stop murdering people and, if possible, to push Somoza out of office. The modified cold warriors' goal was to promote democratization and to prevent instability from growing in Nicaragua, which could allow radical political forces to rise. Their approach to Somoza had been to push for reform and dialogue but not to try to get him to resign. The human rights group could pursue human rights and political reform because they did not fear the USSR, while the modified cold warriors could pursue those same goals because they had no evidence of Soviet or Cuban influence in Nicaragua.

The image each group had of Somoza was that of the banana republic dictator. Hence, maximum U.S. leverage should be used to push him toward a particular form of change. Images of the Nicaraguan people were somewhat different, with the human rights group seeing them as fully complex and the modified cold warriors seeing them as modified dependents. This meant that there was some sensitivity to Nicaraguan nationalism by both groups. The modified cold warriors wanted a policy (which they thought of as strict noninterference) in which the United States would not mediate between Somoza and his opposition (ibid., p. 77). Moreover, to the extent that the United States did get involved, it should be in a multilateral context, so as not to antagonize other Latin Americans. Nevertheless, State Department officials "privately" encouraged the moderate opposition in Nicaragua, which was determined to get rid of Somoza.[26]

The difference in perception about Latin Americans between the human rights group and the modified cold warriors did not generate a policy dispute at this time. They agreed in their perception of Somoza, and the difference in their perceptions of other Nicaraguans was not yet important. Neither wanted to dictate Nicaragua's political future to Somoza's opponents, but they did not recognize that forcing change on Somoza was a hegemonic action and was interpreted as such by Nicaraguans, who expected the United States to push Somoza out and to replace him with someone else. U.S. officials argued that they simply wanted to get him to reform, not realizing that the U.S. use of power was taken by Nicaraguans as a manifestation of traditional U.S. hegemony.

The major disagreement between these two groups during 1977 concerned implementation of the human rights policy, but that disagreement can be traced to underlying differences in image-based goals, to seeing the consequences of rapid, uncontrolled change quite differently. Members of the Bureau of Inter-American Affairs, who were mainly modified cold warriors, argued that human rights reform in Nicaragua could be achieved by combining rewards for reform with punishment for failure to reform. Their concern was partly that the use of punishment alone would only increase Somoza's resistance, but they also argued that security concerns necessitated continuing to send aid to Somoza, including military aid to be used for training and supplies.

In 1977 Assistant Secretary of State for Inter-American Affairs Terence Todman argued in favor of such aid for fiscal year 1978, as follows: "U.S. security concerns in Nicaragua and the rest of Central America relate directly to our need for secure flanks and our commitment to hemispheric collective security under the Rio Treaty. Our objectives include prevention of the introduction of hostile forces and bases into the region, limitation of hostile influences, protection of lines of communication and maintenance of regional stability. We seek to provide the Central Americans with the sense of security essential to social, economic and political development, and to encourage their initiatives toward regional cooperation."[27] In general, the modified cold warriors approved of withholding military aid to Somoza but not of forgoing access to military aid in case traditional tactics for pursuing containment goals were needed. With threat perceptions low, their concern for short-term containment was absent, freeing them to pursue long-term containment goals through slow-acting tactics that, simultaneously, satisfied their concerns about abuses of human rights.

One can also see the importance of self-image in these policy preferences. In the earlier cases, U.S. policy makers perceived themselves as powerful; in the Carter years, this was not always true. Moreover, a powerful self-image was not necessarily associated with the more extreme dependent image. In fact, in the Carter administration some of those with more complex images of Nicaragua and El Salvador also had powerful self-images of the United States. Self-image thus interacts with, but is not determined by, one's image of the other.

There was disagreement among the modified cold warriors about when and to what extent human rights tactics ought to be employed. The difference between Carter's first and second Assistant secretaries for Latin America, Terrence Todman and Viron Vaky, was in the degree to which they believed that aid sanctions would serve U.S. interests. These disagreements are explainable in terms of how "modified" the warriors were. The more modified they were, the stronger their desire for deep implementation. There were also differences in self-image, however. People with a strong positive national self-image tended to believe that sanctions would work.

For members of the human rights group, the goal of terminating human rights abuses required complete implementation of the aid sanctions. They objected to any signal that might be interpreted to mean that Somoza was making satisfactory progress, including requests for aid. In August 1977, for example, Senator Kennedy, argued that the United States had "a special responsibility to dispel any previous misconceptions that the United States supports the Nicaraguan Government's suppression of dissent." Nearly two years later he was still calling for continued suspension of aid and continued pressure (ibid., p. 27175).

The traditional cold warriors saw the whole notion of imposing human rights sanctions on Somoza as dangerous and outrageous. Congressman Kiki de la Garza worried that, if aid to Somoza was terminated, communists would take over in Nicaragua (ibid.). To him, Somoza was a loyal friend, if not an equal, who provided a bulwark against the communist forces perpetually trying to take advantage of any U.S. weakness. Congressman Murphy argued: "Nicaragua physically is the largest of the Central American countries. It extends from the Pacific to the Caribbean. It is a blocking position in Central America against the spread of Communist subversion. This is why it is a target for Communist infiltration from Cuba" (p. 20582).

For this group, an extreme enemy image of the USSR combined with an extreme dependent image of Nicaragua to produce a policy preference of unflinching continuous support for Somoza. Some refused to believe information indicating that Somoza's regime was in fact committing human rights abuses (p. 27175). Congressman O'Brien insisted that freedom was "breaking through in Nicaragua," that the "questionable activities" by the National Guard were being curtailed, and that the United States should encourage this trend by granting aid (p. 20582). This group believed that opponents of Somoza in the human rights lobby were probably communist sympathizers. Murphy placed into the *Congressional Record* "instructions" from the Washington Office on Latin America for people testifying before Congress on human rights in Nicaragua. Murphy called it a "primer for anti-American testimony" (ibid.).

In the summer of 1978, U.S. policy considerations changed. Up until then, the policy debate was over the question of whether aid should be sent to Somoza. In May 1978, the administration succumbed to pressure from Congressman Wilson to provide two economic aid loans to Nicaragua. The administration insisted that these loans did not constitute a change in policy.[28] And Wilson threatened to block the foreign aid bill unless these loans were approved.

PHASE 2: SEPTEMBER 1978–JULY 1979

A number of events combined to change perceptions of the growing crisis in Nicaragua. Between May and August 1978, the opposition reorganized into the FAO. In August a Sandinista force took over the

National Palace, releasing fifty-nine political prisoners, taking posses-
sion of a large amount of money, and broadcasting a political communi-
qué throughout Nicaragua. The action was celebrated in the streets of
Managua. August also witnessed a call by the FAO for a general strike
and the Sandinistas' seizure of the town of Matagalpa. Moreover, the
governments of Venezuela and Panama were openly hostile toward Somoza now, with Venezuelan President Carlos Andrés Pérez telling Somoza point blank to get out of office.

In the midst of these events, a major diplomatic problem erupted
for the United States when a letter from President Carter to Somoza was
made public. The letter, according to its author, was sent to encourage
Somoza to uphold his promises in the areas of human rights. It was
leaked to the press by "a senior pro-human rights official in the Bureau
of Inter-American Affairs" as a congratulatory letter praising Somoza for
his human rights performance (ibid., p. 70). This affair forced Carter
and Brzezinski to pay close attention to Nicaragua for the first time (pp.
70–71). They increasingly marginalized the human rights group, and
the personnel of the Human Rights Bureau became less important in
shaping policy. The administration was surprised by the Sandinista raid
on the National Palace, the degree of popular support for the Sandinistas, and the decline in support for Somoza even in the National
Guard, where a group of officers attempted a coup.[29]

The violence and chaos in Nicaragua activated different components of the modified cold warrior worldview; their efforts to achieve
containment shifted from promoting reform to attempting to guide the
direction of change in Nicaragua to prevent the Sandinistas from winning. The human rights group was replaced in policy influence by the
traditional cold warriors, who shared the containment goals of the modified cold warriors. Once again, debate centered not on goals but on
tactics. This is not to say that the human rights group was silent. After
September 1978, violence increased dramatically as the National Guard
bombed Nicaragua's cities, and supporters of economic sanctions for
human rights reasons continued to press for aid sanctions. The fall of
1978 was a critical period for policy evaluation.

In August 1978, the State Department recommended pushing Somoza out of office to ensure a moderate government after his departure.
The National Security Council and the Pentagon argued in favor of
shoring Somoza up and blamed his regime's instability on the human
rights policy. The administration was slow to recognize that the crisis in
Nicaragua was a revolution rather than a series of random events.[30] In
September, as violence mounted, the administration decided to mediate the dispute between Somoza and the opposition. Important percep-

tual differences influenced the positions of policy makers regarding the growing crisis. The traditional cold warriors regarded human-rights-based sanctions as poor tactics, while the modified cold warriors believed the human rights policy pursued security needs quite well. For both, security concerns were paramount; the issue was what tactics should replace human rights sanctions, which failed to produce reform, stave off revolution, or promote democratic change. The new tactics had to pursue fundamental security goals, which had come to mean preventing a Sandinista victory.

The next tactical debate hinged in part upon the U.S. perception of its own power and leverage and its perception of the moderate opposition in Nicaragua. Policy advocates disagreed on the degree to which the United States could or should directly control events. The United States in this period was commonly accused of being paralyzed, unable to decide what to do. In fact, a policy shift did occur, although the change was incremental and not the product of a major policy debate at the highest levels.[31] Instead, Vaky, Pastor, and Anthony Lake (of the policy planning staff of the State Department) hammered out the strengths and weaknesses of the various options.

In reconsidering U.S. policy, discussions concerned the issue of mediation—whether the United States should act unilaterally or multilaterally (with Costa Rica, Venezuela, and Panama)—and the issue of whether the United States should identify itself more openly with moderate sectors of the opposition.[32] Those members of the administration who perceived the United States as very powerful advocated stronger measures to depose Somoza. Vaky believed that a Marxist victory would result if order was not restored, that the United States could remove Somoza, and that it "should use whatever force necessary—barring assassination" to do so.[33] Others, including Pastor and Lake, believed that the United States should not ask Somoza to resign, since that would constitute old-fashioned intervention. Instead, they advocated that the United States support and encourage a proposal by Costa Rican President Rodrigo Carazo that he act as mediator in the Nicaraguan conflict (pp. 82–83). The difference in these two approaches was tactical and could be attributed to different perceptions of U.S. capabilities. The goals were the same and compatible with the modified cold warrior worldview. The multilateral approach was chosen. Carter supported the Costa Rican offer to mediate and sent former Ambassador to Panama William Jorden to consult with the Central American governments. Meanwhile, during September and October 1978, the traditional cold warriors were calling for renewed support for Somoza. Seventy-eight members of Congress, spanning partisan lines, asked Carter to support

Somoza and accused the opposition of attempting to create another Cuba.[34]

Multilateral mediation proved unsuccessful. After casting about for alternatives, the administration undertook the role of mediator itself, although the Dominican Republic and Guatemala were nominal partners. The position of the United States now was that a civil war could not be avoided as long as Somoza remained in power. Hence, the role of the mediators would be to facilitate his speedy exit. The United States team was headed by William Bowdler. Although Somoza accepted this team of mediators, he refused to resign or lift the state of siege and doubled the size of the National Guard and the defense budget. He did, however, agree to talk about elections. The United States insisted that the main opposition groups in the FAO be included in the negotiations, but it did not include the Sandinistas.[35] The hope was to create a transitional government quickly enough to preclude both a Sandinista victory and a major Sandinista role in the post-Somoza government.

No one was optimistic or enthusiastic about these mediation efforts, although they lasted from October 1978 through February 1979. The FAO just wanted Somoza out. No new government from the established opposition parties was acceptable to the FAO, and the organization would have preferred Latin American, not U.S., mediation.[36] The Carter administration worried about the prospect of a Sandinista victory if the National Guard disintegrated but believed that without such a disintegration Somoza would not leave office. A number of twists and turns took place in the U.S. position as Somoza attempted to maintain his control of the government and the United States was unable to decide how much pressure to apply to Somoza to get him to resign. The United States found the FAO difficult to deal with due in part to its diverse constituencies. The U.S. representative did not speak to the FSLN, and there was a real conflict between the U.S. position and the FSLN position on mediation. The Sandinistas did not trust Americans and disapproved of the mediation in principle, particularly if it resulted in the protection of the National Guard.

Inside the administration disagreement erupted as to how much pressure should be applied to Somoza. Vaky and Bowdler believed that the United States had the power and leverage to push him out quickly, while most others, including Carter, believed the United States could not force Somoza out without serious international and domestic repercussions.[37] To some extent, this difference reflects different perceptions of U.S. power, but it also reflects different perceptions of Nicaraguans, again one of degree. Those with the more complex view, Vaky and Bowdler, were less fearful of what would happen after Somoza was ousted and were more sympathetic toward the position that Somoza should be gotten rid of quickly. Those with a less complex view worried about Somoza's departure in the absence of a transition government.

This perceptual difference reappeared as the negotiations concerning elections evolved. The FAO proposed that Somoza resign, that the National Guard be reorganized, that elections for a Constituent Assembly be held, and that a new government with a Council of State and a three-person junta be formed (ibid., p. 101). Pastor, Brzezinski, General Smith from the Joint Chiefs of Staff, and others believed that Somoza should not be hurried out of office lest the opposition prove too weak to handle the situation, leaving an opening for the Sandinistas. Vaky, on the other hand, favored pushing hard with economic sanctions to force Somoza out *because* the opposition's cohesion was so weak that it might not survive if Somoza rejected the FAO proposal and fighting erupted again. Each feared a Sandinista takeover of the revolutionary momentum. Their disagreement was once again about the most appropriate tactics for preventing such an outcome. Traditional cold warriors, like Brzezinski and the Joint Chiefs of Staff, leaned toward maintaining the bulwark against communism (Somoza) until the alternative was clear. And, given this camp's more contemptuous view of Nicaraguans, they opted to bide for time, during which "the opposition would learn to organize . . . so that when they assumed power, they could govern" (p. 104). A compromise was reached. Some pressure was applied—but not the maximum pressure needed to produce Somoza's resignation.

Somoza's response to the FAO was to propose a plebiscite. The Carter administration discussed the option of using the plebiscite to force Somoza to accept the fact that Nicaraguans wanted him out of office as opposed to the option of applying full sanctions against Somoza to force him to resign. Considerable debate took place among top-level policy makers, including Vance, Brzezinski, Pastor, Vaky, Christopher, and Bowdler, regarding these two options. The division over preferences were between those who were "more attuned to the debate in Managua and more disposed to make the opposition's case for pushing Somoza out" (Vaky and Bowdler) and those who "were more sensitive to developing a policy that was defensible in the United States and more inclined to advocate a North American approach to solving the problem—elections (ibid., p. 107). This fits with the perceptual argument made here, that those with a more complex image of Nicaragua favored a Nicaraguan solution, while those with the more simplified, dependent image assumed that a U.S.-style solution would work best.

Negotiations regarding the plebiscite continued through December. The FAO began to disintegrate, when four of the sixteen groups in the organization left, indicating that the center was falling apart. Yet the Carter administration doggedly pursued the idea that an election could be held and would produce a centrist government. On January 19, 1979, when Somoza attempted to back out of the plebiscite and the FAO declared the negotiations to be terminated, mediation collapsed completely. On February 8, the Carter administration announced the imposition of sanctions against the Somoza regime. They included a reduction in the size of the U.S. diplomatic mission, the withdrawal of U.S. military personnel, the termination of all U.S. military aid (which had been suspended any way), the withdrawal of Peace Corps personnel, and the suspension of U.S. economic aid.[38]

The United States became involved again in events in Nicaragua in June, 1979, when the Somoza government began to fall and support shifted to the Sandinistas. More members of the FAO left and joined the newly formed National Patriotic Front, which was dominated by the Sandinistas. The United States minimized contact with the opposition, did not recognize the tide of popular support for the Sandinistas, and failed to devise a plan for establishing contact with the Sandinistas, despite the endorsement of the FSLN by all of the major opposition groups.[39]

In late May and early June, the Sandinistas launched their final offensive. U.S. policy makers called upon to devise a response included Deputy Secretary of State Warren Christopher, Secretary of Defense Harold Brown, NSC Adviser Zbigniew Brzezinski, and CIA Director Stansfield Turner, in addition to lower level officials such as Robert Pastor. The goal was clear, and it was a containment-based goal. By this time, threat perceptions were high, and although this group of policy makers still did not see the Soviet Union as instigating events in Nicaragua, they believed that the Sandinistas would win if the United States did not stop them and that, if the Sandinistas won, Cuba would extend Soviet influence in the region via the Sandinistas.

U.S. goals had now crystallized at the global containment level. One should expect the modified enemy and dependent images, under threatening context conditions, to produce a preference for fast-acting, coercive instruments in an effort to determine events. This is precisely what happened. Conflict did occur—again between those with a more complex view of Nicaragua and the rest of Latin America and those whose modified dependent view was now pushed closer to the extreme by heightened threat perceptions. Not surprisingly, a member of the options-formulating team with the most stereotyped extreme of the dependent image of Latin America, Zbigniew Brzezinski, came up with the first plan to prevent a Sandinista victory. His plan called for proposing a multilateral peacekeeping force to the OAS, for which the United States would "assume a major part of the responsibility."[40] Somoza would be removed, and order would be restored. State Department officials with the more complex image of Latin America, including Vance and Vaky, warned that the plan would not go over well with the OAS. But Brzezinski and Brown believed without military intervention by the United States, there would be a Sandinista victory.

In addition to the peacekeeping force, the U.S. plan called for direct efforts to shape the future government of Nicaragua. On June 17 the Sandinistas announced a provisional government composed of a five-member junta, two of whom would be from the FSLN. The others were Alfonso Robelo, a leader of the business community, Sergio Ramírez, a member of Los Doce with strong ties to the FSLN, and Violeta Chamorro, widow of Pedro Joaquín Chamorro. The U.S. proposal to the OAS, on the other hand, included the formation "of an interim government of national reconciliation acceptable to all major elements of the society."[41] This provisional government would be a junta appointed by the Nicaraguan Congress and composed of representatives of the major opposition groups. The Sandinistas would negotiate with that junta to form a new government. The United States also planned to "draw international attention to the Cuban role in the conflict," which reflected the unreality of the U.S. perception of the situation. Eight Latin American countries had either condemned or broken relations with Somoza, and Costa Rica and Panama were shipping large amounts of supplies and material to the FSLN, yet U.S. policy makers believed they had to make Latin Americans aware of Cuban support for the FSLN.

The administration had come a long way from imagining itself a neutral, uninvolved party to being a mediator and then to being a kingmaker. Some policy advocates knew that kingmaking could not succeed. Vance was ordered to make the intervention proposal to the OAS, but he doubted it would be accepted. Brzezinski had doubts, too, but set the prevention of the FSLN victory as the highest priority and believed that, as long as the National Guard survived, a peacekeeping force would not be necessary anyway.[42] As the images became more extreme due to the mounting crisis, the behavior of U.S. policy makers typified that of people with stereotyped enemy and dependent images. Gone was the preference for neutrality or even diplomacy. Now they toyed with the idea of using military force—maybe not unilateral military force, but still a force able to achieve the U.S. goal of preventing the victory of the left. Moreover, their ability to empathize with Latin America and to anticipate the nationalistic response to these proposals degenerated as the crisis worsened.

Not surprisingly, the OAS did not approve the U.S. proposal. Moreover, the Nicaraguan opposition endorsed the FSLN's proposed junta. At this point, the traditional cold warriors in the administration adopted the traditional cold war strategy. Brzezinski urged Carter to intervene, a recommendation that echoed the views of the cold warriors in Congress. Vance, Brown, and Carter all opposed the idea. A new search was launched for a diplomatic approach, and the United States ultimately embarked on an effort to get the OAS to approve external mediation. This the OAS did, and it was interpreted as permission for the United States to arbitrate a transition government.

With this new mandate, the administration in late June pressed for the creation of an executive committee that would negotiate with the junta. Bowdler went to Costa Rica, where three members of the Junta waited, and attempted to convince them to broaden the membership of the junta. He also wanted to strengthen the "democratic forces" in Nicaragua before Somoza was forced out in order to diminish Sandinista power and to ensure that the National Guard would not be dismantled after Somoza's departure. The Nicaraguan opposition, however, insisted that the junta be treated as the provisional government and that Somoza be replaced with the new government before negotiations with the National Guard proceeded.[43]

The executive committee alternative and the expansion of the junta were simply different ideas for achieving the same goal: watering down FSLN power after Somoza's departure. Differences over the feasibility of the executive committee did reflect different estimations of the condition of the moderates in Nicaragua and the degree of nationalistic hatred of the United States. Ambassador Pezzullo and Vaky argued that there were few moderates left in the country and that, in any case, the moderates did not want to be associated with a U.S.-sponsored government.[44] Others argued that the Sandinistas would never be convinced to expand the junta, and that the United States should try any other option to prevent a complete FSLN takeover. The debate concerning the nature of the junta revolved around whether it was best to push for an expanded junta or a reorganized one, the latter being a junta that would give a diminished role to the Sandinistas.

This was the final concern of the Carter administration during the Nicaraguan revolution. On July 17, 1979, Somoza resigned. A provisional president, Francisco Urcuyo Maliaños, was elected by the Nicaragua Congress to serve as president for a day and oversee the transition to the junta's rule. The United States hoped for a cease-fire, which would freeze the FSLN's military position. But once Somoza announced his resignation, the National Guard fell apart. Moreover, although Urcuyo decided to stay in office rather than be a transition executive, he fled when it became apparent that the revolution could not be sidetracked. The Sandinistas won the revolution on July 19, 1979, and the junta, which was ultimately expanded to seven members, took over. The Carter administration designed an economic aid program to shore up the Nicaraguan business community and to influence the course of Nicaragua's revolution. It was harshly criticized by members of the U.S. Congress.

EL SALVADOR

The case of El Salvador was heavily influenced by the perceptual shifts that occurred in the Carter administration as the Nicaraguan revolution developed. The actions the United States took in El Salvador were designed in part to prevent another Nicaragua.

At first glance, El Salvador's polity appeared to be the familiar Central American dictatorship: decades of military rule characterized by repeated military coups, fraudulent elections, multiple political organizations, and apparently irremediable class conflict. Traditionally, El Salvador had been ruled by an oligarchy of wealthy families called the Fourteen Families—but really numbering many more than fourteen. The oligarchy formed an alliance with the military, and together they denied the country's rural majority basic freedoms and economic opportunity. The country is and has long been very overpopulated, with a highly skewed distribution of land, wealth, and power. The proportion of the rural population composed of landless peasants rose throughout the twentieth century, reaching 41 percent by 1975.[45]

El Salvador's political scene changed during the 1960s and into the 1970s. New political parties and organizations formed with a wide range of political ideologies. The Catholic church increased its participation in politics as a result of the influence of liberation theology. Finally, the far right had a number of political organizations. The National Broad Front (FAN) was formed by Major Roberto D'Aubuisson, a retired military officer linked with death squads and a leading figure in the National Republican Alliance (ARENA), a right-wing political party. The Organización Democrática Nacionalista (ORDEN), another right-wing (paramilitary) organization, was supposed to ensure stability in rural areas. The government was dominated by the military, which in turn had three factions, a left, a right, and a center. Military officers typically were united by strong loyalty to the military as an institution as well as to their *tandas:* their military academic class. The death squads that operated so openly during the 1970s and 1980s were associated with various branches of the military, particularly the Treasury Police and the National Guard. They also were closely associated with ORDEN.

In the 1970s the political scene was further complicated by the emergence of a number of guerrilla groups. Initially, there were three left-wing guerrilla groups: the Popular Liberation Forces (FPL), the People's Revolutionary Army (ERP), and the Armed Forces of National Resistance (FARN). Two more were established later: the Central American Revolutionary Workers Party (PRTC) and the Armed Forces of Liberation (FAL). They were united in a loose organization known as the Farabundo Martí National Liberation Front (FMLN) in May 1980 (ibid., pp. 53–54).

It is often argued that El Salvador began its long slide into civil war after the 1972 elections, when the presidency was stolen from the Christian Democratic candidate, José Napoleon Duarte, which essentially destroyed the political center as an effective force.[46] With the center destroyed, the polity became more chaotic; some members of the center moved leftward, political activity became more dangerous, and repression and right-wing violence increased. The church became more politicized, and popular organizations and guerrilla groups increased. In 1977 General Carlos Romero took power, and repression grew even more severe.

There were two phases in U.S. policy, which closely followed the two phases of the Nicaraguan case. In the first phase, the Carter administration's policy was an outgrowth of its general human rights policy. The second phase developed after General Romero was overthrown on October 15, 1979, three months after the July victory of the Sandinistas. The Carter administration's policy in El Salvador involved the use of economic instruments and diplomatic pressure to force reforms by the El Salvador governments in power after the October coup. However, the operative images produced policies that promoted containment goals above any specific reform measures.

In general, the U.S. leverage in El Salvador was strong, but much of it was not manipulable. The U.S. had been a very powerful actor in Salvadoran politics historically but also an unconcerned actor, which rarely exerted its power. The United States was the major importer of El Salvador's agricultural exports. Efforts to use U.S. diplomatic pressure upon the Salvadoran regime to implement reforms in 1975 and 1976 failed. The United States could apply economic pressure by blocking aid and grants from international institutions. It also could terminate military aid, but this was not particularly effective in the 1970s, when El Salvador could buy military equipment from Israel and some Western European governments.

Phase 1: March 1977–October 1979

The first phase of U.S. policy toward El Salvador parallels that phase in its policy toward Nicaragua. The same individuals with the same worldviews debated and selected policy. Once again, divisions emerged between those in the Human Rights Bureau and those in other State Department bureaus. As in the case of Nicaragua, the Human Rights Bureau advocated complete human rights sanctions against the regime, while those in Inter-American Affairs Bureau worried about the impact of such a policy on the stability of the regime and the imperialist implications of the policy for Salvadoran nationalists. During phase 1, the conflict among middle-level bureaucrats was crucial in determining the direction of U.S. policy. El Salvador simply was not an attention-grabbing situation until the Nicaraguan revolution made it so in 1979.

The Human Rights Bureau did not win much in the bureaucratic contest to implement a human-rights-based policy in El Salvador. Although pressure was applied to Romero's regime to reduce abuses, that pressure was temporized with inconsistencies in economic aid and loans. Moreover, although military aid to the Salvadoran government should have been terminated due to human rights abuses, that aid was not cut. Congressional hearings in March 1977 made criticism of the Salvadoran government's actions public. The Salvadoran government's response was to refuse military aid rather than comply with U.S. human rights standards. The termination of aid did not include the withdrawal of the U.S. military mission in El Salvador.

Three human-rights-based issues were the subject of disagreement between the two perceptual groups. They included the disappearance of an American under suspicious circumstances, the allocation of funds from the Inter-American Development Bank for a hydroelectric project, and the implementation of a land reform program. In the first case, a young American named Ronald Richardson was arrested; he subsequently disappeared in September 1976. The U.S. embassy pressured the government of El Salvador, then under Colonel Arturo Molina, to provide information concerning Richardson's whereabouts, but the embassy was not supported by the State Department. Not until May 1977 did Ambassador Ignacio E. Lozano Jr. get State Department authorization to threaten the Salvadoran government with a negative vote on its request for a $90 million Inter-American Development Bank loan for a hydroelectric project unless the government provided information on

Richardson. The Salvadoran government only repeated its previous position—that Richardson was no longer in El Salvador.

In March 1977, after the fraudulent electoral victory of General Carlos Romero in the presidential race, frustrated members of the Salvadoran political opposition staged demonstrations that turned into riots. Somewhere between six and two hundred people were killed by security forces, and a state of siege was imposed. These events prompted hearings in the U.S. Congress on human rights in El Salvador, hearings that focused upon a people's right to select freely a government and upon violations of the person. At this point, the Carter administration disagreed internally about the degree of pressure to impose on the Salvadoran government regarding the Richardson case, but this was not a basis for a major debate on the human-rights-based policy of sanctions against El Salvador. Very simply, those who advocated a human rights foreign policy and who saw no threat from instability were building a human rights case on El Salvador. The Molina government saved them the trouble when it refused U.S. military aid. Subsequently, questions concerning economic aid would become important areas of dispute—but not in the first half of 1977.

At the same time, members of the administration who had modified dependent images of El Salvador were not inclined to pursue a human rights policy unless it promoted democracy and, thus, U.S. security interests. In 1977, although they were reticent about openly accusing the Salvadoran government of killing Richardson (not to mention Salvadorans), this group did not see a security problem in El Salvador. When queried by Congress during the March 1977 hearings, for example, Deputy Assistant Secretary of State for Inter-American Affairs Charles Bray stated that there was no revolutionary movement in El Salvador.[47] Thus there was no real conflict concerning policy goals or a definition of the situation. By the summer of 1977 there was some disagreement over tactics. At this point, the Inter-American Affairs Bureau was arguing that the United States ought to ease human rights pressures on the Romero government because time was needed to establish positive ties between the United States and the new regime. Moreover, Romero had ordered his security forces to be more restrained in their treatment of Salvadoran citizens.

The improvement in human rights was due in part to Romero's concern about El Salvador's request for the hydroelectric project loan from the Inter-American Development Bank. The United States cast a negative vote on this project in July 1977 because of human rights conditions in El Salvador. This caused some controversy between the Human Rights Bureau the Inter-American Affairs Bureau. The former argued in favor of economic sanctions against El Salvador, while the next U.S. Ambassador to El Salvador, Frank Devine, and other foreign service officers were in favor of the loan. The loan request was resubmitted by the Romero government in the fall, and in October the United States approved the loan. Other economic aid suspensions were not used to influence the Romero regime. In fact, U.S. economic aid to El Salvador increased from $6.8 million in 1977 to $10.9 million in 1978.[48]

In summary, U.S. policy toward El Salvador during phase 1 barely constituted mild coercion, and it conformed to the type of policy and tactics predicted in the nonthreatened scenario with a dependent. Generally, those with the nonthreatened view were not concerned if instability occurred because they perceived the political actors in El Salvador in full complexity and did not fear leftist forces: if human rights sanctions disrupted military rule, so much the better. Those with the modified dependent image did worry about the impact of human rights sanctions on the stability of the regime, because their less complex image of the rest of the polity led them to fear that Salvadorans would not prevent leftists from extending their influence. As in the case of Nicaragua, the human rights group simplified the right-wing regimes but not the polity as a whole.

There were also significant differences in the assessment of human rights abuses, a reflection of differences in the intensity of the images. The Inter-American Affairs Bureau and the Human Rights Bureau had fierce arguments about the level of human rights abuses, with the Inter-American Affairs Bureau relying upon information provided by the embassy, headed by Frank Devine. This interpretation was patronizing and protective of what they considered a reliable ally. The embassy maintained that Salvadoran security forces were not involved in murders and that ORDEN was not an institutionalized death squad. The security forces were unrealistically described as professional. Human Rights Bureau personnel, particularly Mark Schneider, maintained that the whole security apparatus was corrupt, repressive, and "a bunch of goons and cutthroats."[49]

Both views were simplifications of the Salvadoran situation. This is not to say that the truth lies somewhere in the middle, but that both views, through selective attention to evidence, had very simplified pictures of a polity heading for civil war. The Inter-American Affairs version ultimately became the most simplified, particularly when the Human Rights Bureau view was silenced in 1979. But even so, the latter view was also simplified in that it focused upon the regime itself, which was the stereotyped extreme, and failed to formulate a policy that responded to the Salvadoran political crisis as a whole. The preferred solution became that of getting rid of Romero and the safe haven for murderers and torturers, rather than a solution that addressed El Salvador's very real political problems.

As in the Nicaraguan case, the human rights group in the Carter administration was able to influence policy toward El Salvador during the early Carter years in part because the agencies dominated by the traditional cold warriors were unconcerned about that country. Nevertheless, the Human Rights Bureau was still unable to defeat the Bureau of Inter-American Affairs when it came to a full-scale implementation of the human rights policy. People in the Human Rights Bureau were quite vocal in their criticism of El Salvador, but the administration's actions reflected the views of both groups. Ambassador Devine in particular was an effective lobbyist for the Salvadoran government and persuaded pro-human-rights members of Congress, such as Kennedy and Harkin, to support loans (ibid., p. 32).

PHASE 2: 1979–1981

Repression reached new heights under the Romero regime. Political assassinations were ten times that of the pre-Romero period, and disappearances doubled (ibid., p. 42), causing more guerrilla activity and opposition to the regime. But to speak out against the regime was to risk death, and as the months went by, thousands lost their lives.

Even so, the Carter administration did not become concerned about El Salvador until after the Sandinista victory in Nicaragua, when policy making toward El Salvador gradually shifted away from the middle-level officials toward top-level officials. As in the Nicaraguan case, the human rights group was shoved out of the picture. From late summer of 1979 until the end of the Carter administration, the prevailing worldview on El Salvador in the Carter administration was that of the modified cold warriors. Internal and international contexts added threat to perceptions of the situation, pushing the images to their stereotypical extreme, which affected policy making in several ways. First, as perceptions of El Salvador became ever more simplified, intervention became the logical and unquestioned policy choice. Whereas in the Nicaraguan case there was some debate about the implications of U.S. actions, such concerns were absent here. Intervention was pursued with economic and diplomatic instruments, and when it appeared that a potential for a Soviet-Cuban-Marxist influence was growing, there was a quick switch to military support. The left was seen as extremely dangerous, and the primary goal became containment, to prevent a Marxist victory in El Salvador. There was no interest in negotiating with the left, which was seen as monolithic.

Second, a search was launched for a reform-minded center. When one could not be found, it was assumed that the United States could create one that would hold elections, create a U.S.-style democracy, and govern. Viron Vaky and William Bowdler made secret trips to El Salvador to convince General Romero to resign and hold early elections. Vaky and Bowdler also met with leaders of the Christian Democratic party and the church (ibid., p. 146). On October 15, 1979, to no one's surprise, Romero was overthrown.

The policy makers who had been unable too construct a set of tactics to prevent a Sandinista takeover in Nicaragua were not about to let a similar disaster occur in El Salvador. The policy followed in El Salvador was essentially a continuation of the tactics that were operative in Nicaragua after the fall of Somoza. The United States acted as a political arbiter as El Salvador had a new military junta and then three more juntas in the year and a half after the October 1979 coup. This approach by the United States was consistent with the modified dependent and enemy images. Threat makes images more extreme; but even with low threat, the images of these policy makers called for cautious intervention and containment.

The officers who overthrew Romero on October 15, 1979, were part of the reformist sector of the Salvadoran military. They were led by Colonels Adolfo Majano and René Guerra y Guerra. The ideological bent of these officers could not be called leftist, although some were clearly smypathetic to land reform and the needs of the poor. The plotters included not only military officers but also civilians, who formed a civilian and military coordinating committee. The committee decided upon a five-man junta of two military officers and three civilians. There is no solid evidence concerning the role the United States played. Information from unnamed inside sources indicates that the Central Intelligence Agency pushed for conservative Colonels José Guillermo García and Jaime Abdul Gutiérrez and opposed the more radical Colonel Guerra y Guerra.[50] Others argue that the CIA had too little knowledge of El Salvador during this time to have served in such a capacity and that Guerra y Guerra himself does not believe the U.S. maneuvered this way against him.[51]

The civilian members of the October 15 junta were the rector of the University of Central America, Roman Mayorga; the leader of the Movimiento Nacional Revolucionario, Guillermo Ungo (both of these men were representatives of the Foro Popular, an organization of opposition parties and popular organizations); and Antonio Andino, a fairly liberal businessman. Ministers selected for the new government's cabinet included Social Democrats and Christian Democrats, and they were

endorsed by the Communist party. Colonel García was appointed minister of defense by Colonel Gutiérrez, who did not consult the other
members of the junta on this appointment.

After the coup, the military leaders presented a reform program,
which included an end to violence, guarantees of human rights and civil
liberties (free elections, political organization, amnesty for political exiles and prisoners, and free speech), land reform, and economic reform.[52] The program met with immediate opposition from the far right,
including members of the right wing of the military, mostly senior officers. The junta also faced opposition from the left. The Foro Popular
accepted the junta, as did one of the guerrilla groups and the Communist party, but the other guerrilla groups and some popular organizations
remained in opposition.

The reformist officers and civilians in the October 15 junta had little
chance of initiating their reform programs. The right wing of the military moved into important positions in the junta, and violence mounted
as the military used bullets to quell dissent. More Salvadorans died in
the first month of the October junta than in last nine months of the
Romero regime.[53] Few of the provisions of its program were implemented, and it became clear that the junior officers were being marginalized and that the military, not the junta or the cabinet, ran the
government. In late December, the junta and the cabinet demanded
the removal of García as minister of defense. They were brusquely
informed that the military had given them their positions and that the
military was in command. In early January, the junta resigned en masse,
and a new junta was formed.

The October coup did not precipitate high-level meetings in the
Carter administration. According to one official, "Nobody saw this as a
major problem for which major decisions had to be made."[54] Nevertheless, there was internal disagreement on what the United States should
do. Members of the human rights group argued that the United States
should not provide military aid to the new government. This group did
not fear instability and saw continued demonstrations and discontent in
El Salvador as part of the process of change and an opportunity for the
United States to promote change. It called for political support for the
reformist elements in the new regime.

The modified cold warriors were now much less "modified." They,
and the traditional cold warriors in the Pentagon and the National Security Council, argued in favor of military aid to El Salvador. This position
was supported strongly by Ambassador Devine, who met regularly with
the military men in the junta (but not with the civilians) and who
believed that the military was justified in using force to prevent disor-

der. Moreover, the CIA station chief in El Salvador had termed Mayorga, Ungo, and Majano *leftists,* which was worrisome to the Pentagon and the National Security Council (ibid., pp. 164–65). Many focused entirely on the perceived threat from the left and the growing instability in El Salvador. The use of pressure in the form of economic aid and diplomatic persuasion was deemed appropriate. Simplification of the Salvadoran polity was notable, as was the intention to direct the process of change there. For example, military aid was renewed despite the fact that El Salvador's Archbishop Oscar Romero and a number of civilian political leaders explicitly asked the Carter administration not to give such aid—and that the military had not asked for it. In short, U.S. policy makers assumed that they knew what was necessary for the Salvadorans to fulfill U.S. goals. Furthermore, the left was continuously regarded as a monolith. No effort was made to contact the left or to discern their ideological and political properties and divisions (p. 87). Thus ended the human rights policy in El Salvador. U.S. intervention began in full force as the October 15 junta collapsed.

The puzzle of the Carter administration's approach to the October junta is why it made no greater effort to support the junta and ensure its longevity. To some extent, the flow of information and the attention given to it can be held responsible. First, as mentioned, the local CIA chief had labeled two of the civilians as well as Colonel Majano *leftists,* which caused suspicion among traditional cold warriors. Second, Devine favored the status quo. He even counseled the junior officers to obey their superiors and not press to remove them from power (ibid., p. 167). If Devine's memoirs are reliable, as U.S. ambassador he sat in the embassy, held and attended social functions, and occasionally gently suggested to Romero that he moderate the death squad activities in El Salvador. Not until a regional meeting of ambassadors and State Department Latin Americanists was held in Costa Rica in May 1979 was a fire was lit under Devine to find out what the opposition was doing. With such lack of information, it is not surprising that El Salvador was interpreted as it was by Washington or that there was so little recognition of how close the country was to complete civil war.

In December 1979, Carter sent James Cheek, a career foreign service officer, to El Salvador to attempt diplomatic to stop the growing disarray of the junta's government. Cheek did try to convince the civilians to stay in the junta and the cabinet, but since he could not assure them of U.S. help in taking control back from the right wing of the military, his efforts were of no avail.

As the junta fell apart, the United States began to search for a supportable moderate political center. The problem was that the center had lost its political base by 1977, and during the Romero years, more and more of its leaders were killed. There is a significant problem when the center is not politically organized or cohesive, as was the case in Nicaragua. There is an even bigger problem when many of its leaders are dead and the rest know that they are the next targets, as in El Salvador. The simplified dependent image of El Salvador led the Carter administration to believe that there was a center, that it could be bolstered by the United States, and that it could share power with the military without being politically compromised. The simplified dependent image also correlates with the rest of the interpretation of the U.S. role as the patron of the coming order, which would evolve through civilized discussions of constitutional issues and the eventual selection of democratic representatives through elections. The polity was further simplified and the political problem made easier when the myth was propagated that violence in El Salvador was committed by outlaw extremists on the far right and far left, not by the mainstream security forces and protected and encouraged by the government.

Armed with these perceptions, the Carter administration set about convincing the Christian Democrats to replace the members of the Movimiento National Revolucionario who had left the junta. The makeup of this new junta also changed fairly quickly after the assassination of El Salvador's attorney general (probably by agents of the far right, with the consent of the Ministry of Defense). One week later, seven Christian Democrats resigned from the junta. The new civilian members were led by José Napoleon Duarte. The resignations signaled the end of the Christian Democratic Party, whose political organization had been disintegrating through the deaths of its members or by their defection to the rebels.[55]

In addition to creating a junta composed of representatives of a minute political center and a military establishment, who hated one another, the Carter administration was also determined to ensure that the junta was reformist. To do this, the administration supplied "nonlethal" military aid to prevent the left from achieving military success and to prevent any instability from the massive demonstrations that continued, despite the fierce response by the security forces. This military assistance matched the information the United States received regarding the strength of the guerrilla forces and their support from outside El Salvador. The administration acknowledged that their numbers were small. And because the administration held a modified enemy image of the USSR (although this was rapidly changing), it assumed that the left originated indigenously but that their loyalties, and ultimately their obedience, would be to Moscow.

The administration's goal was straightforward containment—to prevent a leftist victory in El Salvador in order to prevent the spread of Marxism to El Salvador, Guatemala, and Honduras.[56] Because the guerrillas were weak and because the U.S. sense of its own power was strong, nonlethal military aid was deemed sufficient (*nonlethal* meaning communications equipment, transportation equipment, flak jackets, tear gas, etc.). Those with more extreme images, including members of Congress and the Pentagon, called for a larger quantity of lethal military aid.

An important U.S. intervention in El Salvador following the first junta was the promotion of land reform. A land reform program was developed by an American, Professor Roy L. Prosterman of the University of Washington, whose previous experience in land reform programs included South Vietnam's abortive effort in the early 1970s. The American Institute for Free Labor Development, an international affiliate of the AFL-CIO, was brought in to provide technical assistance for the implementation of the land program. The Basic Law of Agrarian Reform that resulted was presented to the country in March 1980, at the same time that the Christian Democrats resigned from the second junta, making way for the Duarte junta.[57]

Another part of the Carter administration's policy in El Salvador was diplomatic. In March 1980, Frank Devine was replaced by Robert White, a tough career foreign service officer. His mission was to force the Salvadoran military to abide by its promises to reform and to live in harmony with, if not obedience to, the civilians in the junta. White was particularly passionate about the need to stop the gross violence. He was a solid member of the modified cold warrior group, and as such was sensitive to some Salvadoran political complexities but not to those of the left, and he was prone to believe any information indicating support for the left from the USSR. He regarded civilian allies of the left, like Guillermo Ungo and Rubén Zamora, as naive and "irrelevant" and easily duped by the leftists. He referred to the left as the "Pol Pot left."[58] "The far Left," he said, "are just totally dedicated revolutionaries who, if they came into power, would reject the United States. Their program would be to eliminate all U.S. power from the area and counter the United States by bringing in Cuba and perhaps the Soviet Union."[59]

Robert White believed that a political center could be created and maintained with U.S. support. His mission was to exercise U.S. influence to the maximum extent and to promote a democratic alternative to the left. According to one analyst, the United States, as represented by Ambassador White "acted as the junta's foreign ministry, close domestic political counselor and propagandist, arbiter of internal disputes, liaison with business, and, increasingly, military adviser."[60] White approved of military aid for the Salvadoran government, first the nonlethal variety and then the lethal variety, after an alarm was raised in January 1981 that Nicaragua was supporting the rebels in El Salvador.

The Carter administration followed this policy throughout its remaining months in office. Nineteen U.S. military advisers were sent to El Salvador, and Salvadoran officers were trained at U.S. bases in Panama in the largest training program ever sponsored by the United States in Latin America.[61] The Salvadoran military was warned against trying to depose the civilian members of the junta, as the United States continued to try to create a reformist political center. The U.S. embassy applied pressure for land reform and insisted that the program was moving ahead successfully.[62] The administration claimed that the land reform program had effectively destroyed both the stranglehold of the oligarchy on El Salvador's polity and the alliance between the oligarchy and the military. U.S. economic and military aid to El Salvador increased: by fiscal year 1980, Carter requested $58.8 million and planned to ask for $63 million for 1981 (p. 6). Throughout, no effort was made to negotiate with the left.

The Carter administration did try to use aid as a sanction to get the Salvadoran military to reduce human rights abuses. In December 1980, El Salvador security forces killed three U.S. nuns and a U.S. lay worker. U.S. aid was suspended until the Salvadoran government made a minimal effort to give an accounting of the murders. Aid was renewed in January 1981, at the same time that reports were issued indicating that Nicaraguan-backed forces were entering El Salvador.

POLICY DISPUTES

The Carter administration's policy toward El Salvador came under attack in the form of packaged criticisms, each associated with different worldviews. Those with the human rights view objected to renewed aid, questioned the wisdom of the administration's fear of the left and its simplification of the Salvadoran polity, and complained about its interpretation of information. Traditional cold warriors complained that the military aid was not enough, that it should take priority over economic aid, and that the value of land reform was dubious and, possibly, communistic. Their primary concern was a communist takeover.

The position of the human rights group reflected their nonenemy image of the USSR and their more complex image of the Salvadoran polity (except for its view of the Salvadoran military). First, they were skeptical of the argument that, if victorious, the Salvadoran left would ally the country with the USSR and Cuba. In questioning White, congressional members holding the human rights worldview indicated they were skeptical of his assessment of the Salvadoran left. For example, Stephen Solarz asked White why his view of the Salvadoran leftist threat differed from that of Mexico and why he believed that a leftist victory in El Salvador would lead to more Soviet influence.[63] White's response was a standard rendition of the "lessons" of history: Marxists just do that sort of thing; and Salvadorans like the "well-intentioned social democrats and others" who think they can ally with the Marxists would "soon realize how impotent they are when the policies of the Government begin to be set" (ibid.). Senator Paul Tsongas questioned White about whether the United States had adequately assessed Salvadoran nationalism and other political complexities in setting its policy in April 1981.[64]

Some members of this world-view group also attacked the Carter administration's notion that the Duarte junta represented a political center. Members of the National Security Council, the State Department, and other government agencies put out a dissent paper complaining that their analysis had been repressed. The Carter administration, they said, misrepresented the Salvadoran junta as moderate and reformist and deliberately discredited "centrist spokesmen of the opposition as puppets of hardline guerrilla leaders."[65] The dissent paper also alleged that the Carter administration was "prepared to . . . use military force in conjunction with others or, if necessary, unilaterally" in El Salvador to prevent a leftist victory" (p. 332). The dissent paper's concluding criticisms focused on poor interpretation of information, the suppression of opposing views, and a simplified understanding of the situation:

> We consider these activities and the policies they imply to be dangerously misguided. Current policy, as we interpret it, is based on inaccurate intelligence, and on the suppression within various bureaucracies of verified contradicting information. The options and recommendations on which policy decisions were made have been based on irresponsibly self-serving evaluations and analyses of intelligence reports available within the agencies. Critiques and dissenting views were systematically ignored. Underlying these apparent bureaucratic maladjustments one finds a fundamental lack of understanding of general conditions and trends in Central America and the Caribbean. (ibid., p. 333)

This analysis of El Salvador was echoed by others, including the director of the American Institute for Free Labor Development in El

Salvador. This group disagreed with the Carter administration's policy on the distribution of aid and hoped that the letter from Archbishop Romero to President Carter begging the United States not to send military aid to El Salvador's military junta would make a difference. They believed, as did some members of Congress, that the administration should not provide aid while the Salvadoran government continued with its miserable human rights record.[66]

The traditional cold warriors were on the opposite side of the policy debate. Brzezinski's office worked hard to get military aid approved. Moreover, members of the Pentagon, another bureaucratic locale of the traditional cold warrior worldview, also supported military aid to the junta. Ambassador White even accused the Pentagon of attempting to undermine his support for nonlethal, rather than lethal, aid. The Pentagon found the perfect opportunity in January 1981, when the myth of the Nicaragua-supported attack in El Salvador was circulating. White claimed that U.S. military personnel pressed the Salvadoran government to request seventy-five U.S. military advisers. "It amounted to a Pentagon take-over of U.S. foreign policy on El Salvador."[67]

Those with this worldview perceived the crisis in El Salvador as a result of Soviet efforts to foment revolution. They did not see the left as indigenous. They feared the consequences of a leftist takeover and saw it as much more likely than did the modified cold warriors. Consequently, they preferred fast-acting instruments of U.S. intervention. The difference in perception is demonstrated in the following exchange between Robert White and Representative Jack Kemp shortly after Ronald Reagan took office:

> MR. KEMP: Given the fact that they are now embroiled in this very difficult conflict, are you suggesting that there be no assistance to El Salvador?
>
> MR. WHITE: The priority for El Salvador should be important amounts of economic assistance. . . . I will repeat the point I made, that the El Salvador military proved itself perfectly capable of handling the leftist threats over the past year.
>
> MR. KEMP: Wait a minute. You just said that they have been capable of handling the insurgency that had taken place. In effect, they must think that they are confronting a military situation, which requires a military solution. . . . I recognize there are political and economic issues involved, but do you deny that there is a military threat to El Salvador posed by this insurgency?

MR. WHITE: There is a threat to El Salvador—there is an authentic insurgent movement. There is no question about that.
MR. KEMP: Would you define *authentic?* Does that mean totally indigenous to El Salvador? Are there any outside elements involved, to your understanding?
MR. WHITE: The insurgent movement in El Salvador would exist whether the Soviet Union or Cuba was lending assistance or not. . . . The Soviet Union, Cuba, and others have reaped enormous advantages around the world by attaching themselves to nationalist revolutions. The importance of what we have done in El Salvador is we have supported a new model for profound social, economic, and social change.
MR. KEMP: I don't disagree. . . . My question though was, if the insurgency should gain, is it not imperative that the Government of El Salvador have the ability to militarily repress it?
MR. WHITE: Congressman, I can guarantee you that there is no possibility of the leftists taking over El Salvador.[68]

The disagreement here was about the degree of threat, the degree of Soviet and Cuban control and involvement, and hence, the appropriate U.S. tactics. It went no deeper than that. But the most extreme traditional cold warriors even saw the land reform program as socialistic.

CONCLUSION

All of the cases discussed so far demonstrate the importance of two images in producing U.S. policy in Latin America. Interaction between a perceived enemy and a perceived dependent is a recipe for quick, coercive intervention, often using military, paramilitary, or covert forces. The two Carter adventures demonstrate that even when those images were only moderately strong they moved to the extreme as threat perceptions increased. The cases also illustrate the extent to which the enemy image was associated with containment as a global strategy. Even under modified conditions, the enemy image was associated with containment. In all of the cases, when threat perceptions increased, goals shifted from bilateral to global containment. When a country perceived as a dependent was associated with the enemy in a particular situation, the assumption was that the United States would have to act, since the dependent could not resist the machinations of the enemy.

U.S. policies toward Latin America illustrate the relation between coercion and the dependent image. They indicate that those policy preferences were not contingent upon a perceived enemy but were associated with the dependent image in and of itself. In the Peruvian case, where no enemy was identified, intervention involved the use of slower acting instruments, but it was coercive nevertheless. In the Carter administration, even those who did not perceive an enemy advocated coercive treatment because of the dependent stereotype. Although the human rights group denied that the USSR was a threat and perceived Central Americans as complex, they had a simplified view of right-wing dictators associated with U.S. imperialism.

These cases illustrate the important relation between images, tactics, goals, and strategy. First, different images produced different goals and policy preferences as shown by the division within the Eisenhower administration regarding Cuba. But the prevailing worldview consistently won the debates in all of these cases concerning definition of the situation and the policy approach. Second, the Carter cases show that underlying disagreements about images and goals could be obscured if a single set of tactics was interpreted as satisfying each goal. Goals were rarely discussed, but tactics were continually debated. One set of tactics could be advocated by groups with different short-run goals. But if the tactics failed to achieve all goals, the goal basis of the conflict might emerge.

The group that most failed to realize its policy preference was the human rights perceptual group. One can attribute this to the fact that they were a minority, but it was also due to their inability to present the administration with an alternative to containment. A global human rights strategy was not seen as an alternative, even by them. But without an alternative global strategy, it is difficult to see how they could have persuaded the procontainment majority to adopt its worldview, even when that majority felt that containment was achievable through human rights tactics.

5

THE LAST GASP OF THE COLD WAR:
REAGAN AND BUSH IN
CENTRAL AMERICA

THE PREVIOUS CHAPTERS EXPLORE THE U.S. USE OF COERCIVE TACTICS IN conflicts with countries perceived as dependents and that sometimes played with the devil—that is, the Soviet Union. The most rapid and coercive tactics were selected when a dependent appeared to be moving toward the enemy. When the enemy was not present, tactics were coercive but less forceful.

The end of the cold war changed some aspects of this pattern. Without an enemy, we would have expected that the tactics used in the Peruvian case would be used in all cases—unless, of course, the end of the cold war also heralded the demise of the dependent image. However, less than two years into the post–cold war era, the United States once again sent troops into a Latin American country, overthrowing and arresting the head of Panama, General Manuel Antonio Noriega.

This chapter begins with an evaluation of the prevailing image of Latin America in the Reagan and Bush administrations. Although there is some discussion of Reagan-era policies toward Central America, the main focus is on U.S. perceptions as the cold war gradually ended. The Bush policy toward El Salvador's peace negotiations are examined in the context of changing perceptions. Chapter 6 examines U.S. intervention in the post–cold war era.

BACK TO BASICS: THE REAGAN ERA WORLDVIEW

The Reagan administration brought in advisers with the classic dependent image of Latin America and the classic enemy image of the USSR. One of Reagan's principle authorities on Latin America was Jeane Kirkpatrick, who blasted assessments of "Latin American political culture [as] neither better or worse than that of the United States—just different." "Nonetheless," she wrote, "it always seems to be the Latin Americans who make a practice of 'the butchering of one's personal and political foes.' We vote; they butcher."[1]

Career foreign service officers who held the traditional cold warrior worldview were called upon to explain the new administration's policy to Congress in 1981. Walter Stoessel's simplified version of the political alignments in El Salvador has already been described. John Bushnell told Congress that the Salvadoran military was dominated by junior officers who had expelled the eighty or so right-wing officers responsible for human rights abuses—and that most of those abuses were committed by the left, anyway. (In fact, the military was severely divided, and its right wing was winning control of the government.) In explaining why El Salvador would never turn into a Vietnam, General Ernest Graves remarked that U.S. advisers should not be active in combat in El Salvador, and furthermore, they were fluent in Spanish and "you don't have the distinction of a Western force coming into an Oriental country. Most of the people [i.e., U.S. advisers] are of Latin extraction."[2]

Before Reagan's election, a group of six advisers met in Santa Fe, New Mexico, to consider Reagan's Latin American Policy. The group included current and future officials as well as private citizens. Their analysis of Central America and Nicaragua, in particular, showed a clear dependent-enemy image. They divided political actors into pro-American and anti-American (hence anti-Soviet and pro-Soviet) groups. The church and human rights groups, for example, were part of the anti-American coalition and, according to this analysis, participated in "overthrowing authoritarian, but pro-U.S., governments and replacing them with anti-U.S., Communist or Pro-Communist dictatorships of a totalitarian character."[3] The Reagan campaign's position on Latin America was also influence by other conservative ideologues, including Jesse Helms, who firmly believed that the Marxists were taking over in Central America.

The administration's early documents on Central America demonstrate the strength of the relevant worldviews. In a 1981 speech to NATO, Secretary of State Alexander Haig discussed the situation in El Salvador: "A well-orchestrated international Communist campaign designed to transform the Salvadoran crisis from the internal conflict to an increasingly internationalized confrontation is under way. With Cuban coordination, the Soviet bloc, Vietnam, Ethiopia and radical Arabs are furnishing at least several hundred tons of military equipment to the Salvadoran leftist insurgents."[4]

This analysis was supported by a February 1981 white paper issued by the State Department. Based upon hastily and poorly analyzed captured guerrilla documents, this white paper became the first major publication on El Salvador by the new administration. It describes the situation in El Salvador as being typical of "Soviet, Cuban, and other Communist military involvement in a politically troubled Third World country," the guerrillas and their Soviet and Cuban patrons cleverly terrorizing and duping the populace into passive acceptance and also deceiving "much of the world about the true nature of the revolution. Their objective in El Salvador as elsewhere is to bring about—at little cost to themselves—the overthrow of the established government and the imposition of a Communist regime in defiance of the will of the Salvadoran people."[5] Moreover, they attempted to disguise these machinations by bringing in, "for appearances sake, three small non-Marxist-Leninist political parties" (p. 232). The administration discounted the possibility of popular support for the guerrillas: "The guerrillas' propaganda aims at legitimizing their violence and concealing the Communist aid that makes it possible. Other key aims are to discredit the Salvadoran government, to misrepresent U.S. policies and actions, and to foster the impression of overwhelming popular support for the revolutionary movement" (ibid.).

The left everywhere was considered to be deceitful. Whatever agreements they made, they would cheat on.[6] Moreover, they were considered to be the same wherever they appeared. "Popular movements elsewhere in the region, for example in Guatemala, were interpreted as co-conspirators in this Soviet plot, the end purpose of which was to gain a foothold in the United States' traditional sphere of influence by establishing ideological loyalists and military bases. With naval and air bases in the Caribbean, the USSR would be in the position to disrupt US oil and shipping lanes, distract US military energies from Western Europe, the Middle East and elsewhere, and make direct attacks on the US mainland."[7]

Latin Americans with different views of the situation in El Salvador were regarded with contempt. Policy makers arrogantly believed that the people would eventually see that the U.S. interpretation of the problem was correct. A report on Mexico's efforts to mediate describes U.S. officials' views as follows: "A broader reason for encouraging Mexican mediation efforts . . . was a hope that if the effort fails, as the Administration expects it will, the Mexican Government will be braced by the rejection and will better appreciate the threat to its security presented by Soviet and Cuban interference in Central America. 'We want them to learn a lesson,' a senior official said."[8]

Salvadorans were also encouraged to adopt the U.S. assessment of the origins of the crisis: "The local, largely pro-Government press rarely dwells on the subject of foreign involvement. . . . Salvadoran officials appear to be under pressure from the Reagan Administration to pursue this line more actively. But according to moderates in government and many other Salvadorans, priority must go instead to ending the wartime killings so that the deep roots of peacetime violence can be attacked."[9] There was a strong belief that the Sandinistas were providing aid to revolutionaries in El Salvador, despite the absence of evidence. The U.S. ambassador to Honduras, for example, remarked that they had found no "smoking gun" but that he was certain that it existed.[10]

There was significant simplification and apparently unnoticed contradiction in the Reagan administration's assessment of the political center in El Salvador and elsewhere in Central America. Assistant Secretary of State for Latin America Langhorn Motley described the political spectrum in El Salvador (excluding the guerrillas) in these simple terms: "On the political left there is the Christian Democratic Party and on the right is the Arena Party. . . . A real democratic situation exists there."[11]

The guerrillas and their external communist supporters were described in highly conspiratorial terms, and the government of El Salvador was described as the only reasonable alternative to left- or right-wing violence.[12] The center—that is, the Christian Democrats—was described as in control and in the process of implementing the necessary reforms. Nevertheless, in the early 1980s the United States issued a national plan for El Salvador, which strongly encouraged the development projects needed to win the support of the people. Without those efforts, it was said, "the war would be lost."[13] In the early years, the left alone was blamed for the death squads, but by 1982 the administration admitted that there were also right-wing death squads. This realization inevitably led to a consideration of the relation between the Christian Democratic center, the military, and the right wing led by the ARENA party and former Major Roberto D'Aubuisson.

One can certainly argue that the obvious simplification of the Salvadoran polity was merely an effort to garner popular support for the administration's policies. However, that argument should not be accepted without careful thought, for the simplified picture of Salvadoran politics was accompanied by policies that required an equally simple reality. Support for the "political center" as represented by the Christian Democrats in El Salvador rested upon this simplification. In interviews in the summer of 1984, for example, U.S. embassy officials argued that the military and the business sector approved of Duarte, that his economic reforms were successful, and that the military was doing well in the battlefield.[14] Death squad activities were attributed to a small cell of the military and civilian right wing and were considered well under control. An interview with the Salvadoran military, including Minister of Defense Carlos Vides Casanova, painted a very different picture.[15] Vides Casanova said that reports of atrocities committed by the armed forces were leftist propaganda and that the death squads had nothing to do with the armed forces. An interview with the elite business organization ANEP (Asociación Nacional de la Empressa Privada) also reflected a different view of Salvadoran politics.[16] One ANEP official argued that few business people belonged to the Christian Democratic party because it was antagonistic to the private sector. He further described the country as divided into two camps, conservative (ARENA) and center-center-left. He also stated that the two most important instruments of power in El Salvador were the U.S. Embassy and the Salvadoran military.

The simplification of the U.S. assessment of Salvadoran politics can also be observed in statements made by Ambassador Dean Hinton when discussing the difficulties of achieving a political consensus in El Salvador: "I'm afraid it may be the hardest goal to reach. . . . I say that because of the polarization in this country, coupled with what I see as an extreme lack of tolerance for the other person's point of view. So many Salvadorans seem to see issues in strictly black and white terms. People are loath to compromise and so quick to question their opponents' motives."[17] This evaluation appears to be in stark contrast with the U.S. belief that elections, even in wartime, could bring democracy to El Salvador. In terms of image analysis, however, it makes sense. The administration believed at one and the same time that Salvadorans did not have a democratic mentality but that they could be transformed through U.S. tutelage. This accounts for the differences between the Salvadoran and U.S. assessments of the political situation and the U.S. stereotype of Salvadoran politics.

Underlying this perception was an overall perception of U.S. cultural and political superiority. Thomas Enders argued: "Rather than sacrifice either our interests or our values, either support for democracy or defense of our security, we must find a way to assert both so that we can check the Communist drive for power in the region, yet help the region develop in a humane and democratic way."[18] The policy dilemma was as follows. The Christian Democrats were considered the only reasonable leaders for El Salvador. However, the Reagan administration insisted that the conflict with the rebels be won militarily, and thus it needed to support the Salvadoran military, which both sponsored death squads and was close to the wealthy elite. The elite, in turn, supported ARENA, and both the military and the elite despised the Christian Democrats.

This dilemma was simplified by the Reagan administration worldview: the center was good, the left was bad. What to do, though about the far right, a far right containing both the military and the business elite? The answer was to compartmentalize and deny reality. This is illustrated by the gradual change in the administration's acknowledgment of right-wing death squads. In the first two years of the administration, their existence was called leftist propaganda. Ambassadors White and then Hinton were punished for denouncing right-wing death squads. Yet in 1983 Ambassador Thomas Pickering was joined by other officials in warning the Salvadoran government that right-wing death squad activity had to cease.

An important element in this view of the situation and actors in Central America was the assumption that U.S. aid and advice were necessary for Central American governments to stay in control or to gain victory. U.S. military and economic advisers were sent to El Salvador, and they advised, cajoled, and even threatened the Salvadoran military to improve the military performance and reduce human rights abuses. The U.S. Southern Command (Southcom) in Panama came up with the economic plan mentioned above. The contras, in Nicaragua, to give another example, were recruited and trained by U.S. advisers. U.S. training of Central American police forces to monitor and contain leftists while also promoting "democratic policing" is another example of the administration acting as though the United States knew the best way to teach others about democracy and to eliminate leftists.[19]

The administration repeatedly emphasized the necessity of democratic pluralism and of "an end to support for terrorist and insurgent groups in other countries of the region" for the institution of peace in Central America.[20] Pluralism was to be achieved through elections; and if elections were held, no matter what the context, and if U.S.-favored parties won, then democratic pluralism was said to exist. "Pluralism" in El Salvador excluded the left and major portions of the country and "democracy" required voting with ballots that could hardly be called secret. The National Bipartisan Commission on Central America in its *Report to the President* described political conditions in El Salvador as follows:

The coup d'état carried out by young officers in October of 1979 put an end to the brutal regime of General Romero and opened the way for . . . revolution. In the years since, even in the midst of escalating violence, the struggle for basic reform and a democratic transformation has continued. A sweeping program of land reform, now affecting 20 percent of the country's arable land, was launched; a Constituent Assembly election was held in which about 80 percent of those eligible went to the polls under very adverse circumstances; a new constitution has now been written and the country is preparing to elect a president in March.[21]

The narrow terms in which the United States defined political participation can be seen in the U.S. response to a 1984 proposal by Salvadoran guerrillas regarding power sharing. The guerrillas proposed sharing power with the government of El Salvador while negotiations ensued regarding the future of the country. The proposal was totally unacceptable to U.S. policy makers and to the Bipartisan Commission. First, despite their interest in subsequent elections, "the insurgents [did] not view power sharing as merely an interim measure needed in order to hold elections" (p. 110). Second, the commission concluded: "power sharing as proposed by the insurgents is not a sensible or fair political solution for El Salvador. There is no historical precedent suggesting that such a procedure would reconcile contending parties which entertain such deeply held beliefs and political goals, and which have been killing each other for years. Indeed, precedent argues that it would be only a prelude to a take-over by the insurgent force" (pp. 110–11).

What is amazing about this evaluation is, first, that it argues that conditions were not appropriate for power sharing in El Salvador but at the same time insists that elections could be held—and failed to notice that elections are supposed to distribute political power. Second, it states that the left could not be trusted to participate in the political system. Thus participation in El Salvador was never intended to include left-of-center political groups. Nevertheless, in the next paragraph, the report maintains that "a true political solution in El Salvador [could] be reached only through free elections in which all significant groups [had] a right to participate" (p. 111).

Similar simplifications of political participation were evident in descriptions of other countries. The military regime in Guatemala was praised for scheduling elections and promising to stay out of the political process, a promise not fulfilled (ibid. pp. 29–30). Political participation in Nicaragua was denounced as only one element of the repressive apparatus of a "Cuban-style regime," which caused poverty and despair in that country (p. 30). The simplification pattern in the dependent image often involves the assumption that there are good guys and bad guys and that the United States can find and support the good guys. This was evident in the Bipartisan Commission's description of political conflict in El Salvador:

> In El Salvador two separate conflicts have raged since 1979. One conflict pits persons seeking democratic government and its associated rights and freedoms against those trying to maintain oligarchical rule and its associated privileges. A second conflict pits guerrillas seeking to establish a Marxist-Leninist state as part of a broader Central American revolution against those who oppose a Marxist-Leninist victory.
>
> In each of these conflicts one of the parties has pursued its goals by violence. Both traditionalist death squads and murderous guerrillas have attacked political party, labor and peasant leaders working to establish and consolidate democratic institutions, killing them and dismantling their efforts to build democracy (p. 85).

This passage demonstrates the assumption that there was a clear political and institutional distinction between the right wing bad guys and the government of El Salvador. But anyone familiar with Salvadoran politics would agree that there was a link between the rightist death squads and the government. Although the United States advised President Duarte to break with the far right and periodically threatened to terminate aid if rightist death squads were not reined in, this did not happen. Even so, the Reagan administration continued to argue that Duarte and the Christian Democrats constituted a political center, which was clean despite its long history of compromise with the military right wing, dating from 1979, when it drove the reformist officers from power, until Duarte's ascent to the presidency in 1984. This political center never did defeat the far right or delink its control over policy.

The same report has an equally intriguing discussion of Guatemala, in which the Guatemalan armed forces are described at once as having a "long tradition" of "civic action" and as engaging in the "brutal behavior" that fuels revolution (pp. 99–100). This picture was combined with ideas about the role the United States had played in the past and should play in the future in Central America. The role was that of patron, the big brother helping the younger to understand democratic values and U.S. morality. *The Report to the President* emphasized that the "strategic and moral interests" of the United States coincided in Central America—that U.S. goals required the preservation of "the moral authority of the United States," the promotion of "the cause of democracy," and the prevention of "hostile forces from seizing and expanding control in a strategically vital area of the Western Hemisphere," (pp. 37–38). The report advocated that the United States help create an electoral process through advice and funds.

The characteristic impact of the dependent image on diplomacy emerged quickly in the new Reagan administration. In 1981 the United States did engage in some talks with Nicaragua, involving little diplomatic interaction and bargaining but a great deal of coercive ordering about. In Thomas Enders's initial approach to Nicaraguan negotiators in 1981, he demanded concessions from Nicaragua concerning its relations with Salvadoran guerrillas but did offer some U.S. concessions in return, such as pledges not to invade Nicaragua, to reconsider the activities of the counterrevolutionaries, and to consider resuming aid. These initial talks were not mild exchanges, and Enders came across to some Nicaraguans as taking a very rigid line, informing Nicaraguan officials in one exchange they should "never forget that the United States [was] exactly 100 times bigger" than Nicaragua.[22] And Daniel Ortega remarked that Enders was "as arrogant as he was tall" (which was six feet eight inches).[23] Nevertheless, some in the Reagan administration found Enders's approach much too soft. In the next negotiating effort in August 1981, Enders did not repeat that mistake: he issued a statement declaring that the termination of Nicaraguan support for insurgents in the region was a precondition for negotiations. Meanwhile, others in the administration were working to overthrow the Sandinistas by supporting the contras.

Subsequent exchanges further inflamed the situation. In September a declaration of nonaggression was composed, but it was followed two days later by joint U.S.-Honduran military exercises. There were humiliating U.S. demands that Nicaragua return new military equipment to its source (ibid. pp. 74–76). Roy Gutman's interviews with informed observers (and critics) of this approach to negotiations describe an approach to negotiations typical of those with the dependent image:

> Enders has been criticized by some Latin American experts for his style before the commandantes, which was cold and confrontational. One long-time participant in U.S.–Latin American negotiations commented: "Whatever their faults or virtues, you are talking to guys that have faced death, that have killed and that have exposed themselves. To threaten them is counterpro-

ductive. You can't expect them to say, 'OK, you're right, we're scared.' He backed them into a corner. It's an approach that never works."

And another U.S. official said: "Enders humiliated them. Threats would not work. The way to deal with them was to compliment them and face them with facts they could not cope with. Moreover, he didn't have the tools in his hands at the time to carry out the threats. It wasn't coercive diplomacy. It was bullshit diplomacy" (ibid., p. 77).

The pattern was repeated in subsequent diplomatic efforts. The Manzanillo talks, in which the U.S. team was led by special envoy Harry Schlaudeman, were opposed in principle by the hard right in Reagan's administration. Those who did favor proceeding with negotiations made demands concerning Nicaragua's internal political system that were bound to be unacceptable to Nicaragua and, more important, reflected the dependent image. In return, the United States promised to consider rethinking its policy toward Nicaragua. For example, in the timetable of reciprocal unilateral measures, the United States

called for specific Sandinista concessions over a ninety-day pe-riod in return for an undefined U.S. response. For example, it proposed that one third of the Cuban and Soviet military advis-ers be removed from Nicaragua within thrity days, the second third within sixty days, and the remainder within ninety days. After thirty days, "the U.S. military presence in Central Amer-ica will take Nicaraguan actions into consideration." After sixty days, "the U.S. continues to take Nicaraguan actions into con-sideration." And after ninety days, "the U.S. presence in Cen-tral American will have taken Nicaraguan actions into consider-ation" (pp. 219–20).

The United States also called for redesigning Nicaragua's internal political system; this proposal gives some insight into the U.S. percep-tion of Nicaragua's political center. Reagan's advisers universally be-lieved that Nicaraguan elections could not be fair. However, they split on the question of whether a candidate for the political center should participate in this election: one faction believed that participation amounted to sanctioning the process, the other argued that, even though the center had no chance of winning, it would be in a position to criticize the Sandinistas or to benefit from the public repression the Sandinistas were expected to impose (p. 239).

Two important pieces of information can be inferred from the Reagan administration's response to Nicaraguan elections. First, Reagan's advisers believed the elections would not be free and fair, demonstrating the strength of their image of the Sandinistas as dependents under hostile influence. Second, the U.S. approach to the centrist candidate, Arturo Cruz, reveals the administration's simplification of Nicaraguan politics. He was also supported by the faction of Reagan advisers who believed that participation in the elections would be beneficial. Cruz was chosen in a highly undemocratic process by two members of the Nicaraguan opposition group, the Coordinadora Democratica. The Coordinadora was an amalgamation of a broad variety of organizations opposing the Sandinistas, and the nine points of its platform included negotiation with the contras, which the Sandinistas did not regard as reasonable. The United States did then provide Cruz with a revised platform, dropping the more offensive provisions. But Cruz did not have a domestic constituency; he lived in Washington, D.C., and there was no local organization to run his campaign. And Cruz himself was reportedly highly uncertain about running for office (p. 241), failing to take advantage of the growing discontent with the Sandinistas in Nicaragua to form a popular support base.

Ultimately, the United States encouraged the center and the right to boycott the election. The missing element in the U.S policy was any understanding that domestic support for the opposition candidate had to be genuine and had to be organized in Nicaragua itself. Instead, the United States regularly interfered in the opposition's decision making and consistently acted as though this political center could be shaped and guided by the United States.

REAGAN ADMINISTRATION POLICIES: AN OVERVIEW

Once Reagan took office, top-level officials ensured that their image of Central America was shared throughout the administration. William Bowdler and Robert White were dismissed. Moreover, the Reagan team that replaced these career Latin America experts lacked expertise in the region (ibid., p. 27). This is not to say that the administration had no Latin Americanists: its conservative specialists included Jeane Kirkpatrick, Otto Reich, Roger Fontaine, and Constantine Menges. But all of these individuals shared dependent and enemy images of Latin America and the Soviet Union, respectively. Consequently, there was fundamental agreement on policy: Marxist revolutionaries in

El Salvador and elsewhere in Central America had to be opposed and defeated. The Sandinista government had to be destroyed. The disputes that did exist among these advisers concerned tactics. Some—including those with less expertise on Latin America such as Richard Allen—opposed land reform, saw centrists like President Duarte as weak, and advocated the elimination of the left. Alexander Haig, for example, is famous for announcing that the administration would "go to the source" of leftist insurgencies in Central America, which he believed was Cuba. Some tended to favor a policy of rollback (overthrow of leftist governments). Others, such as Thomas Enders, assistant secretary of state for Latin America (who was not a Latin America expert), favored containment.

The first clear tactical decision by the Reagan administration regarding Central America, and Nicaragua in particular, was that negotiations would not be relied upon. Military aid to El Salvador was increased almost immediately. Ambassador Lawrence Pezzullo's use of diplomatic leverage to shore up domestic opposition to the Sandinistas and attempts to moderate tensions between the United States and the new Nicaraguan government (with, among other things, aid funds) were discarded (ibid., p. 36).

From 1981 until the ouster of Thomas Enders as assistant secretary of state for Latin America, the central debate within the Reagan administration concerned what kinds of and how many U.S. resources should be devoted to Central America. Enders advocated the containment of Nicaragua (which is to say, Cuba and the Soviet Union) and a negotiated defeat of the left in other countries. He was opposed by the hard-line group associated with Jeane Kirkpatrick and National Security Adviser William P. Clark, who advocated rollback—that is, the overthrow of the Sandinistas—and extensive military aid to the rest of Central America to defeat the leftist rebels. After months of maneuvering and bureaucratic infighting, Enders lost the policy battle and his post.

The Reagan administration's regional policy can be described as a mixture of containment and rollback, depending upon the country in question and the faction dominating policy making at any given time. In general, the trends were as follows.

EL SALVADOR

Reagan's policy toward El Salvador sought to realize a military defeat of the rebel FMLN coupled with the establishment of democratic institutions through elections. This required support for the Christian Democrats and a combined effort to both restrain the right wing and mend relations between the Christian Democrats and the right wing. The latter goal was essentially impossible, since the right wing believed that the Christian Democrats (and often their U.S. supporters) were taking the country down the path to communistic ruination.

The military U.S. objectives in El Salvador were easier to achieve, although defeat of the rebels was never possible. First, the Reagan administration sought to improve the equipment, training, and fighting ability of the Salvadoran armed forces so that they could contain and then defeat the FMLN. Second, the administration sought to transform the character of the Salvadoran armed forces from defender of the oligarchy to a professional national army subordinate to civilian authority. To accomplish this, the administration pumped aid into El Salvador. By the mid-1980s almost 31 percent of this aid was direct war-related aid, about 44 percent was indirect war-related aid, while the rest was economic development aid.

The administration counted among its successes in the military sphere an improvement in the performance of Salvadoran troops. They actually engaged the rebels in combat and began to use more effective tactics. Several key officers closely associated with the oligarchy were removed, and the security forces, closely associated with the death squads, were reorganized. But in the end the military did not become the apolitical professional force envisioned by the Reagan administration. Many of the changes at the top were cosmetic, and the military remained the final arbiter in the political arena. Moreover, although combat in the rural countryside may have become more efficient, peasants living in rebel-controlled areas were still considered guerrilla sympathizers and, therefore, legitimate targets. The military failed to win hearts and minds in this war.

The political U.S. objectives were more difficult to address and impossible to achieve. By 1984, with Duarte's election the Reagan administration's policy looked like it could start counting successes; when he was elected, Duarte and the U.S. policy gained significant support, particularly in the United States, where he was well liked on Capitol Hill. The elections were widely regarded as fair despite important criticisms. But as time passed, the prospects for the Duarte government deteriorated. Popular support diminished as he failed to end the war and as his administration was increasingly criticized for corruption. By the late 1980s the right wing began to make significant gains in the electoral process; it took the presidency in 1989. Thus the United States lost control of the electoral process that was once seen as the channel for the political center and the best path to centrist control of the political system.

NICARAGUA

U.S. policy toward Nicaragua was designed to promote the collapse of the Sandinista government, using diplomatic, economic, and military pressure. Diplomatically, the Reagan administration tried to isolate Nicaragua, complaining that Nicaragua consistently refused to negotiate. Nevertheless, serious talks were held in 1981 and 1983. In August 1981 the Sandinistas agreed that Nicaragua would limit its military buildup and pledged not to assist the guerrillas in El Salvador in exchange for a U.S. pledge of nonaggression. The State Department ultimately scuttled this agreement by rewriting it in an insulting and unacceptable form. Verbal U.S. support for negotiation efforts by the Contadoras and by Costa Rican President Oscar Arias was accompanied by behind-the-scenes maneuvering to prevent those negotiations from succeeding. When the Contadora effort approached a successful conclusion in September 1984, the Reagan administration announced that it found the agreement acceptable but that it doubted that the Sandinistas would agree to sign. When they did, the United States suddenly found serious flaws in the agreement and began consultations with Costa Rica, El Salvador, and Honduras to get them to back out.

Military pressure was applied in a variety of forms. The United States created and supported the Nicaraguan Contras. It also conducted joint military maneuvers in Central America with a number of Nicaragua's neighbors. Finally, it placed an economic embargo against Nicaragua and used its leverage in international aid-granting institutions to destabilize the Sandinistas.

HONDURAS AND COSTA RICA

U.S. policy toward Honduras and Costa Rica followed a similar line. Both were encouraged to join the U.S. effort to contain Nicaragua militarily. Honduras was encouraged to see its internal problems as resulting from international subversion. It was militarized as part of the effort to train Salvadoran forces and the contras. As a consequence, Honduras began to experience political disappearances, increased repression, and a new threat to its stability in the form of thousands of contras living illegally in the countryside. In Costa Rica, the United States attempted to transform the police into an anticommunist paramilitary force.

REGIONAL POLICY

U.S. regional policy in Central America became one large exercise in containment. The policy followed the worldview of the Reagan administration perfectly, a logical response to the world as this administration saw it. The Central American people and governments were seen as dependents, with one government having been overtaken by agents of the Soviet Union. The conflict was seen as having global implications, and U.S. regional goals were derived from perceptions of threat to U.S. global goals. As Alexander Haig stated in 1982, "Salvador is at once a global, a regional and a local problem. In solving it we have to act in all three areas."[24] This is not a difficult development to understand or explain from a perceptual standpoint.

THE BUSH ADMINISTRATION: WHAT HAPPENED TO THE ENEMY?

Perceptually, the Bush administration resembled the Reagan administration except that ideological hard-liners advocating a rollback policy toward Nicaragua were absent. This camp was largely discredited by the Iran-contra scandal, and most remaining members departed with Ronald Reagan. Bush was left with advisers with the standard cold warrior view, who saw Central America through the dependent image and the Soviet Union through the enemy image. U.S. policy toward Central America would not change with the Bush administration unless the images supporting that policy changed, and change they did. As the enemy image of the Soviet Union disintegrated, policy toward Central America began to be shaped by the dependent image alone.

What happens when one's worldview falls apart? Images are difficult to change, particularly images as threat filled as the enemy image. The need for change produces a sense of loss of control, and so this change is resisted psychologically. The enemy image of the USSR, while threatening, also offered the psychological assurance of knowing the enemy; explanations and predictions of Soviet behavior were easy and were made with confidence. Then came the rapid change in the USSR and in the U.S. image of it. Official resistance to changing the image was rapidly overcome by events. The impact of the change in the enemy image of the USSR extended to Latin America, even though there was no evidence that the Bush administration had changed its dependent image of these countries. Without an enemy, the motivation for coercive intervention in response to extreme threat perceptions coupled with containment goals disappeared. But because the U.S. dependent image of Latin America did not change, the potential for coercive intervention remained. It simply was no longer linked to global strategic considerations.

What this means is that, although there is no longer a threat-based justification for using coercion in Latin America and there is no containment strategy to guide U.S. policy in Latin America, nevertheless, because the image has not changed and because U.S. power vis-à-vis Latin America remains the same, there is no reason to expect a critical reevaluation of U.S. tactics. However, the United States, as one would expect in a chaotic system, will not return to the pre–cold war era of U.S.–Latin American policy. The Cold War altered forever the path to be taken, yet one causal factor did not change: the U.S. dependent image of Latin America.

THE BUSH ADMINISTRATION: PROSPECTS FOR PEACE IN EL SALVADOR

The Bush administration began its approach to Central America with strong remnants of the cold war worldview in place. In the early days of the administration, for example, Secretary of State James Baker "acknowledged that the Soviet Union was changing in profound ways, although then, and throughout the year, he called on Gorbachev to prove his 'new thinking' by resolving regional conflicts like those in Central America."[25] Gradually, the change in the U.S. perception of the Soviets affected its perceptions of the left in Latin America. Bush administration policy makers remained consistent in perceiving leftist forces in Central America as dangerous and untrustworthy, but without a Soviet sponsor, their ability to threaten U.S. interests in the region were considered minimal. Moreover, the Soviet Union had now become a friend, meaning that the Soviets would not only be neutral but helpful in dealing with the left in Central America.

The post–cold war images produced two policy patterns, one reflecting the changed perceptions of the Soviet Union, the other reflecting the unchanged perceptions of Latin America. Crises in Central America associated solely with the U.S.-Soviet rivalry were quickly redefined. The Bush administration clearly wished the problem to disappear and had no desire to expend valuable leverage with Congress to continue the Reagan administration's Central America policy. Elliot Abrams, a hard-line Reaganite ideologue, was replaced by Bernard Aronson, a pragmatic conservative, as assistant secretary of state for Latin America. Bush pushed Speaker of the House Jim Wright to meet with the secretary of state and forge a bipartisan accord on Central America, in an effort to escape a repetition of the strain on executive-legislative relations caused by Central American policy during the Reagan administration (ibid. p. 9). In contrast to Reagan, Bush supported Costa Rican President Arias's Esquipulas peace plan for Central America.

At the same time, Bush saw no more complexity in Central American politics than did Reagan. Bush tried "to effect a political escape from the morass of Nicaragua, but it was hardly a solution. A solution required delicate negotiations between the Sandinistas and the internal opposition in Managua, not between Democrats and Republicans in Washington nor, for that matter, between the US and Soviet governments. . . . Instead of going to Managua to negotiate or to Latin America to consult, Aronson's first trip abroad as Assistant Secretary of State was to Moscow" (ibid, p. 10). In other words, the assumption was that the United States and the Soviet Union, not Central Americans, were the crucial actors determining events in Central America. The administration's frustration over the inability of the Soviet Union to affect the behavior of its alleged dependents in Central America failed to elicit a reexamination of the recipe for effective tactics.

Although the Soviets and the United States became friends, the Bush administration still had a strong distaste for the left in Latin America. In 1989 the administration strongly distrusted the Sandinista election plan and accused the Nicaraguan government of running a dishonest election—until the opposition won. In El Salvador, the rebels were consistently blamed for breakdowns in their peace negotiations with the Salvadoran government and were accused of attempting to maneuver for control of the country. But in early 1992, a peace accord was signed between the right-wing government, headed by President Alfredo Christiani, and the FMLN guerrillas, the best hope for peace in El Salvador in twelve years. Between late 1988 and early 1989, four important events influenced the momentum toward peace negotiations. First, there were crucial changes in the makeup of El Salvador's right wing. Second, the Christian Democrats, upon whom the United States had placed great hopes for military defeat of the rebels, fell apart in a sea of corruption and internal disputes. Third, the cold war started to collapse. And finally, George Bush replaced Ronald Reagan as president. These changes meant that, by the time Salvadoran presidential elections rolled around in March 1989, the United States was more disposed to urge negotiation with the rebels, particularly if negotiations meant that the rebels might participate in the election.

In early March, the United States supported the postponement of the election scheduled for March 19 in response to the rebels' suggestion that negotiations and a postponement of the election might convince them to participate. The reason for U.S. support was clear: the right wing seemed likely to win the election, and a six-month delay might forestall that victory (the Bush administration being concerned with congressional reaction to a right-wing victory). The rebels made some demands unacceptable to the El Salvadoran military (including a cut of 80 percent in the armed forces)—and the elections were held. The right wing ARENA candidate, Alfredo Cristiani, won. The Christian Democrats did very poorly. And the left did not participate. Cristiani immediately announced he would negotiate with the rebels, but for the first year of his presidency he did not follow up on this promise. In fact, ARENA's supporters, particularly the wealthy business elite, wanted to defeat the rebels militarily and to end programs such as land reform. Freedom was restricted, and repression—including death squad activity—increased.

A number of factors helped change this. First and foremost was a change in the support base of the ARENA party, which gave Cristiani greater domestic political leverage. This change happened when the behind-the-scenes strongman and arch right-winger who had run ARENA during most the 1980s, Roberto D'Aubuisson, contracted terminal cancer. As his followers squabbled about the leadership of the party, Cristiani took the opportunity to get out from under these extremists and build up a support base of conservatives who believed that the war would not end without negotiations.

Cristiani himself was an important ingredient in the change. Forty-one years old when he became president, he was a member of a very wealthy coffee-growing family of the oligarchy. Politically, he was conservative—more conservative than the Christian Democrats, certainly—but he was not a murderer. He was a founding member of a conservative economic think tank in El Salvador called FUSADES, and after he became president, he appointed members of this organization to advisory positions involving economic progress. But for the first year he was in office, Cristiani had little control over the antidemocratic faction in ARENA and the military. With D'Aubuisson's illness and the inability of that faction to pull together behind another leader, he gradually gained more power.

Second, and very important in convincing the right that negotiations were necessary, was the change in U.S. policy. At first, after the election of Cristiani, the Bush administration's goal to keep the right wing in check while pressing the war against leftist rebels to convince them they could not win militarily and must participate in the electoral process. As the peace negotiations reached a critical juncture in late 1991, U.S. officials pushed the right wing to conclude the agreement. Central to this was the change in the administration's belief that the Soviet Union sought to take over Central America.[26]

Why, given its hostility toward the left, did the Bush administration push the Salvadoran right to negotiate? One answer is that, with the end of the cold war, funds for El Salvador to fight a seemingly endless war against its rebels was less and less politically feasible for the United States. Many members of Congress had never shared the Reagan-Bush perception of the left in Central America, and those who did had changed their perception with the end of the cold war.

More important, however, was the change in the Bush administration's perception of the rebels: without their alleged Soviet patrons, they posed no real threat, despite their evil intentions. They were now viewed—as were other members of the Central American political spectrum—as childlike. How could a childlike guerrilla force win against forces supported by the United States unless they had a patron? The Bush administration's diminishing interest in El Salvador made it possible for neutral actors, like Costa Rican President Oscar Arias and the United Nations to step in as mediators. The UN-sponsored negotiations began in February 1990.

The role of the United States in these negotiations was primarily to press the Cristiani administration to stay at the negotiating table. In 1990, half of U.S. aid funds for El Salvador were frozen as a result of the Salvadoran military's murder of six Jesuit priests. Military aid was used as leverage to convince the government to negotiate with the left. Half of U.S. military aid was frozen in January, 1991 to promote the negotiations and a cease-fire. At the same time the United States provided new planes and helicopters to the Salvadoran military to replace those shot down by guerrillas. U.S. Assistant Secretary of State Bernard Aronson defended the Cristiani government against human rights abuses charges, but he also visited the rebels in guerrilla-held territory to try to convince them that the United States supported the peace process. In April 1991, Aronson and Joint Chiefs of Staff Chairman Colin Powell "reminded President Cristiani and Salvadoran military chief General René Emílio Ponce that the U.S. Congress could refuse military aid for next year's budget if they appear too intransigent."[27] U.S. officials periodically sat in at the negotiating table at the United Nations, and as the negotiations reached their final days in late 1991, these officials participated intensely in behind-the-scenes efforts to "soften positions on the Government side."[28]

As the talks progressed, the Salvadoran right split into more and more factions. The business sector divided on the importance of peace versus continued warfare. The military divided into four groups: one opposed negotiations because it saw the outcome as a loss of the military's traditional economic and political privileges; the second believed negotiations were dangerous but, rather than oppose them publicly, prepared a paramilitary apparatus to be put into operation after a cease-fire was signed; the third saw the negotiations as the only institutional alternative and as a way to allow the armed forces to gain professionalism and legitimacy; and the fourth was the majority of rank and file, who were uncertain, being ignorant of the details of what was being negotiated.

U.S. pressure was probably particularly effective with the military. A year of the United States giving and withdrawing military aid made it clear that the military could not expect aid without progress in the negotiations. By February 1991, Defense Minister General René Emílio Ponce stated: "We cannot go against changes which are taking place regionally, nationally, and internationally. The Armed Forces cannot go against the tide of historical changes. We believe it is necessary to readjust our organization and carry out the reforms that would allow us to have a strong professionally organized Armed Forces, and that in the future it will fulfill its role within a democratic community at peace.[29] His statement reflected both the end of the cold war and the change in U.S. perceptions of the left in El Salvador. The conditions that had permitted U.S. support during the 1980s had changed.

Some of most important elements of the peace accords were a 50 percent reduction of the size of the Salvadoran military and the substitution of a national civilian police force for the police forces, which were institutionally tied to the military. Military officers found guilty of human rights abuses by an independent commission were to be removed. The government promised to attempt to purchase land occupied in the rebel-controlled zone and turn it over to the squatters. The United Nations agreed to provide a four-hundred-troop peacekeeping force.

In general, U.S. behavior was that associated with the dependent image without the enemy image. U.S. leverage was applied to get the Cristiani government to negotiate and to agree to the peace accords. All sides, including Cristiani, claimed victory, but in the end it was the United States that achieved its desired ends. Salvadoran interests were forced to comply with U.S. interests.

The Salvadoran peace accords would not have been possible during the cold war. Many regard the agreement as providing the guerrillas the victory they could not have achieved in the battlefield, that although the guerrillas made concessions, the Cristiani government made more. This too would not have been possible during the cold war. Interestingly, the United States seems to regard the accords as a success for both the United States and Cristiani.[30] If so, the significant concessions made by both sides will get little consideration, and any potential lessons from the U.S. involvement in a twelve-year civil war that could not be won through the tactics preferred by the United States will be missed. This blindness is likely to be another long-term pattern of the post–cold war.

CONCLUSION

The Reagan administration's policies in Central America were classic cold war image-based policies of intervention to prevent a perceived Soviet effort to extend its influence in the region. The policies involved all of the cold war tactics except one, outright military intervention (although that did take place in Grenada in 1983). It is legitimate to ask why the administration did not take the extra step and use direct overt military force to eliminate the Sandinistas in Nicaragua and the FMLN in El Salvador. Is this something that one should expect, given the operative images?

The administration did not use direct military force in Nicaragua and El Salvador for two reasons. First, there never was an internal U.S. consensus on the need for military force. In the first Reagan term, bureaucratic battles were waged between those who favored containment and those who favored rollback, but even those who favored rollback believed that U.S. support for the contras and other covert operations would suffice to destroy the Sandinista government and the FMLN. It was rumored in Central America in 1984 and 1985 that the United States expected that the Sandinistas would eventually respond to contra attacks by invading Honduras, the contra's sanctuary. This would then invoke the defense commitment of CONDECA, a regional defense organization that included Central American military governments, which the Reagan administration had resuscitated after years of torpor. These forces would do the ground fighting, while the United States provided the air power that would defeat the Sandinistas. Once the Sandinistas were gone, the FMLN would follow, since it was firmly believed that the FMLN depended upon Sandinista support. This scenario is believable. The Reagan administration was hampered by public opinion opposing U.S. military intervention in Central America; a certifiable Sandinista assault against a neighbor would overcome much of that opposition.

Second, the policy the administration followed was incremental, and it often appeared to be working better and better with each escalation. The cost was relatively low; the Sandinistas were hurt both by the contras and by U.S. efforts to isolate them internationally. Meanwhile, in El Salvador during the mid-1980s, with Duarte in office and the Salvadoran military becoming a more effective fighting force, things appeared to be going quite well from the Reagan perspective. More-over, advocates of this policy would probably look at it in the post–cold war context as a cold war success: the Sandinista revolution was largely destroyed, and the guerrillas in El Salvador laid down their arms.

Should the Reagan administration have launched an outright overt military assault on Nicaragua, given the high threat with which they saw Central America? Domestic opposition made that a nonoption in 1981 and 1982. The Reagan worldview may have been the prevailing one, but these policy advocates were not about to fight a very contentious battle with opponents in Congress and the public, particularly when the administration had bigger concerns in Europe and with the arms race. After those early years, they probably thought they were on the right course anyway and did not need to invade unless provoked—which they did think a real possibility.

The perceptual changes that accompanied the end of the cold war shifted the pattern of U.S. intervention in Latin America. The Salva-doran case demonstrates how quickly and profoundly the elimination of the enemy image in the Central American context changed U.S. goals and negotiating behavior. This change was not accompanied by a reflective examination of the costs and consequences of containment-based intervention in Latin America, however. The absence of change in the dependent image of Latin America provided no motivation to reexamine intervention in principle. Thus, the emerging post–cold war U.S. approach to Latin America was destined to be different but still interventionist.

U.S. policy toward Panama, which is examined in the next chapter and which also took place during and after the cold war, gives us an opportunity to explore both the impact of a pure dependent image on tactic selection and possible trends in post–cold war U.S. policy toward Latin America. U.S. policy toward Panama during the late 1980s fol-lowed the pattern usually associated with the dependent image, support-ing the theory that the dependent image alone, without an added threat perception from the enemy image, produces the most severe form of coercive policy. The United States had no hesitation in using military force once other coercive tactics failed to achieve its goals. Moreover, the inadequacies of U.S. policy leading up to the U.S. invasion demon-strate the impact of the dependent image along with powerful self-image. U.S. policy makers simply believed that Noriega could be dis-posed of easily; however, the absence of an enemy led to the absence of a recipe for dealing with this Panamanian fly in the ointment. Policy was uncoordinated, bureaucratic conflict was rife, and the personal pride of a U.S. president was permitted to play an important role in the decision to invade another country.

Interestingly, while the end of the cold war terminated the U.S. propensity to use military force to prevent a perceived Soviet opportunity, it opened the door to the U.S. use of military force to achieve other goals. U.S. policy makers are now freer to consider military attacks, not because the fear of escalation to a superpower conflict is gone but because the difficult trade-offs need no longer be made. Panama was, after all, a transition case. It may have been the first post–cold war invasion by the United States, but the problem originated from the common cold-war-based tactic of using military strongmen in Latin America as a vanguard against leftists in the region. This is the role Noriega played throughout his years of cooperation with the United States. Once that role was no longer necessary, it was also not necessary to put up with his drug dealing or his insults. The Bush administration did not need to decide between a guarantee against leftist influence or a democratic government allowing free speech and open political participation.

One final element should be considered as a potential factor in influencing post–cold war policy—the U.S. self-image. Despite political changes in the former Eastern bloc, despite claims that the West "won" the cold war, and despite the euphoria over the success of U.S.-led military operations in the Persian Gulf, the basis for U.S. domination of the international theater is clearly changing. A nuclear arsenal is increasingly meaningless as a source of power and leverage, and U.S. economic might is declining relative to other countries. The United States will be decreasingly able to set international agendas, and this is producing some deep changes in the U.S. self-image.

Several patterns are possible if the U.S. self-image is challenged. There will be efforts to bolster that self-image to keep it positive. If the collective self-image does ultimately degenerate into a negative one, the country's policy makers will manifest the kinds of behaviors observable in defeated or downtrodden countries: a decline in the ability to see alternative sources of leverage or alternative policies; an unwillingness to take risks; a preoccupation with demonstrating competence; and an excessive attention to information. Similarly, people will attempt to retain control when its loss seems possible, particularly when the situation they are in is highly threatening. Loss of control hastens loss of self-esteem and the emergence of a negative self-image.

The U.S. self-image has been intricately tied to its international role as superpower. The end of the cold war has threatened this self-image and role. A central policy-related question concerns what the

U.S. response to this loss of control will be. Self-image bolstering is expected to some degree, yet there was early post–cold war evidence that policy makers were not engaging in denial. They did recognize that the era of superpower dominance was over in some domains, particularly those related to the nuclear arms race and alliances. Bush and his aides indicated as much at the end of the Houston economic summit in the summer of 1990.[31]

It seems likely that any U.S. effort to maintain a sense of power will shift from a perception of military might to a perception of economic might. Because Americans have seen their country as a military power first and foremost, the increasing irrelevance of military might holds serious consequences. Not only is the major instrument that gave the United States power becoming passé, it is being replaced by instruments that the United States not only has less of but that it has little control over in comparison to other industrialized giants: economic power and political power. This will pose a serious challenge to the U.S. sense of control. However, at least one portion of the U.S. role as global protector could be salvaged by directing U.S. military power to some other important global obligations like the drug war or operations to support humanitarian relief.

6

THE NEW WORLD ORDER:
INTERVENTION IN
POST-COLD WAR LATIN AMERICA

As the cold war ground to an end in the late 1980s a new U.S. policy toward Latin America emerged. Guided by the dependent image of Latin America prevalent in the Bush administration, cold war tactics were employed to direct change in the region but with no overriding general strategy such as containment. The U.S. approach to Latin America was familiar but new, at the same time. Its efforts to employ the traditional tactics of the cold war were tempered by the absence of the enemy image. Although coercive treatment of Latin Americans remained, the urgency was gone, largely because neither drug lords nor small bands of leftists posed a perceived threat.

Despite the diminished sense of threat, the passing of the cold war does have serious implications for the United States. The cold war produced repression in many parts of the Third World, caused the United States to ally itself with repressive governments in Latin America, and transformed the legitimacy of governments in that region. Countries perceived as having served the interests of the United States rather than those of their own people were bound to become unstable as the restraints imposed by the cold war disappeared. Just as U.S. policy makers found the Latin American left less threatening, these groups could see that U.S. support for rightist regimes had also changed. These governments would have to respond to demands from sectors that had been neglected or repressed during the cold war.

The cold war contributed mightily to the U.S. propensity to ignore the political realities in Latin America. Continued reliance on cold war goals and tactics allowed the United States to ignore impending political crises, particularly crises of legitimacy. This chapter examines two cases of U.S. policy toward Latin America in the post–cold war era. The first is Panama, which illustrates the continuing presence of the dependent image in producing coercive interventionist policies. The second is Peru, which provides a glimpse of the future.

PANAMA: RETURN OF THE BANANA REPUBLIC

Panama has been viewed as a dependent throughout its history; the United States has been intricately involved in Panamanian politics since its beginning as a country. The Panama canal was built and owned by the United States and became a major campaign issue in Ronald Reagan's first run for the presidency in 1976. The canal and the Canal Zone were regarded as U.S. property. During and long after the canal treaty negotiations, Americans expressed concern about the ability of Panamanians to run the canal. Moreover, a U.S. presence in the Canal Zone was also seen as crucial to the U.S. war against communism. George Bush expressed this position in 1972.[1] Thus the initial worldview that guided U.S. policy toward Panama was the traditional cold war worldview. The Panamanians were dependents, they held an important geopolitical position due to the canal and its importance in the cold war, and they could not be relied upon to conduct their part in the cold war without U.S. leadership. This led to a preference for pro-U.S. strongmen in Panama, including General Manuel Noriega.

During the Carter administration, Panama was led by General Omar Torrijos, who, although from the traditional mold of the military dictator, was a nationalistic populist. He called for the return of the canal to Panama and had a receptive audience in the Carter administration. Lacking a strong traditional cold war worldview, the Carter administration was more responsive than other administrations to nationalism in Latin America. Concerns about potential sabotage against the canal were important considerations in Carter's efforts to negotiate a treaty (ibid., p. 92).

But Carter did not win reelection, and Torrijos was killed in a plane crash in 1981. The Reagan administration did have the traditional cold war worldview and accepted Torrijo's replacement General Manuel Antonio Noriega, as leader of Panama. Noriega soon maneuvered himself into position as Panama's de facto head of state. The United States was contemptuous of Panama under Noriega, who was seen as a manipulative, dishonest dictator who sold information to both the United States and Cuba and who participated in shady operations, some of which involved drugs. Interestingly, this knowledge did not alarm the United States. He gave information to Cuba, the hemispheric agent of the evil empire, but U.S. officials who dealt with him were seemingly confident that opportunism was his motive and that he could be controlled and manipulated to serve U.S. ends. This is typical of the dependent image: dependents are corrupt and we know it, but we are superior, and we call the shots.

This image can be seen in numerous statements by U.S. officials. An intelligence officer who worked with Noriega for ten years said, "I personally was glad he died. . . . Torrijos was a pain in the ass. He once told me he didn't care a stitch for the U.S. except its women and money. Sure, Noriega worked for the Cubans, but we calculated he belonged twenty percent to them and eighty percent to us."[2] Officials like John Negroponte also acknowledged that Noriega "played both sides" of the political fence (p. 122). And Oliver North knew that Noriega was "double dipping" but that "Noriega was an ally" in North's war against the Sandinistas (p. 158). State Department officials took to calling Noriega a "rent-a-colonel" (ibid.). In 1986 Elliot Abrams, assistant secretary of state for Latin America, described Panama under Noriega as the typical cold war dependent ally: "We have never lacked a sympathetic hearing for our views from Panama's government. . . . There has been no dispute concerning U.S. military bases in Panama. In a region where we have too many problems, the virtual absence of difficulties about our most significant military bases is notable and beneficial to us."[3]

Once Noriega's participation in the international drug industry became common knowledge, Abrams was anxious to get rid of Noriega and advocated his overthrow or kidnapping in the spring of 1988. Yet even when Noriega was generally recognized as a liability to the Reagan administration, he was not considered a threat. The dependent image was not accompanied by a perception of the enemy's presence, and a political liability is not as alarming as a threat. One administration official, interviewed for the *Miami Herald*, said, "We do not see Noriega abandoning the U.S. sphere. . . . He likes the good life and we do not see him joining the East just to spite the U.S. And at the same time, we do not see the Soviets warmly embracing Noriega because they understand that challenging the U.S. in Panama could create a crisis between Washington and Moscow."[4]

The dependent image was certainly reflected in the Reagan administration's (and the the Bush administration's) view of the political arena in Panama. Although Abrams described Panama in 1986 as "one of the most open societies in the hemisphere, with pluralistic social and economic institutions [and a] genuine freedom to express political dissent and the legal rights of individuals are generally respected" when pressed, he admitted that the military really did control political decision making in Panama.[5] Opposition to Noriega was discounted, especially before the Reagan administration reached a general consensus that Noriega should be removed from office. The U.S. embassy chose to ignore Panama's electoral fraud in 1984, for example, being more concerned with rallying any Panama president to the anti-Sandinista campaign. Anyway, the United States preferred Nicolás Ardito Barletta, who benefited from the electoral fraud. The opposition in Panama required a careful and complex analysis, a kind of analysis impossible in the Reagan administration.

Many of the strongest opponents of Noriega's regime were middle-class businessmen, while his supporters were the poor. Some members of the opposition were nationalists who despised General Noriega but were hostile toward middle- and upper-class *rabiblancos* as well. Moreover, Noriega was able to arouse anti-American passions among the poor in part as a result of the civic projects provided by the Panamanian Defense Forces (PDF) and in part by appealing to nationalist sentiments. Thus the opposition had a significant amount of fence-mending to do among Noriega's supporters and would have had to provide a policy alternative to Noriega that satisfied some of their needs. This they did not do.

This lack of an alternative may have contributed to the U.S. lack of support for them. Yet the U.S. tendency to support totally illegitimate, civilian puppet presidents makes it more plausible that the United States presumed that the opposition was malleable and that a Panamanian solution to the Noriega problem was relatively unimportant. In fact, members of the Panamanian middle-class opposition may have fed this assumption by privately expressing the wish that the United States would intervene militarily.[6] Noriega played on Panamanian nationalism in his effort to resist U.S. pressure to resign, and there is little evidence that the United States considered this important enough to be addressed with countertactics.

In June 1987, for example, after Noriega's opponents rioted in Panama, U.S. officials complained that Panama lacked a Corazon Aquino who could replace Noriega. One official remarked: "We face a . . . dilemma in Panama where a powerful leader is at the end of his rope and no one there or in our government has the guts to tell him to his face that it's time to go."[7] This statement followed the worst riots in Panama in twenty years. Many voices were calling for Noriega's resignation, but U.S. policy makers wanted an individual whom they could promote as the leader of the opposition.[8] Without one, they would have to face the chaos of open and uncontrolled democratic participation—which was to be avoided at any cost. At the same time, U.S. officials were seriously underestimating Noriega's staying power.

Two hundred organizations were united in the National Civic Crusade, an umbrella opposition group. There were political figures on Panama's electoral scene as well, including Arnulfo Arias, leader of the Authentic Panamenista Party. Arias was not acceptable to the United States because he was an ultranationalist. In fact, he was the probable winner of the 1984 election, which, because it was fraudulent, resulted in Barletta's ascent to the presidency. The United States did not oppose the electoral fraud because it did not want Arias in the Panamanian presidency. According to one official, "The Panamanian military wanted Barletta to win as much as we did. . . . The reason was that the military, like Washington, feared that a victory by Arnulfo Arias would bring an undesirable ultranationalist brand of politics to power."[9]

There were also divisions within the PDF and among civilian supporters of the Noriega regime. Some divisions involved outright rejection of Noriega. The important instances reflecting this division included an attempted coup in October 1989 and an incident in June 1987, when Colonel Roberto Díaz Herrera went public with accusations against Noriega. Díaz Herrera was considered to be the keeper of the Torrijos flame and, therefore, had serious potential as an opposition leader. As conditions deteriorated in Panama and instability increased, Arias held talks with Díaz Herrera, and the possibility emerged of a united opposition front.[10]

But potential leaders such as Díaz Herrera were anathema to the United States because of their suspected leftist tendencies. Torrijos was regarded as a leftist by the Reagan administration, and nationalism fell under the banner of Torrijismo was as well. In fact, Díaz Herrera and Arias were exactly the type of the political figure who could unite both the middle class and the poor. Discounting the power of the opposition, the Reagan administration held that the PDF would have to oust Noriega. Yet "civilians had flocked to Díaz Herrera . . . but not one of the six colonels, thirteen lieutenant colonels, and sixty-five majors who comprised the senior officer corps followed him. The crisis had created an opportunity for dialogue between some elements in the government and the opposition, but the PDF appeared to remain solidly behind Noriega. The administration's objective could not be attained by Panamanians at this time because the military appeared unwilling and the civilians, although stronger than before, were not in a position to overthrow the regime" (ibid., p. 114).

In addition to factions within the PDF that sought Noriega's ouster, there was a complex web of power sharing within the PDF-civilian ruling group. Noriega was not an absolute dictator. He was supported by promilitary political parties, which formed coalitions with military officials representing PDF factions. There is no evidence that the Reagan or Bush administrations attempted to use these complexities to achieve U.S. goals. In fact, the United States was incapable of aligning itself fully with the anti-Noriega military officers, as witnessed by its failure to support Díaz Herrera and, more significantly, its failure to support the attempted coup of October 1989.

The Reagan administration's response to developments among the opposition reflects the dependent image in several ways. Rather than using diplomacy to urge a united front among the opposition, the administration believed that the PDF would have to get rid of Noriega. The administration also tried to make the civilian president chosen by Noriega act like a real president. This is particularly interesting in light of the fact that the president, Eric Arturo Delvalle, was soundly disliked by Noriega's opposition.

Elliot Abrams and others alternately saw these civilian presidents as weak puppets and as holding political power. Of President Delvalle, Abrams said, "I always liked him . . . I found him very personable and I liked him and I liked his wife. . . . We had a good relationship. But I though of him as a weak man. I though of him as a man who would never take on Noriega. I thought of him as kind of a playboy business-man."[11] However, when Delvalle was fired by Noriega, the Reagan administration strongly supported him, as though he had actually been a popularly chosen civilian president who was tossed out of office by the military. The State Department insisted that Delvalle was still the president of Panama and that only an election could replace him. The CIA, however, found Delvalle's replacement, Manuel Solias Palma, to be "not a bad fellow. . . . He is a typical upper-class Panamanian. He's not some kind of leftist or something" (p. 129). Meanwhile, President Delvalle had approved attacks on opposition demonstrators shortly before he was deposed.

The dependent image view of Panamanian politics had an important impact on the first serious U.S. effort to remove Noriega from office. When the Reagan administration became convinced that Noriega should go, its officials attempted to convince Noriega to leave office. Delvalle was supposed to oversee Noriega's departure and to return to power as the president. The Panamanian opposition played little role in negotiating Noriega's departure. Panamanian opposition activist Gabriel Lewis said in frustration, "The U.S. should consult us before closing a deal about the fate of our country" (ibid., p. 143). But to argue that U.S.

policy makers decided Noriega's fate regardless of the wishes of the Panamanians is to paint too simple a picture. Long before it tried to depose Noriega, the United States helped establish and maintain his power and made it impossible for the opposition to get rid of him without U.S. approval and participation. Thus by treating Noriega as the head of state of a banana republic, the United States created an atmosphere in which Panamanians acted as citizens of a banana republic, simultaneously expecting, demanding, and resenting the U.S. role in the termination of Noriega's rule.

A final interesting manifestation of the dependent image was the absence of threat perceptions. Noriega was certainly disliked by officials in Washington, but the lack of anxiety about the situation, even given the growing hostility between Noriega and the Reagan administration, indicates that the threat was not perceived. As the situation deteriorated in the spring and summer of 1988, only Eliot Abrams consistently maintained that this was a crisis that the United States should respond to immediately and forcefully. He was opposed by overwhelming bureaucratic alignments, including Joint Chiefs of Staff Chairman Admiral William Crowe and CIA Director William Webster. He failed to convince Secretary of State George Shultz to take the situation as seriously as he did, and as a consequence he did not have the bureaucratic ammunition needed to win policy debates on Panama. Crowe objected strongly to military intervention, arguing that, if the Panamanians did not have the drive to remove Noriega, the United States should not. At one point after the United States recognized only the Delvalle presidency, Webster did not even know who the officially recognized president of Panama was.[12]

Given the dependent image of Panama, we would expect that U.S. behavior would be that associate with the prototypical dependent alone, without the complicating presence of a perceived enemy. Therefore, U.S. negotiations would be zero-sum, the United States setting the conditions and expecting the opponent to accept them. There would also be a willingness to use economic or military force if negotiations failed. Throughout, there would be a tendency to assume that the United States held all the power and could unquestionably achieve its goals.

The evolution of U.S. policy toward General Noriega shows the extent to which policy toward a dependent alone, in the absence of a perceived enemy, is both rudderless, in that containment does not apply, and of low priority, even when the problem is extremely annoying. Neither Reagan nor Bush had a consistent strategy. The Reagan administration did little for months after Noriega became a political liability to the United States. It finally regarded Panama as a serious problem area after domestic instability in Panama reached new heights in June 1987.

Hypothetical plans to remove Noriega began as early as 1985, when National Security Adviser John Poindexter reportedly asked Noriega to step down. That same year the U.S. Southern Command presented a concept called "systemic change," which, it was suggested, could be applied to Panama as a test case. Systemic change "could 'modify or remove' unwanted 'elements' in a given country. . . . Changes were needed in Panama because some government activities there posed actual or potential threats to vital U.S. interests or were 'repugnant to U.S. values.' "[13]

However, by the summer of 1987 U.S. foreign policy bureaucracies were divided over Noriega's fate, as his reputation in the United States deteriorated with the drug indictments and the accusations against him of human rights abuses. The questions became, Should the United States continue to use Noriega as an agent in the contra war against Nicaragua? Or should the United States avoid the embarrassment of being publicly associated with the general? Gradually, a consensus developed within the Reagan administration that Noriega would have to go. But a consensus on how to do this was never achieved: a division emerged between the State Department and the White House, on the one hand, and the CIA and the Pentagon, on the other. The former advocated public denunciations of Noriega coupled with behind-the-scenes efforts to find a temporary replacement for him from the PDF until an elected government took its place. The CIA and the Pentagon, however, were worried about political chaos in Panama once Noriega was out of office.[14] A related issue concerned whether the drug indictments against Noriega should be dropped as part of a deal to convince him to leave office.

REMOVING NORIEGA 1: THE BLANDÓN PLAN

The first efforts to negotiate Noriega's departure occurred in the summer of 1987. From the beginning, Panamanian opposition leaders asked for U.S. participation in their plots to depose the general. Leading opposition figures, such as Gabriel Lewis, attempted to use contacts in the United States to promote a joint action between the United States and the opposition to Noriega. The first meeting with the Reagan administration was a disaster.[15] The representative from the National Security Council suggested that the opposition ought to solve its own problems, reflecting the belief that Lewis was engaged in a personal vendetta against Noriega. Lewis responded that it would be impossible for Panamanians to unseat

Noriega as long as he remained on the payroll of the CIA: "You are the source of his power. . . . You have to cut yourselves off from Noriega" (p. 220). Lewis was able to persuade the Senate to pass a resolution calling for Noriega's resignation.

Consultations between Panamanian political figures and U.S. policy makers grew more serious in October 1987. Noriega's emissary, José Blandón was instructed to find an alternative that would allow Noriega to remain in Panama after leaving office. Blandón did more than that. In meetings with Gabriel Lewis, Deputy Assistant Secretary of State William Walker, and others during late October, the Blandón plan was developed. It was presented to Noriega as a package prepared by the general's people (not the opposition or the United States) to permit Noriega to leave office without facing an indictment on drug charges. In Washington, it was presented as a basic strategy for removing Noriega from power (ibid., p. 229). It involved manipulation of the Panamanian opposition and signals from the U.S. Department of Defense to Noriega indicating that his time was up. The true plan was quickly apparent to Noriega.

The plan was implemented for the United States by a personal friend of Vice President Bush, retired admiral Daniel Murphy, who went to Panama and discussed Noriega's future with him in a number of meetings. Murphy's exact message is in dispute: Murphy claims he clearly explained to Noriega that he had to leave office; others maintain that Murphy delivered a message the opposite of that intended by the Blandón plan. He certainly set a different departure date: February 1989, as opposed to April 1988. Murphy described the opposition as inflexible: "Their reaction was vehement. They wanted Noriega out now—no negotiation, no room for compromise."[16] Murphy gave Noriega the impression that his opponents in Washington were unimportant and that his departure was not necessary.[17]

This was the one moment in the Panamanian episode in which the United States worked with Panamanian political figures, and even then it was not a coherent, systematic effort to support the Panamanian opposition. Instead, it was an ad hoc interaction between several important Panamanians and U.S. representatives. Moreover, some of the most important Americans involved in the negotiatiion of the Blandón plan were not officials at all (one central figure was a private political consultant named Joel McCleary). Nevertheless, "Gabriel Lewis described the plan as 'the only serious blueprint to emerge in the whole crisis. . . . Its value,' he emphasized, 'was that it was developed by someone in the government.' "[18] It was the closest thing to a Panamanian solution to come along.

What is important about this episode is the behavior of the United States. First, the plan demonstrates a general lack of interest in assessing and working with the Panamanian opposition. While on the one hand, no leader could be identified with whom the United States could work, on the other hand, any opposition figure with personal contacts in the United States might serve as the de facto leader of the opposition. What this indicates is that the opposition was not taken seriously as a political movement and that there was no comprehensive search by the United States for a Panamanian soulution to the growing crisis.

Second, it reflects a U.S. lack of concern about the situation in Panama. Had the United States been more serious about the instability there, it would not have permitted unofficial emissaries such as Murphy to present the government's position. This lack of concern was reinforced by the interagency debate about the utility of Noriega as an informant and contra supporter versus his liability as a participant in the drug industry.

Third, it is not clear who in the U.S. government approved of the U.S. role in the Blandón plan. That Murphy's activities were not those of a private individual acting on his own is clear from the fact that he was briefed both before and after he went to Panama by representatives of several agencies (ibid., p. 122).

REMOVING NORIEGA 2: LITIGATION AND SANCTIONS

These patterns were replicated in the Reagan administration's next step. After Noriega rejected the Blandón plan in January 1988, President Delvalle was encouraged by Elliot Abrams to fire Noriega. Noriega's response was to fire Delvalle. The United States supported Delvalle and maintained that he was the legal president of Panama. Meanwhile, the United States still did not believe that the opposition was a force capable of forcing Noriega out of office. As one U.S. official remarked, "No one is happy that we are virtually powerless to do anything and there is no strong, viable opposition in Panama" (ibid., p. 132). The fact is, the opposition was quiet when Noriega fired Delvalle, which is not surprising given the fact that they considered Delvalle Noriega's puppet and strongly disliked him. Therefore, there were no widespread demonstrations in opposition to Delvalle's ouster, although the opposition did plan strikes for a later period. Moreover, in March a coup attempt occurred, further indicating large fissures in Noriega's support.

In March, the United States cut military and economic aid, and Noriega was formally indicted on drug trafficking charges. In February, Lewis, Blandón, and the civilian U.S. citizens who worked with them had instituted lawsuits that froze Panamanian assets in the United States. Thus the most effective force working against Noriega was an odd couple from the opposition, Lewis and Blandón, who disliked each other, and private U.S. citizens, many of whom had important government connections (such as William Rogers, former assistant secretary of state for Latin American affairs). The State Department was blocked by the Treasury Department and the Federal Reserve from promoting an even stronger anti-Noriega stance, but it did facilitate the litigation strategy by recognizing Delvalle's administration as the legal government of Panama (ibid., pp. 135–36). It also encouraged New York banks not to disburse Panamanian funds to General Noriega. Nevertheless, this was not a coordinated effort between the Reagan administration and the Panamanian opposition; the United States was "simply reacting to events controlled largely by Delvalle and his political associates based in Washington."[19]

In April 1988 the State Department's preferred tactic was selected: declaration of a national emergency and the invocation of the International Emergency Economic Powers Act. By this time, the earlier economic tactic was causing serious economic problems for Noriega, prompting requests by some of his opposition for increased international pressure on him. Delvalle's associates even called for an international police action against Noriega. Such requests must have reinforced the dependent image. Some Latin American diplomats and former U.S. officials certainly saw it as such, remarking that they found the Panamanian demands for intervention appalling. Former U.S. Ambassador Ambler Moss was "dismayed to see Sosa [Delvalle's ambassador to the United States] 'yelling for US intervention. This is the legacy of the old colonial mentality, to expect Big Daddy to solve your problems,' he said, noting that so far Noriega's only response has been to dig in his heels and protest against US interventionism."[20] Critics also argued that Noriega might be more inclined to release his hold on Panama if the United States stopped raising his nationalistic dander.

Washington's response to such criticism reflected the power of the dependent image: it rejected the criticism and dismissed Latin American concern about the U.S. action being a dangerous precedent. Moreover, U.S. officials noted that the only countries to support Noriega were Cuba, Nicaragua, and Libya, the Reagan administration's favorite agents of evil. They also repeated the argument made after the Grenada invasion of 1983: despite public protests, Latin American governments actually privately approved of U.S. actions (ibid.). The dependent image continued to blind U.S. policy makers to the importance that nationalism played in the crisis in Panama.

The nationalistic component of Noriega's opposition began to split off from the National Civic Crusade as a result of U.S. support for Delvalle and its complicity in the economic sanctions against Panama. In April 1988 leaders of the Popular Action party and the Authentic Panamanian Party—the party of Arnulfo Arias and the largest political party in Panama—formed a counteropposition group, the Popular Civic Movement. As one of the leaders of the Popular Action Party, Mauro Zuñiga, explained, "For us, no recipe that comes from Washington has been favorable to the Panamanians. The people of the world know that the recipes formulated in the imperial capitals, the United States and the Soviet Union, never are favorable to the interests of the people. . . . It is absolutely necessary for General Noriega to abandon his post. For us, this is fundamental."[21]

Thus the U.S. officials who complained about a lack of leadership among the opposition were by 1988 quite correct. U.S. policy had helped produce that lack of leadership by failing to understand the complexity of the Panamanian opposition. As the spring of 1988 wore on, the United States continued its efforts to negotiate Noriega out of office, further dividing the opposition in the process. Divisions appeared within the opposition concerning whether the best tactic was to negotiate with the Noriega government or to maintain staunch opposition without negotiations until Noriega was out of office. The United States chose the former approach, which aroused the fear among the opposition that Panama would be left with "Norieguismo without Noriega."[22]

REMOVING NORIEGA 3: SELECTING TACTICS WITHOUT THE OPPOSITION

The next series of steps by the Reagan administration are typical of tactics associated with the dependent image in that they manifested an overestimation of U.S. power and a quick readiness to resort to coercive action. From late March onward, the administration essentially abandoned any approach that would give the opposition a role in determining Noriega's fate. The administration had assumed that partial economic sanctions would cause serious economic dislocations in Panama, resulting in a mass uprising to oust Noriega. This did not happen. The sanctions did cause the Panamanian banks to close and prompted wealthy Panamanians in the opposition to call for Noriega's ouster. However, the U.S. Treasury made it possible for cash to continue to flow into Panama; it sent $40 million into Panama each month to pay military and canal personnel. Moreover, the policy did not require U.S. businesses to withdraw from Panama, and those businesses, along with Panamanian businesses, brought money from the United States into Panama to sustain their operations. Thus, although the economy was hurt, U.S. officials vastly underestimated their own ability to cause an economic crisis large enough to provoke mass protests against Noriega.

As economic measures were put into place in March 1988, Shultz and Abrams advocated a military attack against Noriega that would be swift and sure and that would extract him from Panama. This was opposed by the CIA, the Joint Chiefs of Staff (under William Crowe), and the National Security Council. Crowe objected to putting U.S. forces at risk for the sake of wealthy Panamanians who wanted Noriega out; he also worried about the impact of such an action on other governments in countries where the United States had military bases. Crowe asked, "How do you expect those governments would react to the specter of the U.S. using its bases to overthrow a country's leadership?"[23] Reagan declined the military option but did send additional troops to Panama and continued to imply through his press spokesman that a military option was being considered.

Reagan did approve a series of talks between the United States and Noriega. Initially, the United States took a tough, no-compromise, position: Noriega had to resign and leave the country, the drug indictments in the United States would not be dropped, and the PDF would have to leave politics.[24] But General Noriega was a skilled negotiator and squeezed important concessions out of the United States. State Department representative Michael Kozak, acting as the Reagan administration's negotiator, met with Noriega three times during April and May of 1988. In May President Reagan gave Kozak permission to include the drug indictments as bargaining chips. This was essential for any agreement, since Noriega most feared the indictments once he was out of office. By May 15 an agreement had been reached that included Noriega's resignation and temporary departure from Panama (he could return after the May 1989 election). Most important, the indictments would be dropped. This was opposed by many of Reagan's closest supporters, including Senator Robert Dole and Vice President George Bush.

The agreement was scuttled when the State Department set a deadline for signing the agreement. Secretary of State Shultz delayed his departure for a summit with the Soviet Union to await the signed document. Noriega refused to sign at the required time, arguing that he needed more time to bring the PDF behind the agreement. The talks were then terminated. This was the last major episode in the Reagan administration's approach to Panama.

Did the Reagan negotiations follow the pattern expected in the perceptual context of the dependent image? For the most part, the answer is yes. Throughout these negotiations the United States issued ultimatums to Noriega, many of which were deflected by Kozak.[25] These negotiations were also an attempt to single-handedly remove the leadership of another country, and they did not include any of the Panamanian opposition. The odd aspect of U.S. behavior concerns its willingness to concede on the drug indictment issue. Reagan reportedly did so because he knew the indictments were meaningless if Noriega remained in power. This is an anomaly, it does not conform with the behavior usually associated with the dependent image, and it certainly did not conform with the wishes of most policy advocates at the time. Bush was particularly appalled by the offer, since he was in the middle of a campaign for the Republican nomination for the presidency. However, it might be attributed to Ronald Reagan's personality and political style. Usually uninterested and indecisive in policy issues regarding Panama, he reportedly waxed eloquent on this particular decision. He "wasn't letting off a drug dealer," he said, he was getting rid of a dictator" (p. 310).

The decision could also have been the result of political expedience pure and simple. There were many reasons for Reagan administration officials to not want to see the drug indictments go to trial. Trials would risk revelations about the CIA's long-time support for Noriega, early information about his drug involvement that the United States ignored, and George Bush's knowledge of Noriega's activities. The Bush group was, of course, most concerned about the immediate impact of Reagan's decision on Bush's campaign. But in fact Bush could have his cake and eat it too on this issue by publicly disagreeing with Reagan yet benefiting from the decision itself. Thus the convenience of this "concession" for domestic political concerns for many figures in the administration made it less of a concession. Moreover, the lack of threat generated by the dependent image permitted policy makers to place short-term domestic political considerations above foreign policy issues.

Diplomacy was also supplemented by five covert plans (called Panama 1 through 5) to get rid of Noriega. The relations among the plans is not clear, and they were developed both before and after the Kozak negotiations. One of the early plans proposed establishing a residence for a Delvalle government-in-exile at a U.S. military base in Panama. Panama 3, a plot to overthrow Noriega, was cooked up in part by a Panamanian military officer, Colonel Eduardo Herrera Hassan. It was presented to (and rejected by) the Senate and House intelligence committees and to Delvalle in July 1988. The plan was for Herrera Hassan and others in the Panamanian military to "enter Panama clandestinely, and 'from safe houses on American military bases or other U.S.-controlled territory' operate a campaign of increasing pressure on Noriega. Their activities would include sabotage operations and propaganda. . . . The main objective was to incite a counterattack by Noriega against those areas; Noriega's attack thus would allow the United States to intervene for the reason the administration had been stating all along—to protect U.S. lives and property."[26] The plan was rejected because of the prospect of the U.S. government being involved in an assassination attempt.

When it was leaked to the press, Panama 3 set off a protest by the National Civic Crusade, which said that it made the Civic Crusade appear to be a puppet of the Reagan administration. A series of sharp exchanges occurred between the Civic Crusade and the administration. One Civic Crusade leader, Aurelio Barria, stated, "These leaks create the expectation here and in Panama that someone else will solve Panama's problems"; the response to this remark by one Washington source was, "The nerve of those people! They want the US to take care of 'its monster' Noriega, but as soon as the plans become public . . ."[27]

Panama 3 was the final Panamanian effort by the Reagan administration. Diplomatic and economic pressures had failed to remove Noriega from office, and the U.S. election loomed. According to one Reagan administration official, "[w]hen negotiations broke down, there was a conscious decision by the political staff of the White House to remove Panama from the agenda"; the administration muffled discussion of Panama to such an extent that senior aides in the Pentagon and the CIA "assumed that the initiative to oust [Noriega] had ended. The State Department demanded and received clarification from the White House that the initiative was on and that only the publicity was off."[28]

REMOVING NORIEGA 4: THE PANAMA 4 PLAN AND THE ELECTION

As U.S. president elect George Bush prepared to take up the reins in late 1988, the Panamanian opposition divided and disintegrated further. The largest anti-Noriega party, the Authentic Panamanian Party, split into two factions in December 1988. Several smaller parties had split in the previous months. Many in the opposition blamed Noriega for the divisions, citing a divide-and-conquer strategy.[29] Meanwhile, deposed President Delvalle, after ten months in hiding, threatened to resign. He was frustrated over the impact of economic sanctions, which he said hurt the Panamanian people rather than the Noriega regime. He also reportedly asked for a military operation by the United States to remove Noriega from power.[30]

Attention in the new Bush administration was directed toward the Panamanian election scheduled for May 7, 1989. The election was for the president, two vice presidents, and the entire legislature. Naturally, the opposition and Noriega regarded these elections as crucial. The opposition offered a unified ticket led by Guillermo Endara, a former aide to Arnulfo Arias. The vice presidential candidate, Ricardo Arias Calderón, came from the Christian Democratic party. The second vice presidential candidate, Guillermo Ford, came from the Liberal Republican Nationalist Movement. The opposition united behind these candidates under the banner of the Alliance of Democratic Civilian Opposition (ADOC).

The Noriega ticket consisted of a coalition of eight pro-Noriega parties united as the Coalition of National Liberation, COLINA. The presidential candidate was Carlos Duque, a businessman; the vice presidential candidates were Ramon Sieiro, Noriega's brother-in-law (with whom his relations were poor), and Aquilino Boyd, former ambassador to the United States.

The Bush administration regarded the elections as crucial. The administration resurrected the Panama 4 plan, which involved assisting Noriega's opponents in the election scheduled for May 1989. "President Bush authorized Panama 4, one of his first covert operations, in February 1989. The operation had a dual focus: to get the candidates and their message across to generate votes, and to publicize and minimize opportunities for fraud by the government and PDF. This finding reportedly continued a program authorized by President Reagan in 1988. Bush 'personally lobbied' congressional committees and gained their support for $10 million for the opposition campaign, principally for printing, advertising, transportation and communications."[31] The Bush administration's interest in the successful election of the opposition naturally led to accusations by Noriega supporters that the opposition was merely a puppet of the United States.

As elections neared, it became clear that hopes for a peaceful electoral transition would be dashed. Polls were attacked, candidates were attacked, and the vote was annulled by Noriega, as his candidate, Carlos Duque, faced certain defeat. After vote counting was suspended, civil disturbances erupted, ending in the beating and arrest of hundreds and brutal attacks on ADOC candidates.

The Bush administration responded with a series of tactics. Additional troops were sent to Panama, Southcom moved off-base personnel and their dependents to the safety of military installations, military exercises designed to frighten Noriega were scheduled, and Bush called for the Panamanian military to overthrow Noriega, saying, "They ought to do everything they can to get Noriega out of there. . . . He's one man and they have a well-trained force."[32] The Bush administration continued economic sanctions and recalled the U.S. ambassador to Panama. The United States also supported OAS efforts to convince Noriega to leave office.

REMOVING NORIEGA 5: HOPING FOR A COUP—TACTICS IN SEARCH OF A STRATEGY

The response of the Bush administration to the electoral disaster in Panama were a collection of tactics unrelated to one another and accepted because Panama was viewed through the dependent image. From the May election through the October coup, the Bush administration used tactics that relied primarily upon the threat of military force. The emphasis was on the threat part of military force, the administration being not ready to pursue a military overthrow.[33] Instead, it attempted a psychological approach, by signaling to Noriega that the United States had the military power to depose him. For example, the administration publicly announced that U.S. troops were being increased to protect American lives; this was followed by statements that it was "not ruling out any options."[34] The hope was that the PDF would get rid of Noriega. The formula was augmented by an additional tactic, targeting Noriega's closest supporters for economic sanctions in an effort to turn them against him.[35]

Did this policy approach reflect the dependent image? "U.S. intelligence agencies weren't sure how or when this strategy would work, but they had no other strategy: their own intelligence contacts were so poor and their knowledge of the PDF so limited that they could only hope that their show of military power, the increased international criticism of Noriega, and the new sanctions would convince officers that Noriega was more of a cost than a benefit" (ibid., p. 367). It is important to ask why they had no other strategy and why they had such poor information about the PDF. Were they unable to get better information, or did they simply not look for it? Again, the perceptual image of Panama leads to the argument that they did not look for better information or a better strategy because they had a highly simplifiied view of Panamanian politics. The assumption that the PDF was a military force that could undertake a cost-benefit assessment of Noriega is an example of this simplification, in that it existed amid some real information about the complexity of the Panamanian situation.

First, one should examine the belief that the PDF could be convinced that Noriega should be overthrown and that democracy should replace him. This assumes that the PDF could act as a monolith and that it had a single interest—probably its survival as a military institution. Bush indicated this perception of PDF interests when he emphasized that the United States objected to Noriega but not to the PDF. He stated that "a professional Panamanian Defense Force can have an important role to play in Panama's democratic future."[36] However, neither Noriega nor the PDF ruled Panama alone. They existed in an intricate coalition with civilian factions, which had a real stake in the continuation of the regime, if not of Noriega. Reports published after the attacks on the opposition candidates indicated that Noriega did not order them but that they were ordered by "members of his political entourage who [were] trying to prevent a negotiated solution to the crisis."[37] Leaders of the Pala Party, headed by Noriega's brother-in-law Ramon Sieiro, were cited as likely suspects. Sieiro, in turn, had close ties with several high-ranking PDF officials. Moreover, diplomatic sources were aware of "a deep split within the ruling coalition" (ibid.).

The important point here is that, whether or not Noriega personally ordered the assault on opposition political leaders, there were central members of the ruling coalition who would not consider a negotiated transition to a new ruling elite. Those individuals, both civilian and military, would therefore be quite unlikely to respond to U.S. encouragement to overthrow Noriega and open the system up to democratic elections. Yet the Bush administration continued to maintain that Noriega was *the* problem and that no solution was possible without his immediate departure.

This simplification of Panamanian politics not only led the Bush administration to hope that the PDF would rise up and overthrow Noriega, it also led the United States to constantly criticize the efforts of the Organization of American States to negotiate a way out of the political crisis. OAS negotiations began shortly after the May election was annulled. A number of alternatives were being considered in Panama, including a power-sharing junta with the ADOC. Both Noriega's coalition and the opposition had internal splits, with some factions supporting power sharing, others refusing to deal with the opposing coalition. When the OAS negotiators arrived, the most promising compromise was "a junta headed by Endara, and Noriega's retirement within two years."[38] The OAS attempted to negotiate an agreement through two rounds of meetings. When the first round resulted in failure, the Bush administration regarded the OAS's willingness to try a second round as a "setback," hoping instead for an OAS resolution that would demand Noriega's resignation.[39] U.S. officials believed that Noriega was using the talks as a delaying tactic and had no expectation they would succeed.

In the end, the OAS efforts failed. The OAS blamed that failure in part on U.S. military exercises, which the OAS considered "inopportune" and dangerous.[40] Noriega's opposition argued that these exercises permitted Noriega to portray Panama's crisis as a result of conflict between Panama and the United States, rather than as a result of internal conflict.[41]

In early October the Bush administration appeared to be on the verge of getting just what it had hoped for, a PDF coup. On October 1, 1989, a meeting was held between U.S. officials and Major Moises Giroldi Vega. Major Giroldi informed the United States that a coup was being plotted and asked for limited help in the form of road blocks to prevent Noriega from bringing in reinforcements. Giroldi, representing junior PDF officers, described the coup as "strictly a military movement and not a political act."[42] It was not a widespread action by the PDF—and it was not in support of democracy. In fact, it involved only around 240 anti-Noriega soldiers, and coup leaders initially intended only to "retire" Noriega, not to punish him for internal abuses of power nor to hand him over to the United States for prosecution on drug charges.

The coup failed quickly, and the Bush administration was roundly criticized for doing too little too late. The criticism came from the press and from congressional Democrats and Republicans. This in itself deserves comment, since it reflects the extent to which the dependent image of Panama was shared. Rather than being criticized for participating in the attempted overthrow of another government, the administration was lambasted for *failing* to participate. In fact, the Bush administration had quickly agreed to Giroldi's requests. There is no evidence of a debate within the administration concerning the appropriateness of becoming involved in Panamanian politics. Instead, there is evidence only of confusion over tactics and the reliability of Giroldi.

Giroldi informed the CIA on Sunday, October 1, that the coup would take place the next day. When Monday passed without a coup, U.S. officials began to worry. Giroldi had been a central figure in putting down a coup attempt against Noriega in March 1988, and there was concern that Noriega was using Giroldi to lay a trap for the United States, giving Noriega an opportunity to expose U.S. participation in an attempted overthrow.[43] Moreover, Giroldi did not meet U.S. demands that his request for aid be made publicly and that he commit himself to the establishment of a democratic regime.

Despite these concerns, when the coup began on Tuesday, the United States did as it promised: two roads were blocked, preventing some loyal troops from coming to Noriega's aid; U.S. helicopters swooped over the city in a show of support for the rebels; and U.S. soldiers sealed off Fort Amador, mistakenly believing that Noriega was there. As the coup faltered, the rebels requested additional help from the United States, although exactly what kind of help they asked for is still unclear. What is clear is that they did not offer to give Noriega to the United States but instead wanted him to retire.[44] This was not satisfactory to President Bush, who first offered to capture Noriega through a covert military operation and then authorized the development of a plan for capturing Noriega "even if this meant the use of force."[45] Meanwhile, loyal troops took advantage of an alternate route to go to Noreiga's defense. Just before their defeat, the rebels did ask for U.S. intervention and agreed to give up Noriega. But by then there was too little time left, and the coup collapsed.

Overall, there was confusion and poor intelligence, as information was channeled from Panama to Washington. The coup was over in five hours, permitting little time for decision making in Washington. In addition, decision makers were not confident of the coup's leaders. For these reasons, President Bush did not authorize a full-scale use of U.S. forces. But at no time did his decision making contradict the patterns associated with the dependent image. Reluctance to support the coup more forcefully was not a result of conflicting perceptions and internal debate but of too little time and and a lack of enthusiasm for the leaders of the coup.

From Panama 5 to Invasion

The failed coup galvanized the Bush administration to be rid of the Noriega pest. Two contingency plans were developed: Panama 5 was a covert operation that prepared for and attempted to advance the prospects of another coup by the PDF. It was supported by a congressionally approved budget of $3 million and a weakening of the ban on assassination. The plan was reported in the press in mid-November. The administration acknowledged that it was "an unimpeded effort to try to topple Noriega . . . with the understanding that there may be loss of life."[46] Panama 5 was supplemented by contingency plans for a military invasion to oust Noriega.

The military plan was ultimately invoked. The invasion of Panama took place on December 20, 1989, after weeks of increasing tension, harassment, verbal conflict, and finally the death of one off-duty U.S. military officer and the beating of another. The precipitating incidents were merely catalysts for the moment of invasion rather than causes of the invasion. In the final days of decision making about the invasion, Bush met with top-level advisers, including National Security Advisor Brent Scowcroft, Generals Colin Powell and Thomas Kelly, White House Chief of Staff Jon Sununu, Secretary of Defense Richard Cheney, and Secretary of State James Baker.[47] Their decision to launch the invasion was made without sharp dissent or debate. The president reportedly "offered no high-flown reflections and did no last-minute agonizing." Moreover, Bush's advisers stated that there had been a "sense of inevitability around the White House for the last two months, since the Administration had been criticized for an ineffectual response to the failed Panamanian coup attempt on October 3."[48]

What is striking about the decision is that it was so easily made. Bush wanted to "get" Noriega because Noriega was "thumbing his nose at him" and was getting "more and more abusive." "Here are my objectives," he said: "I want to get Noriega. I want to be able to have Endara and Calderon and Ford establish themselves as leaders of a democratically established government. I want to, as a result of that, insure the safety of American lives." (ibid.).

The invasion is a very clear illustration of the tactics traditionally used to control an unruly dependent. One government was overthrown and another was put in its place. And no attention was paid to internal political conditions. In fact, the new president of Panama, Guillermo Endara, did not speak to the nation until the second day of the invasion. He was not informed about the invasion until shortly before it began. Moreover, Endara, Ford, and Calderón were sworn in at a U.S. military base, Fort Clayton, and the international community was informed of the Endara government via a U.S. government "fax" machine.[49]

There was also no question that the Bush administration wanted Noriega in U.S. custody and that it intended to punish him. Strong-arm tactics were used to try to get the papal nunciature to turn Noriega over to U.S. forces after he took refuge there on Decemeber 24. President Endara wanted to keep Noriega in Panama—but gave up in the face of technical and political obstacles.

After the invasion, the Bush administration set about building a suitable "democratic" government in Panama. Having put the Endara administration into office, the next immediate tasks were to do something about the PDF and the structure of the Panamanian state. The PDF was to be replaced with a new quasi-military police force, the Public Force. In its first days, the new Panamanian government had to operate out of the Foreign Ministry, because the presidential building was occupied by U.S. military personnel.

PANAMA: CONCLUSION

In the case of Panama—in line with the general model—intervention was conditioned by the presence or absence of the enemy. When the enemy was present, Noriega played a role in containing the enemy in the battle with Nicaragua and, hence, was protected. Then the cold war wound down in Central America, the Iran-contra scandal was exposed, support for the contras waned, and containment became less relevant. Without an enemy, the administration had no strategy and drifted from day to day in making a decision regarding Noriega. Moreover, personal animosity made a large impact on policy, as George Bush came to dislike Noriega intensely, believing that Noriega had humiliated him.

The absence of containment guidelines also opened the situation up to bureaucratic politics, which created a dilemma about the proper U.S. role in ousting Noriega. The State Department at first supported him (as an ally against the Sandinistas) then opposed him (because he was a thug and a drug smuggler). The Pentagon, among the last to give up a concern about a Soviet presence in Central America, was hesitant to lose Noriega. The Drug Enforcement Agency was divided: some officials wanted to get rid of him for his drug activities, others wanted to keep him because he helped nail other drug runners.

The Panama case shows the impact of containment and of the enemy image on intervention. It also demonstrates that intervention can occur even without the perception of an enemy. The enemy image simply conditions the nature of the intervention; the dependent image ultimately causes the intervention. With containment, one can predict the intervention to be violent. Without containment, the manner of interference is less predictable. Situational conditions—including the perception and evaluation of the dependent regime and polity and U.S. domestic and bureaucratic conditions—take on much greater importance. The instruments, on the other hand, still resemble those of the cold war and pre–cold war eras: gunboat diplomacy.

The simplification of domestic political elements has always been part of U.S. perceptions of dependent countries. In the post–cold war era, the danger in this simplification is much greater. This, combined with the cold war pattern of selecting coercive instruments and lack of an overriding strategy (containment), has the potential to lead the United States into a quagmire in Latin America.

THE WAR ON DRUGS IN PERU

Are drug lords the new enemy? General Paul Gorman, former head of Southcom in Panama, certainly seemed to believe this: "The American people must understand much better than they ever have in the past how our safety and that of our children is threatened by Latin drug conspiracies which are dramatically more successful at subversion in the United States than any that are centered in Moscow."[50] A major report by the Senate Subcommittee on Terrorism, Narcotics, and International Operations notes the danger to U.S. security posed by drug cartels. It adds that the cartels formed alliances with left-wing guerrillas, including the M-19 in Colombia and the Sendero Luminoso in Peru, and have been aided by Fidel Castro in a continuing effort to undermine the United States (ibid., pp. 11, 65).

Nevertheless, there is little to indicate that drug cartels are perceived as the new enemy. Instead, the War on Drugs represents a post–cold war policy toward a stereotypical dependent. The tactics, as in the case of Panama, come straight out of cold war lesson books. Moreover, the War on Drugs shows how the end of the cold war has promoted internal bureaucratic bickering.

A CRISIS OF LEGITIMACY

Peru is involved in a serious civil war, a civil war sparked by a notorious guerrilla organization called Sendero Luminoso, or the Shining Path. The story of this crisis is a complicated one, and it cannot be understood without an examination of identity factors and the way the Shining Path and others exploit the people's disenchantment with the government.

Roughly 60 percent of the able work force in Peru is unemployed or underemployed. Malnutrition rose from 7 percent in 1970, to 23 percent in 1989.[51] Peru's economic growth declined by 20 percent between 1988 and 1989, and its foreign debt reached $19 billion. This economic and political structure, in which many are deprived of the most basic economic necessities, leads the poor majority to conclude that they are being victimized by an alien aggressive entity, the Peruvian state.

The identification of the villain is augmented by the ethnic and class characteristics of Peru. The lowest rungs of the social and economic ladder are occupied by Indians, who were a majority of the population until the 1970s. In general, Indians are subjected to racial prejudice, they are poor, and they even speak a different language, Quechua. They hold the most menial positions in society, and the only way out of this condition is to integrate into Spanish society. Peru now has a largely Indian and mixed-race population. There is little similarity between conditions in Lima and other urban centers and the rural areas.

The Peruvian political scene is characterized by a number of political parties with wide-ranging ideologies and complex internal factions and alignments. The military is a central political actor. It controlled the state from 1968 until 1980 and has a nationalistic view of Peruvian politics and the destiny of the state.[52] The military is demoralized and corrupt, as are police agencies and many other institutions. Due to the civil war against the Sendero Luminoso, the military is in formal control of half of the country. The military is beyond civilian control, since it is capable of overthrowing the government at its convenience.

While there is a strong basis for nationalism built upon ethnic identity and deprivation in the Indian and mestizo population, the politically and economically dominant Spanish elite is also driven by nationalistic antiimperialist sentiments. From the military governments of the 1960s and 1970s to the civilian governments of the 1980s, nationalism has been emphasized in periodic state-building and antidependency drives. President Alan García was particularly notable in this regard when he refused to commit more than 10 percent of Peruvian revenues to debt payments.

The Sendero Luminoso and coca production have separate but related origins. The Shining Path got its start in the Southern Andean highlands, where the peasants, particularly in Ayacucho Province, have experienced a serious decline in living standards since the 1970s. Its people earn little, die young, are mostly illiterate, and have few basic human services. Its peasants earn much less than coastal dwellers and somewhat less than peasants in the northern highlands. The southern highlands are primarily agricultural, even though they are poorly suited to agriculture. The Sendero Luminoso was organized by a philosophy professor from the University of Huamanga. It is hardly populist: it is an ideologically extreme, purist, and puritanical Maoist guerrilla organization. It is exceptionally violent and has killed many peasants suspected of supporting the government. It receives no outside support from foreign governments, nor is it supported by other Marxist parties in Peruvian politics. It has incorporated symbols from the Incan insurrectionist tradition and identifies with the indigenous people.

The movement grew gradually. In 1980 it had only a few hundred members; at that time, it went underground, recruiting followers among the Quechua-speaking inhabitants of Ayacucho. The Sendero expanded into the neighboring provinces of Huancavelica and Apurimac and now operates in half of Peru, including the sprawling slums of Lima. Why does it receive so much support? For one thing, the area where it began has been neglected by virtually every Peruvian government; second, it appeals directly to indigenous history and identity and emphasizes that the government of Peru is alien—unrepresentative of, and uninterested in, highland dwellers.

"Shining Path's revolution derives much of its power, as well as its cruelty, from the pent-up resentment among Peru's downtrodden majority Indian population, which until 1980 was effectively denied a vote. The racist character of Peruvian society—where economic power has been in the hands of a white elite for hundreds of years—is such that upward social mobility entails a corresponding denial of all things Indian."[53] And the government itself has fueled support for the Sendero by responding to the insurrection with both retreat and violence. Government efforts to establish military control of the highlands have brought increasing human rights abuses: suspected guerrilla sympathizers have been tortured, murdered, and "disappeared." In the periods when the military simply abandoned the highlands, the inhabitants were left to defend themselves with peasant patrols, since the Shining Path took advantage of this lull to attack villages that had cooperated with government forces.

Over time, the military adopted a "strategic hamlets" program backed by peasant patrols, literally picking up and clumping together whole villages, believing they would be easier to protect if they were not scattered. The government thereby managed to further alienate the people, most of whom had not moved from their land for generations. The Shining Path then attacked these new settlements.

Pressure from both the Sendero Luminoso and the military only add to the worries of a people in desperate economic conditions. This is where cocaine enters the picture. There is nothing new or unusual about the growth of coca in Peru: coca leaves have been grown and used by indigenous Peruvians for centuries. The increase in production was merely a response to demand: the hunger for cocaine in the United States and elsewhere has been a godsend for hungry Peruvian peasants. Peru produces about 60 percent of the world's coca. Coca production not only provides a living for a significant portion of the Peruvian population, it has also become a crucial source of foreign exchange for Peru. Peruvians process coca leaves into a paste and send it to Colombia, where it is processed into cocaine. The coca plants in the Upper Huallaga Valley can produce five crops a year and are easily replaced if destroyed by government eradication efforts.

The upper Huallaga Valley is extremely remote and has never been economically integrated into the central Peruvian economy. Trade from this valley went eastward through the Amazon, rather than westward over the Andes, and then across the Pacific Ocean like the rest of Peru's export. The valley experience an influx of southern highland Indians in the 1940s but remained scarcely populated until recently, when large numbers of poverty-stricken peasants from the coastal lowlands move into the valley. The Sendero Luminoso sent agents into the region in the early 1980s and established ties with the locals. When the Peruvian government implemented programs designed to reduce or eradicate coca production in the Upper Huallaga, it provided an opportunity for the Sendero to act as the protector of the *cocaleros*. The action also gave credibility to the Sendero argument that the Peruvian government is controlled by the United States, since the United States strongly encourages eradication efforts.

The guerrillas also represent themselves as protecting the peasants from the cocaine syndicates. Colombian cocaine cartels have, or course, infiltrated into the Upper Huallaga Valley, since it is such a rich source of coca. They use bribes and force to disarm the local police and political authorities. Before the Sendero showed up, growers were at the mercy of these drug traffickers: peasants who refused to grow coca were likely to wind up dead, floating down a river as examples to other peasants. Sendero soldiers provide military backing for farmers who organize against both the police and the traffickers. They also push peasants to demand higher prices for their product.[54]

The relation between the guerrillas and the cocaine cartels is rather mysterious. They do cooperate at times, but in general their aims are very different. The Sendero Luminoso is the prototypical extreme left-wing guerrilla organization, and the cocaine cartels are almost as prototypically capitalist business organizations. Their interests overlap at times, but in essence they are mutually exclusive. As Pablo Escobar put it, "You can accuse me of being a narcotics dealer, but to say that I'm in league with the guerrillas, well, that really hurts my personal integrity" (ibid., p. 156). There is reason to believe that nothing more than a temporary marriage of convenience exists between the Sendero Luminoso and the drug cartels. The guerrillas are not armed with advanced, sophisticated weaponry, while the drug traffickers and *cocaleros* often are, suggesting that the Sendero is not extorting vast sums of cash from the drug cartels (p. 176). The guerrillas are reputed to extort some money from drug traffickers, as well as from other businesses. They purchase some weapons on the black market, but most of their weapons are taken from the security forces.[55] In general, the guerrillas' focus is on recruiting peasant support.

THE DEPENDENT IMAGE

There is not a great deal of evidence in the form of policy statements, interviews, or writings that can provide details on the prevailing U.S. image of Peru, but the Bush administration approach to Latin American drug producers indicates behavior typical of those holding the dependent image. The administration ignored suggestions that the drug problem can be effectively addressed only by attacking the demand side of the equation. Instead, the administration insisted that eliminating the supply was enough to end the problem.

The Bush administration went far beyond offering to help Latin American countries reduce the production of drugs and has "employed diplomatic pressures, public rebuke, and even threats to cut off economic assistance and market access to force Latin American acceptance of U.S. personnel and programs" for the drug war.[56] U.S. internal political considerations were considered vastly more important than those of Latin America, a war on drugs in the United States being much more expensive and polticially risky than a war on drugs abroad. Thus the United States has forced Latin American governments to spend their scant resources fighting drug production, which can account for 20–30 percent of their foreign exchange.

The Bush administration's reaction to the Sendero Luminoso may also be considered evidence of the dependent image, the dependent image being devoid of considerations of nationalism as a political force in the dependent country. The Sendero Luminoso, by appealing to ancient identities, arouses Peruvian nationalism, delegitimizes the Peruvian government, and supports antiimperialism. The Bush administration's response to the Sendero Luminoso indicates it is blind to this basis for Peruvian nationalism and to the Sendero's appeal.

In 1990, the Bush administration began to face the fact that it could not fight the drug war in Peru without addressing the problem of the growing strength of the Sendero. It viewed the Sendero only as an obstacle in the drug war, but not as a threat to the very survival of the Peruvian state. In April 1990, the administration decided to provide military assistance to the Peruvians to fight the guerrillas. The assistance would come in the form of training and supplies, the construction of a base in the central coca-growing region, and aid for the Peruvian air force and navy. The purpose of this aid was explained by Assistant Secretary of State for International Narcotics Matters Melvin Levitsky: "I want to be very frank in saying that where the insurgency and the drug traffickers are inextricably bound together, we have to deal with them together. . . . We have an interest in helping them fight that insurgency. Sendero Luminoso is a major part of the drug picture. . . . They protect the drug traffickers. They negotiate between the growers and the traffickers and increasingly they are engaged in drug trafficking themselves."[57]

Thus, rather than fearing the Sendero Luminoso for their Maoist ideology, the administration perceived them as agents of the drug cartels. Moreover, the administration rejected arguments from Peruvians and from members of Congress that U.S. military aid and military personnel would impinge on Peru's nationalistic sensitivities. Gustavo Gorriti, a Peruvian expert on the Sendero, argued that it would be like "throwing gasoline on a fire. The bases will be converted into visible symbols for Shining Path recruiting propaganda."[58] Some U.S. officials, notably Representative Peter Kostmayer, argued against military involvement, saying "I continue to have grave doubts about the militarization of the Andean anti-narcotics effort. Are we getting the United States involved through the back door in fighting guerrilla wars?"[59] In the prevailing U.S. image of Peru, there was no recognition of the relation between nationalism, the Sendero's popularity, poverty, and the production of coca. Instead, the insurgency was to be dealt with as drug traffickers; they were lumped together as the common problem, which would be met and defeated by U.S.-directed military and law enforcement programs.

Another important aspect of the U.S. perception of Peru can be seen in the Bush administration's response to the self-coup by President Alberto Fujimori in April 1992. Citing the need to combat the growing strength of the Sendero insurgency, Fujimori suspended constitutional rights, dissolved the Parliament, and threw opposition leaders in jail. Bush's reaction was to condemn Fujimori, to threaten to terminate aid, to suspend some aid, and to call upon the OAS to convince Fujimori to restore democracy. Bush said, "We can't sit by without registering our strong disapproval about the aborting of democracy in Peru. We want it restored."[60]

What is intriguing about Bush's statement is not so much that pro nouncement that "we want" the Peruvian political system to have a certain appearance—that type of statement is typical of the dependent view—but the fact that the internal coup was condemned, particularly considering that its justification was the growing strength of a very left-wing guerrilla movement. Such a coup would have been widely welcomed during the cold war, but by 1992 it was seen as a miscarriage of justice and a blow to democracy. Later, in a more restrained and diplomatic assessment of the situation, Secretary of State Baker announced that the United States sympathized with the stresses faced by the Peruvian government but that that was not an adequate justification for the coup. Baker declined to impose complete sanctions on Peru but did announce that no new aid would be provided.[61]

In a broader sense, the administration's reaction to President Fujimori's coup demonstrates that it had not developed post–cold war tactics for dealing with crises in Latin America. During the cold war the group would have been welcomed with the usual platitudes about democracy having a chance only when the Sendero was defeated. But the administration could not explain why democracy should be restored or why democracy would work in Peru this time around. Secretary of State Baker proclaimed, "you cannot destroy democracy in order to save it" (ibid.), but the administration failed to explain how its policies would be altered to prevent the restoration of the status quo that had already failed in Peru. State Department officials merely referred to ongoing programs which, they argued, if properly implemented would solve Peru's problems.[62] A *New York Times* correspondent concluded, "Those arguments sound similar to ones used by Administration officials months ago, when asked why they were not doing more to aid the former Soviet Union. They would point to the long list of things they were doing, even while acknowledging privately that they knew they were not sufficient. Indeed, American officials dealing with Latin America often sound like their European affairs counterparts, worrying aloud that neither Congress nor the upper reaches of the Administration are ready to focus on the tremendous problems of Latin America in this election year" (ibid.).

This apparent division in perception in the policy-making hierarchy helps explain why the administration continued to emphasize a military approach to the eradication of coca and why the administration paid little attention to Latin America's insistence that economic conditions was the first priority, guerrilla insurgencies was second, and drug production was third at best. Although in report after report one can see that both that State Department and and the Congress understood the political and economic instabilities in Latin America, U.S. policy continued to focus on the drug war as its and Latin America's first priority.[63]

THE ANDEAN INITIATIVE: TACTICS

The international component of the war on drugs has a long history; its Andean front has been in existence since the early 1980s. Of particular interest here is the Andean Initiative, because it is a post–cold war example of the direction of U.S. policy. I focus on Peru, one of the three central countries in the Andean Initiative, because Peru is facing a serious crisis, which could be replicated in other Third World countries in the post–cold war era.

The Andean Initiative became the central component of the Bush Administration's war on drugs in 1989 and 1990. It was described in a House of Representatives report as "a broad program of military, law enforcement, and economic assistance to the cocaine-producing countries of Colombia, Peru, and Bolivia, designed to reduce the supply of cocaine to the United States. With a total budget of over $231 million for the fiscal year 1990, the strategy seeks to disrupt cocaine production and trafficking operations through crop eradication, interdiction, and enforcement measures in the Andean source countries" (ibid., p. 3). The Andean Initiative involved $35.9 million in U.S. military aid and $19 million in law enforcement assistance for fiscal year 1990 (Peru declined the military aid); $34 million in military aid, $19 million in law enforcement aid, and $60 million in economic aid for fiscal year 1991; and $40 million in military aid, $19 million in law enforcement aid, and $100 million in economic aid requested for 1992.[64]

The stated goal of the Andean Initiative is to support the cocaine producing countries "in their efforts to control and defeat the drug trade" in order to achieve "a major reduction in the supply of cocaine from these countries to the United States through working with the host governments to disrupt and destroy the growing, processing, and transporting of coca and coca products."[65] Despite this declaration, the policy was planned to suit U.S. interests, goals, and tactical preferences even in the face of widespread disapproval by Peruvian officials. The Bush administration emphasized the military and police component almost exclusively, despite increasing allocations for economic assistance. (In fact, those funds were not allocated for economic development in the coca producing regions of Peru, as will be seen below.)

Another important aspect of this policy is that it, like the policies that preceded it, shifted tactical focuses several times. In the beginning of the 1980s the focus of the drug war was on training and improving the law enforcement capabilities of the Andean police forces. This did not meet with much success. The emphasis then turned to the militarization of those police. When that did not achieve the desired goals, U.S. officials focused on each country's own military force as the security branch most capable of fighting the drug war. These troops were trained and equipped by the United States. In 1989 the U.S. approach shifted from eradication of coca fields and growers to interdicting trafficking. It was not until 1990 that the economic aid component of the policy began to increase significantly, from about $3 million in 1989 to $60 million in 1990.

Another central characteristic of the U.S. drug war is the increased role of the Department of Defense and the Central Intelligence Agency. Initially, the Defense Department strongly resisted any involvement in a drug war, maintaining that it was a law enforcement problem, not a military security problem, and that it would divert attention from the real security missions of the military. But by 1990 Secretary of Defense Richard Cheney had come on board, and he announced that the drug war was a "high priority national security mission."[66] The U.S. military was to assist the Andean military forces, whose inclusion in the drug war was now seen as essential.

In 1989 President Bush signed a national security directive that authorized U.S. military personnel to leave secure areas and enter areas where they could encounter guerrillas or drug traffickers. The training program was developed jointly by Southcom and the Army Air Force Center for Low Intensity Conflict. According to the congressional report, "Teams of military advisers will remain in-country with each battalion and police unit/staff for eighteen months or longer, if necessary, upon completion of the training program. 'The degree to which the advisory teams would be operational is unspecified,' notes a DEA summary of the SOUTHCOM strategy. In addition, Mobile Training Teams will offer standardized progressive training to host country personnel, both in the region and in the United States."[67]

Thus U.S. forces were deeply involved in fighting in Peru, despite stipulations that Special Forces units would not go into combat with Peruvian forces.[68] In July 1991, the State Department proposed sending fifty U.S. Special Forces instructors to Peru as part of a $94 million antidrug program. For the first time, U.S. forces would work directly with the Peruvian military, training them to fight the guerrillas. During the preceding two years, a visiting fifteen-man Special Forces unit trained Peruvian police in jungle warfare. For more than six years armed agents of the Drug Enforcement Agency operated in the Upper Huallaga Valley. In 1989 guerrilla forces attacked the Santa Lucia Base in the Upper Huallaga valley; this base had been built with U.S. funds and housed both Peruvian and U.S. personnel.

The tactics selected to fight the drug war in Peru are typical of those associated with the dependent image. The United States provides the funding and training, the Peruvians do the legwork. The preferred tactics are military or paramilitary. Economic aid and general diplomacy were not tried. This is, however, a simplification: the Bush administration recognized early on that the Andean countries lacked the commitment or the will to play their role in the drug war—the institutional infrastructure necessary was lacking. So the Bush administration formed the "belief that the United States [could] manufacture the institutional capability needed for Andean governments to carry out U.S. objectives. [This] provides the rationale for the current strategy."[69]

In short, the selection of this strategy followed the logic commonly associated with seeing through a dependent image prism: the United States knows what is best and how to do it and therefore designs the plan without consulting the governments involved.[70] The dependent has a role to play, but its internal conditions are insignificant in designing the plan. The impact of such a plan becomes clearer as its implementation is explored.

THE ANDEAN INITIATIVE: IMPLEMENTATION

From the beginning, Peruvian political officials had profound objections to the Andean Initiative. The similarity between the Peruvian-U.S. debate concerning the U.S.-favored policy and U.S.-Vietnam debate over similar policies are striking. The Andean Initiative spanned the presidencies of Alan García and Alberto Fujimori, both of whom argued that the initiative would not work if it continued its emphasis on military and law enforcement aid. President García ultimately concluded that the antinarcotics program, which initially emphasized coca eradication, was fueling peasant support for the Sendero Luminoso, and he canceled the program for seven months in 1989. When Fujimori was on the campaign trial in 1990, he stated that he opposed military and law enforcement antinarcotics aid from the United States unless it was accompanied by an economic aid program. He complained that proposed economic aid for 1990 would not be targeted at the Upper Huallaga Valley, where it was needed if it were to reduce coca production, and that the proposed figure, $63 million, was not adequate anyway.[71]

In 1990, two months after he was elected, Fujimori refused the U.S. offer of $36 million in military aid. In late February 1992, he rejected a U.S. plan for coca reduction unless economic aid was increased. But the United States ultimately forced Peru to go along with the U.S. program.

First, the Peruvian request for increased economic aid to accompany military and law enforcement aid was stonewalled. Although the administration stated that it recognized that economic aid was indispensable and that economic aid was not attached to acceptance of the military aid, its actual distribution of economic aid was not in response to the Peruvian assessment of the causes of increased coca production nor was it unrelated to military aid. The State Department stated that economic aid would flow only when the Andean countries cooperated in the drug war, and *cooperation* was "defined by the involvement of their armed forces and acceptance of U.S. military aid."[72] Melvin Levitsky put it as follows: "Let me be precise on this, because we have not linked economic assistance to the provision of military assistance. What we have linked it to is counternarcotics performance, so if they could do the job without the military, and could perform up to a standard that would allow the keying in of economic assistance, that would be fine. Our assessment of this is that, given the task and the huge distances involved and our experience thus far where they have gotten better but where the situation could be improved, they could not do it without some infusion of armed forces support for this effort" (ibid.).

The U.S. explanation of how the economic aid was to be used reflects an additional aspect of the perceptual problem. When Peruvian officials complained that the economic aid program would do nothing for the 200,000 peasants growing coca in the Upper Huallaga Valley (and that without some other livelihood, they would continue to grow coca), State Department official Cesar Bernal responded, "The people who have arrived in the last five to ten years are not traditional farmers who changed from coffee or cacao to grow coca. They came from the cities just to grow coca on virgin land."[73]

A less empathetic view can hardly be imagined, and it demonstrates an inability to understand that people grow coca in order to live a marginally decent life—whether they came from Lima or the southern highlands. What did Mr. Bernal think these folks did for a living five years ago in Lima? In addition, U.S. policy has been to forgo economic development programs in the Upper Huallaga Valley because it is not safe for USAID officials, who would supervise the expenditure of the funds. The argument is that security has to be established first, then the money can be given. Again, this is the U.S. view, and it ignores the Peruvian view that the security problem is a *result* of the economic problem.

The Bush administration took an equally hard line on the reluctance of the Peruvian military to become involved in the drug war. But, although Peru's police units favor the Andean Initiative, its military favors pursuing the war against the Sendero, since it does not want to drive coca growers into the arms of the Shining Path. General Alberto Arciniega, in command of the Upper Huallaga Valley region, noted that the *cocaleros* join the Sendero after eradication efforts and thus there is a question as to whether the army will support eradication: "There are 150,000 *campesinos cocaleros* in the zone. Each of them is a potential *subversivo*. Eradicate his field, and the next day he'll be one. . . . Most of my men from this area. In effect, the police were wiping out the livelihood of their families, while I was asking them to fight Shining Path, which was sworn to protect the growers. Shining Path looked like heroes."[74]

Nevertheless, the Bush administration pushed hard for a change in the Peruvian military perspective. In an interview with a *Los Angeles Times* reporter, Levitsky smeared Arciniega's integrity by saying that there had been uncorroborated allegations that Arciniega took payoffs from drug traffickers and colluded in other ways. Levitsky drew back from publicly accusing Arciniega of corruption but did state that the disagreement with him was strong: "[Arciniega] himself is a very honest man. He is very driven, very dedicated. And we believe it is a good strategy to draw the campesinos away from Sendero Luminoso. But the problem is time. When do you start addressing the other part of the problem? Six months is already too far down the road. We strongly disagree with his approach, and we are trying to look for common ground."[75]

The United States won this conflict as well. Arciniega lost his post as commander of the Upper Huallaga Valley region, and the Peruvian military acquiesced to the counternarcotics war along with the counterinsurgency war. President Fujimori ultimately did accept military aid, and the United States made a concession by adding counterinsurgency training to the aid package. The aid package for 1991 included training and equipment for six army battalions, money for six river patrol boats, and refurbishing funds for twenty A-37 planes, and the Bush administration accepted as inevitable that "counter-narcotics activities [would] at times require counter-insurgency efforts."[76] The United States thus found itself at the top of the slippery slope that could lead to involvement in a guerrilla war.

Nevertheless, the military was entirely capable of accepting military aid but continuing to drag its heels in the drug war. The General Accounting Office cited the Peruvian military's "minimal commitment to coordinate and cooperation with the police in counternarcotics missions" as a troubling and debilitating element in the Andean Initiative.[77] Moreover, the noncoup coup of 1992, when President Fujimori suspended the constitution but the military did not take over, was designed to provide a basis for the defeat of the Sendero Luminoso. The coup would hardly have occurred without military encouragement, support, and even insistence.

The Bush administration's pattern of behavior is associated with the dependent image: U.S. policy makers maintained that their evaluation of Peru's problems was superior to that of the Peruvians and that, therefore, U.S. policy preferences must be followed. Compromise was negligible, and the full weight of U.S. leverage was used to force Peru to accept this policy. All of these factors are common in the treatment of countries viewed as dependents.

THE POST–COLD WAR DIFFERENCE

In many respects, the Andean Initiative is consistent with policies toward the dependent during the cold war. However, there are some important differences. First, U.S. policy makers did not regard the

Sendero Luminoso as the threat it would have been during the cold war, nor did they share the tremendous concern of the Peruvian government regarding the Sendero's ability to undermine the government's legitimacy. This merely reflects the absence of the enemy image from the scene, however, since contempt for the Peruvian evaluation of their own internal situation is consistent with the dependent image.

Second, the Andean Initiative was not part of a containment strategy, since containment was a result of the presence of an enemy. The absence of that overriding strategy left the Bush administration unable to explain why Peru should do as the United States demanded and also reduced the administration's capacity to think in the long term. During containment, U.S. policy makers may have been incorrect in their predictions of how democracy would be achieved and that it would do for a people, but they did have a prediction, bolstered by a psychologically logical explanation. Now they could not predict what good a reinvigorated democratic system would do. Without such a "vision," to use one of George Bush's favorite terms, policy was destined to be ad hoc and incremental. Policy was also likely to be the object of tremendous bureaucratic battles: without containment, bureaucratic players were less united behind a single policy front and much freer to compete. This was certainly evident in the case of Peru.

The principal U.S. agencies involved in the Andean Initiative are the Department of State's Bureau for International Narcotics Matters, the Drug Enforcement Agency, and the Department of Defense. There have been reports of serious competition and conflict between these agencies. Defense Department Special Forces and the Drug Enforcement Agency disagree about mission, training, areas of responsibility, and the relative capability and effectiveness of the other. DEA agents believe coca production to be a law enforcement problem not amenable to a military solution and regard the Special Forces as "arrogant young brats with no understanding of intelligence or law enforcement"; conversely, military personnel see the DEA agents as "city cops" out of their element in conditions of jungle warfare.[78] Meanwhile, the Department of State has been criticized for not assigning a high priority to a counternarcotics policy.[79]

The bureaucratic competition is related to the diminished sense of threat cause by the absence of a perceived enemy. The end of the cold war has also created institutional problems for the defense establishment, which in turn fuel bureaucratic conflict. Although initially reluctant to get involved in the drug war, the Pentagon came on board after discovering that the drug war was a potential source of future missions. The drug war was described by a congressional aide as the Pentagon's "new meal ticket now that the commies are not their big threat."[80] The point was also made by Admiral William Crowe: "Certainly I think we'll put more emphasis on the drug war. And if there are resources tied to it, you'll see the services compete for those, and probably vigorously. We take some pride in being accomplished bureaucrats, as well as military men. And I think it's legitimate for military men to try and perpetuate their institution."[81] The drug war provides a basis for military budgetary requests, but it also provides the military with the opportunity to test its post–cold war tactic of low-intensity conflict, a popular approach to warfare in the early 1990s, particularly in Southcom.

At the same time, there is deep military skepticism about the appropriateness of the Pentagon role in the drug war (ibid., p. 33).

CONCLUSION

This chapter traces some emerging patterns of policy decision making toward Latin America in the post–cold war era. It explores the impact of the dependent image in the absence of the enemy image on policy and tactic selection. Would U.S. policy makers have acted differently toward Panama and Peru if it had a different image of Latin America countries? Images that accommodated the political complexities of these two countries would have produced different policies. In these early years of the post–cold war era, there appears to be ample time to reconsider these policy decisions. After all, few Americans were killed in the invasion of Panama (even if hundreds of Panamanians died to catch one drug trafficker). And even though the Andean Initiative did not reduce the flow of cocaine, it was a low-cost operation—what could the United States lose by giving the initiative a chance?

Time is short—the golden opportunity offered by the end of the cold war for a different Latin American policy is quickly slipping away. Peru's situation, in particular, is being replicated in varying forms throughout the Third World and even in Europe. The power of the dependent image outside of the cold war context is such that U.S. policy makers might fail to recognize the crises of legitimacy in the Third World. If the United States continues to respond to those crises with cold war tactics, the new world order will likely be one of continued violence and loss of lives.

The broad patterns of post–cold war policy are more difficult to speculate about. The behavior that the United States accepted and even approved of—vast human rights abuses, official corruption on any scale so long it was committed by an anticommunist government—may not be acceptable in the future. Or will it? The United States has not established any clear policy about such things. The most important factor may be whether an interest group in the United States is willing to challenge such U.S. foreign policies. Even that challenge would be tempered by the basic U.S. image of Latin American countries: public opinion polls show that Americans are concerned about drugs and are willing to use sanctions and other forms of force to get other countries to solve the U.S. drug problem. The challenge, therefore is to change the U.S. self-image and its image of other countries.

CONCLUSION: NO MATTER HOW
MUCH THINGS CHANGE . . .

IT IS DIFFICULT TO ARGUE THAT U.S. POLICY TOWARD LATIN AMERICA HAS served U.S. interests well. Acting as though a red pervert was loose in a children's playground, the United States fueled Latin American hostility toward itself and diverted U.S. attention from the important issues of economic growth and political change in Latin America. Unfortunately, there is little indication that the end of the cold war has heightened U.S. interest in these problems, nor will the end of the cold war change the pattern of U.S. policies toward Latin America in the absence of image change.

The cold war case studies illustrate the role the dependent and the enemy images played in conflicts with Latin American countries, which in combination produced a perception of threat. U.S. decision makers used containment as their guiding strategy in those situations and regarded the goal as containment. Alone, the dependent image resulted in the selection of coercive tactics but without the heightened sense of threat; goals were seen as bilateral, and time was not of the essence. This provided opportunities to use economic pressure rather than military or covert pressure to achieve U.S. goals.

In either case, bargaining was minimal. U.S. policy makers chose their preferred solution and expected it to be accepted by the Latin American country. The United States seldom compromised. And why should it, since its short-term goals could be achieved without compromise? The answer, of course, is obvious: treating countries like dependents produces long-term wounds, like U.S.-Cuban relations. However, from a psychological standpoint, the failures were few. Often, particularly in the early years of the cold war, U.S. policy makers got what they wanted, so there was no psychological incentive to change the image of Latin American countries as dependents.

A profound change in the image of the countries of an entire region usually requires a terrible policy failure. Vietnam was a failure large enough to change many people's image of the Third World to a worldview that incorporated the neutral-nonaligned image. The dependent image was used for fewer and fewer of these countries. Other people, although probably few in number at the highest policy-making level, reverted to piecemeal evaluation of the Third World.

The use of the dependent image as the perceptual guide for U.S.– Latin American relations appears to be particularly difficult to change, however. How many serious policy disasters were there in Latin America? Cuba was a problem, Chile an embarrassment, and there was not much support for Reagan's policy in Central America, but nothing happened that even remotely resembled the disaster of Vietnam. Thus, the psychological incentive for altering the images used to understand Latin America was weak and remains so in the post–cold war era.

Some administrations certainly had a wider array of worldviews than others, particularly during the 1960s and 1970s. In the policy debates among those with different worldviews, we can see the relation among images, goals, and tactics. The Carter administration is the best example of diversity in images, probably because Carter's own worldview regarding the dependent image of Latin America and the enemy image of the Soviet Union was less extreme than his predecessors and successors. However, because Carter was president during the cold war and because he was a modified cold warrior himself, his administration included traditional cold warriors and followed a policy of containment. The differences between classic cold war containment and Carter's were differences only of degree, reflected in his policy toward Nicaragua and El Salvador.

While Carter's policies were dominated by modified and traditional cold warriors, his was a unique administration in the number and power of those with either modified cold war or human rights worldviews. Had these types of advisers been plentiful in the Reagan and Bush administrations, we might have seen a different pattern of behavior toward Central America, the Nicaraguan revolution, the Salvadoran peace process, Panama, and the drug war in Peru. No doubt periodic factors caused the end of the cold war, but random, aperiodic factors, such as the election of Ronald Reagan after Jimmy Carter, knocked the emerging post–cold war system onto a path quite different from what it would have been had Jimmy Carter won reelection. The Reagan and Bush administrations were populated by individuals with worldviews like those of the Eisenhower administration, with few people disagreeing about the categorization of Latin America. Replete with advisers with the prototypical dependent image, these two administrations fell into the classic pattern of U.S. policy making toward Latin America.

The fact that the Reagan and Bush administrations occupied the presidency at the time of the end of the cold war had an effect on the image of Latin America among all Americans, exemplified by the lack of protest over the invasion of Panama and the lack of interest in the Andean Initiative. The accident of the Reagan-Bush presidencies at the end of the cold war pushed U.S. post–cold war policy toward Latin America in a particular direction and, in the process, lost opportunities for a reconsideration and redefinition of U.S. policies in Latin America. Therefore, even with the Vietnam generation controlling the White House and a number of Carter administration foreign policy officials in top-level positions, the approach to Latin America advocated by the human rights group during the Carter administration may still not be adopted. Moreover, even that group had a dependent image of some Latin American leaders. No one is immune to the image, and the Reagan-Bush era has left its mark on the transition from the cold war.

However, chaotic systems do not repeat themselves exactly, and the United States will never return to a pre–cold war policy toward Latin America, despite the fact that the dependent image of Latin America exists today as it did in 1900 (although it differs in kind and is certainly not as widely shared as it was in 1900). The use of the dependent image as a guide to policy during the cold war influenced the nature of the image itself. Tactics associated with the cold war containment strategy are now associated with the dependent image in and of itself. In every previous era there was a perceived enemy to guard Latin America against. Now there is none, and therefore the sense of threat is likely to diminish—until and unless a new enemy emerges. Thus, however the dependent image was influenced by the cold war, its use as a guide to policy in the post–cold war era cannot be exactly as it was during the cold war.

Another important question with implications for U.S. policy toward Latin America concerns the U.S. self-image, the challenge to which is global. Where else but in Latin America can the United States demonstrate with impunity that it is still a superpower and that its military might makes it so? This was the approach taken by the Bush administration to Panama and Peru. However, it is probably too early in the post–cold war era to argue that this trend will continue. If economic problems continue to challenge the U.S. self-image and if political economic issues continue to rise to the top of the international agenda, they may strongly influence the direction of U.S. policy toward Latin America.

Nevertheless, without a change in the image of Latin America, U.S. policy making can be expected to continue to rely on the use of coercive instruments to achieve U.S. goals. It is also possible that the dependent image itself protects a positive U.S. self-image by justifying and giving righteous value to coercive interventionist behavior. If so, threats to the U.S. self-image from economic problems and the loss of international meaning to the superpower status will only contribute to the continuation of a dependent image of Latin America.[1]

Post–cold war U.S. policy must also be placed in the context of the problems and opportunities the United States will be called upon to deal with in Latin America. Here again there is little cause for optimism. There was no indication that the Bush administration's policy toward Peru was designed to respond to the crisis of legitimacy the government of that country faced. The responsibility for addressing these complexities was left to middle-level bureaucrats, who were not heard at the top during the Bush administration. With the Soviet threat gone, top-level policy makers did not ask what was going on in Peru, let alone why; the existence of a powerful, violent, and ideologically pure Maoist revolutionary group there was no longer important.

Cold war case studies permit the study of the dependent image and the self-image in the context of threat and fear. The post–cold war era will provide an opportunity to see these images affect policy in the context of threatless conditions, with its opportunity to achieve something perceived as beneficial for the United States. There is, after all, no enemy left in Latin America. If the dependent image does not change and if the self-image is protected by the dependent image, these situations may result in the usual coercive treatment and possibly return to a manifest destiny self-image. Under such conditions, an imperial policy toward Latin America can easily be perceived as good for the United States and good for the dependent as well.

The demise of the cold war also permits some conclusions about short-term post-cold war policy patterns. During the cold war, containment, as poor as it was as a strategy, gave U.S. policy whatever coherence it had. Today, that is gone, and policy is thus most likely to be ad hoc and the subject of bureaucratic battles. Unfortunately, the absence of containment and the ad hoc nature of policy has not meant that policy is now more sensitive to the complex political, economic, and social realities of Latin American countries. Instead, it is more sensitive to the political, economic and social realities of the United States, pursuing goals that reflect narrow U.S. interests (e.g., a cheap drug war that attacks only the source), public opinion (e.g., fear of being humiliated by a fellow like Noriega), and the desires of bureaucracies to feather their own nests and increase their jurisdictions (e.g., competition over control of the drug war). The ease with which the Latin American components of the drug war are being abandoned by the Clinton administration demonstrates the same pattern. The drug war in the Andes did not achieve the goals of the United States so it is dropped and forgotten without consideration of or concern about the political trends it may have set in motion in the Andes.

This too is unlikely to change without a fundamental alteration of the U.S. self-image and its image of Latin America. U.S. interests are defined by the prevailing image of the other country. If this country is considered inferior, then its concerns will not be taken into account as the United States assesses its own interests. Unless policy is placed in a larger strategic framework, it will continue in this ad hoc pattern. As long as the other country is seen as inferior, the United States will continue to use coercive tactics even when other alternatives are available and would produce a successful outcome.

How would policy change if the dependent image changed? The case studies here suggest, first, nationalism would be recognized as a driving political force in Latin American and that it manifests across the political spectrum. Second, one could expect a reversion to piecemeal examination and interpretation of a country's political system, particularly in short-term decision making, since the dependent image makes policy makers oblivious to the political divisions, alliances, and interests of these countries and makes them focus on individual personalities. This occurred again and again in the case studies: Arbenz, Castro, Somoza, and Noriega were seen as the absolute directors of political events in their countries. Depose those individuals, and the political system would become whatever the United States wanted it to be.

Third, the United States would recognize the power and capability of countries that were heretofore seen as weak and incompetent. Power may always be asymmetrical, but capability is not the same thing. Fidel Castro survived U.S. attempts to get rid of him, and many other political forces in Latin America have suffered tremendous deprivation and suffering as a result of their resistance to U.S. policy. Neither the Sandinistas nor the Salvadoran FMLN were destroyed, despite a decade of U.S. pressure. U.S. recognition of this internal strength and potential for resistance would lead to two changes: a refusal to waste U.S. resources trying to attain the unattainable and a new willingness to engage in mutually beneficial negotiations with Latin Americans. Finally, U.S.

policy makers and the public alike would abandon the idea that they are or should be masters of the universe.

How probable is this change? Sadly, if past trends are used for prediction, not very—unless another foreign policy disaster occurs that forces change. Worldviews change when the environment they organize changes and when people recognize that the mismatch between their images and their universe makes them unable to achieve their goals. Theoretically, images can change through an examination of reality, but this has not changed U.S. policy in the past. Instead, U.S. images changed when they were forced to by failures. The drug war is the most likely U.S. adventure in Latin America to lead the country toward disaster.

This will be Bill Clinton's first challenge: Can his administration, which seeks a pragmatic, realistic approach to policy problems through learning, study, and examination of options, use that process to change its image of Latin America? Such a task is phenomenally difficult. It requires critical self-reflection and the ability to see and accept nonconscious attitudes. It is unlikely that any member of the Clinton administration would be pleased to discover that his or her image of Latin Americans is that of the dependent. Such a revelation would certainly go against the self-image of Clinton's advisers. That first step, therefore, should be a conscious reexamination of the political complexities in Latin America, acceptance of these complexities, and the construction of new policy and negotiation practices that recognize these complexities.

Moreover, the administration will have to reshape the U.S. self-image to fit a more modest concept of the U.S. global role and will have to end the assumption of U.S. cultural superiority. Human psychology, pressure to deal with more immediate domestic and international crises, and bureaucracies with vested interests in continuing existing policies make this a daunting task. But change is possible.

APPENDIX

NOTES

BIBLIOGRAPHY

INDEX

Appendix

RESEARCHING IMAGES

Developing the operative images in a single policy maker's worldview or a group's shared worldview is best done through qualitative analysis. The survey instrument is useful, but its utility in images research is limited for several reasons. First, the concern in this study is with the operative images of policy makers, not of the mass public. Some of the policy makers under examinatin are dead, and others may not be inclined to respond to a survey. Second, and most important, images are nonconscious psychological devices, and people cannot easily discuss their worldviews. Moreover, questions prompt them to examine their simplifications, and they are then inclined to question their own judgment, or to rationalize their worldview, or to become uncomfortable when they see their simplifications, or to refuse to answer.

Personal interviews are also useful in eliciting information about policy makers' images, but this research technique has limitations, too. Access to policy makers is a problem, and reliance upon interviews alone for information would provide a skewed body of information—derived only from those willing to talk. Further, one cannot ask direct questions about images. Asking a policy maker if he or she views Nicaragua as a dependent is certain to bring the interview to an abrupt end. Questions must be constructed that permit the analyst to infer the operative images, since they cannot be directly examined.

Given these difficulties, this research relied upon a looser scheme for collecting and analyzing data. Raw data concerning perceptions were gathered from my interviews with some policy makers, interviews published in the press (both attributed to specific individuals and to "officials" working in a policy area), written or oral comments in the *Congressional Record*, written works by policy makers and by participant observers, speeches, and hearings before Congress in which policy makers and advisers answered questions and exchanged views.

Worldview images cannot be inferred solely on the basis of verbal evidence, however. In fact, given any official's natural inclination to avoid a bad press, one must routinely examine verbal statements with skepticism. Analysis of verbal expressions of perception must be accompanied by analysis of behavioral patterns that reflect, and are explained by these verbal expressions. If there is a contrast between what the policy maker says and what he or she does, it is best to assume that the action rather than the statement reflects the perception.

Finally, in the effort to establish the operative images in policy makers' worldviews, the researcher must be aware of, and avoid the danger of, tautology. It is important to gather verbal and action data using material outside the specific decision that one is attempting to explain.

These verbal and behavioral data were examined in a systematic manner, although the inference scheme was not as tight and systematic as that typical of operational coding research. The research agenda called for accumulating as much material on the policy makers and the case as was available from the sources mentioned above. Images were operationalized and the indicators developed by breaking down an image into its component parts and developing indicators of those parts.

Images are composed of (1) perceptions of a country's capability, culture, and intention; (2) event scripts, reflecting lessons from history that policy makers use to understand the behavior of a country or to predict its behavior; and (3) response alternatives that were consistently considered appropriate for use vis-à-vis a country. The attributes of capability, culture, and intention could not be operationalized at those levels of abstraction and were therefore broken down into smaller components. (Whether any of the statements were accurate is not relevant.)

IMAGE INDICATORS

The capability attribute was derived from statements about the following:
1. Military strength and capability
    a. The country's offensive and defensive military potential
    b. The government's control over the military
    c. The likelihood that the country would resort to the use of military force to achieve its goals
    d. Whether the country's military force was superior, equal, or inferior to the U.S. military force
    e. The country's capability of using, and willingness to use, military force
2. Domestic policy
    a. The country's government structure (open or closed)
    b. The government's effectiveness and efficiency in implementing policy
    c. The organization, size, and strength of the government's opposition
    d. The government's ability to carry out a policy, achieve a goal, or abide by an agreement
    e. Whether the decision structure was multitiered or monolithic (monolithic countries are assumed to be more capable since they do not have to please their publics, interest groups, or bureaucratic interests)
3. Economic characteristics
    a. The capacity and stability of the country's economy (industrial potential, agricultural self-sufficiency, growth rate, potential for growth and development)
    b. The interaction between the U.S. economy and the other country's economy (permeability of other economy; threat to or opportunity for the United States)
    c. The country as recipient or provider of international aid

The culture attribute was derived from statements about the following:
1. Comparison of culture to U.S. culture
   (perception of similarity implies a positive affect with low or no threat)
2. Cultural sophistication
   (includes social norms, literacy, religion, standard of living, scientific and technological capabilities, racial composition, nationalism and the public-mindedness of citizens)

The intention attribute was derived from statements about the following:
1. Goals and motives
   a. Leaders pursuance of their goals
   b. Leaders' and citizens' motives
   c. Compatability of goals with U.S. goals
2. Flexibility
   a. Leader's willingness to bargain, change tactics, and shift policy in response to U.S. initiatives
   b. The country's flexibility
   c. The linking of flexibility with cause (nationalism, imperialism, etc.)
3. Supportiveness of U.S. goals and policies
4. Whether decision structure is multitiered or monolithic (those seen as multitiered are seen as less threatening)

Event scripts were derived from statements about the following:
1. Lessons from history
   a. Historical incident used as analogy to explain current conflict
   b. Historical incident used as lesson regarding appropriateness of techniques for dealing with conflict or issue at hand
2. Predictions about country's behavior or the outcome of conflicts

Response alternatives were derived from statements about the following:
1. Instruments deemed appropriate for use in a conflict with the country (includes military threat or actual force, economic incentives to economic sanctions, diplomatic protests, bilateral and multilateral negotiations, or simply doing nothing; those perceived as weaker are dealt with in a more coercive fashion)
2. Bargaining (those considered equal are dealt with as equals; inferiors are not bargained with)

THE PROTOTYPICAL DEPENDENT

The prototypical dependent is always described as poor in terms of resources and capability. The dependent's military is weak in resources, inadequate in training, and unable to win with maximum effort. It cannot defeat anyone—a guerrilla organization, a neighboring country, or a drug cartel. Military officers are corrupt, stupid, brutal, and power hungry.

The domestic polity of the dependent image is also characterized in highly simplified and patronizing terms. A small elite runs the country, and that elite is manipulable and purely self-interested. This elite has no real concern for the population, which is not particularly troublesome, since the population is simple, childlike, and passive. Any opposition to the ruling elite is either entirely self-serving or under the influence of an alien force, such as an enemy. Neither the elite nor the populace is capable of developing and implementing policy programs. Neither is capable of understanding or responding to the machinations of a superior force, such as the enemy. The state is inherently weak because the people are inherently inferior.

Assessments of capability in the economic realm follow the same pattern. Whatever the country's resource base, the assumption is that it cannot grow and prosper without outside assistance. The dependent cannot extract, refine, or market its resources without the United States. And even though the United States needs those resources, the dependent needs the United States to make a transaction possible. This leads to the assumption that the United States essentially owns the resources in question.

Characterizations of culture are surprisingly easy to find. Contemptuous descriptions of a dependent's culture seem to pop out of the mouths of even cautious officials. Dependent's are described as culturally inferior and simple. Their political culture is composed of individual self-interest, with no sense of right or wrong (except for primitive and quaint characteristics, which have no place in the modern world). Nationalism is not a motivating characteristic of the dependent.

Descriptions of the dependent's intentions are equally simplistic and self-serving. The dependent is flexible, malleable, and shares U.S. international goals—being incapable of constructing any international goals of its own. The elite is simple and nonnationalistic, so it will not counter resistance from internal groups to carry out U.S. wishes. The U.S. response to a dependent is that of a parent toward a child: spare the rod and spoil the child. The dependent is not treated as an equal but is given a complete package of solutions to a problem. Resistance is dealt with coercively, which is assumed best for all concerned.

THE STRENGTH OF AN IMAGE

The concept of images assumes that there is an prototypical image for each category. But the assumption is also made that not all policy makers place each country at the prototypical extreme of its image. Images are continuums, ranging from the prototypical extreme to perceptions that only loosely fit the image. In fact, the differences in the strength of policy makers' images of any country are extremely important in explaining differences in the tactical preferences of policy advocates.

The data were therefore examined with two questions in mind: In which image was the state placed? And how close was that state to the prototypical extreme? To answer the second question, a theoretically based description of the prototypical image was compared to the description of a country found in the data. Typically, policy makers were consistent in their departures from the prototypical description when they did not place the country at the extreme. Interestingly, departures from the extreme tended to begin with a recognition of nationalism as an important element of the dependent's political culture.

Departures from the extreme image of the enemy tended (when the USSR still existed) to begin with a diminished perception of capability, particularly in terms of the military subattribute. Tactical preferences followed suit: policy makers aware of nationalism as an important factor in a country's polity begin to caution against the use of tactics that would be perceived as patronizing or coercive. they also began to predict a country's adverse reaction to those tactics, regardless of the cost to that country.

Notes

INTRODUCTION

1. Martha L. Cottam and E. Thomas Rowe, "Intervention Decisions: The Interaction of Situational and Psychological Factors," paper prepared for the 1987 Annual Meeting of the American Political Science Foundation, Chicago, p. 2.

2. Cole Blasier, *The Hovering Giant* (Pittsburgh: University of Pittsburgh Press, 1976); Robert Pastor, *Condemned to Repetition* (Princeton: Princeton University Press, 1987); Martin Diskin, ed., *Trouble in Our Backyard: Central America and the United States in the Eighties* (New York: Pantheon, 1983); Guy Poitras, *The Ordeal of Hegemony* (Boulder, Colo.: Westview, 1990).

3. See, for example, Jeane Kirkpatrick, "Dictatorships and Double Standards," *Commentary* 68 (November 1979): 34–45; Edward Luttwak, "The Nature of the Crisis," in Joseph Cirincone, ed., *Central America and the Western Alliance* (New York: Holmes and Meier, 1985); James Michel, "Defending Democracy," in Cirincone, ed., *Central America and the Western Alliance;* Morris Rothenberg, "The Soviets and Central America," in Robert Leiken, ed., *Central America: Anatomy of Conflict* (New York: Pergamon, 1984); Pedro Sanjuan, "Why We Don't Have a Latin American Policy," *Washington Quarterly* 32 (Autumn 1980): 28–39. Classics include Thomas Bailey, *A Diplomatic History of the American People*, 7th ed. (New York: Appleton-Century Crofts, 1964).

4. Rothenberg, *The Soviets and Central America*, p. 131.

5. Stephen Krasner, *Defending the National Interest* (Princeton: Princeton University Press, 1978).

6. Poitras, *The Ordeal of Hegemony;* Abraham Lowenthal, *Partners in Conflict: The United States and Latin America in the 1990's*, rev. ed. (Baltimore: Johns Hopkins University Press, 1990); and Harold Molineau, *U.S. Policy Toward Latin America: From Regionalism to Globalism*, 2d ed. (Boulder, Colo.: Westview, 1990).

7. Poitras, *The Ordeal of Hegemony*, p. 157.

8. On interventions, see Julio Cotler and Richard Fagen, eds., *Latin America and the United States: The Changing Political Realities* (Stanford: Stanford University Press, 1974); Walter LeFeber, *Inevitable Revolutions: The United States in Central America* (New York: Norton, 1983); Richard Fagen and Olga Pellicer, eds., *The Future of Central America* (Stanford: Stanford University Press, 1983); and Stanford University Action Network, ed., *Revolution in Central America* (Boulder, Colo.: West-

view, 1983). Classics include Theotonio dos Santos, "The Structure of Dependence," *American Economic Review* 60 (May 1970): 231–36; Osvaldo Sunkel, "Big Business and 'Dependencia,' " *Foreign Affairs* 50 (April 1972): 517–31; Raymond Duvall, "Dependence and Dependencia Theory," *International Organization* 32 (May 1978): 51–78; Ronald Chilcote and Joel Edelstein, eds., *Latin America: The Struggle with Dependency and Beyond* (New York: Shenkman, 1974).

9. Robert Pastor, "U.S. Policy Toward the Caribbean: Fixed and Emerging Images," *World Politics* 3 (April 1986): 491–92.

10. Reviews of dependency theory include Steven Hughes and Kenneth Mijeski, "Contemporary Paradigms in the Study of Inter-American Relations," in John Martz and Lars Schoultz, eds., *Latin America, the United States, and the Inter-American System* (Boulder, Colo.: Westview, 1980); and John Gitlitz and Henry Landsberger, "The Inter-American Political Economy: How Dependable Is Dependency Theory?" in Martz and Schoultz, eds., *Latin America, the United States, and the Inter-American System.*

11. Examples include Jerome Levinson and Juan de Onis, *The Alliance That Lost Its Way* (Chicago: Quadrangle, 1970); Lars Schoultz, *Human Rights and United States Policy Toward Latin America* (Princeton: Princeton University Press, 1981); Pastor, *Condemned to Repetition;* Blasier, *The Hovering Giant;* Howard Wiarda, *Finding Our Way? Toward Maturity in U.S.–Latin American Relations* (Washington, D.C.: American Enterprise Institute, 1987).

12. Diskin, *Trouble in Our Backyard,* p. xvi

13. Kenneth Coleman, "The Political Mythology of the Monroe Doctrine," in Martz and Schoultz, eds., *Latin America, the United States, and the Inter-American System,* p. 97.

14. John Martz, "Democracy and the Imposition of Values," in Martz and Schoultz, eds., *Latin America, the United States, and the Inter-American System,* p. 147.

15. See especially Lars Schoultz, *National Security and United States Policy Toward Latin America* (Princeton: Princeton University Press, 1987).

16. See, for example, Ole Holsti, "Cognitive Dynamics and Images of the Enemy: Dulles and Russia," in David Finlay, Ole Holsti, and Richard Fagen, eds., *Enemies in Politics* (Chicago: Rand McNally, 1967); Keith Shimko, *Images and Arms Control: Perceptions of the Soviet Union in the Reagan Administration* (Ann Arbor: University of Michigan Press, 1991); and John Dower, *War Without Mercy: Race and Power in the Pacific War* (New York: Pantheon, 1986).

17. There were several disagreements within several cold war administrations concerning exactly how prototypical an enemy the Soviet Union was. Moreover, while a full-intensity enemy image was dominant during the 1950s, the last half of the 1960s, and most of the 1980s, a modified enemy image, wherein the Soviet Union was perceived as less aggressive due to its diminished capabilities but as still being opportunistic and dangerous, emerged during the Kennedy years and again during the 1970s. Both enemy images provided a logic for NATO's existence but caused disagreement about the appropriate nuclear policy—flexible response or assured destruction. The modified enemy image, particularly in association with the

modified dependent image, had important implications for policy toward the Third World, as well. In combination, the two images resulted in increased tolerance for nationalistic, reformist, and even left-of-center regimes in the Third World, particularly when the Third World country in question was stable.

The importance of distinguishing trends and variations in containment, and in avoiding the oversimplification of containment as a strategy, was pointed out to me by Ole Holsti, who noted that these variations were evident from the beginning of the cold war, especially between George Kennan and John Foster Dulles. For analyses that cover many central perceptual trends during the formation of containment, see Robert Jervis, "The Impact of the Korean War on the Cold War," *Journal of Conflict Resolution* 24 (1980): 563–92; and John Lewis Gaddis, *Strategies of Containment* (New York: Oxford University Press, 1982). Trends in public opinion are discussed in Ole Holsti, "Public Opinion and Foreign Policy: Challenges to the Almond-Lippmann Consensus," *International Studies Quarterly* 36 (1992): 439–66.

1. IMAGES, STRATEGIES, AND TACTICS

1. Portions of this chapter are in M. Cottam and Rowe, "Intervention Decisions."

2. There are many personality studies. Some of the more informative include Alexander George and Juliet George, *Woodrow Wilson and Colonel House: A Personality Study* (New York: J. Day, 1965); and Betty Glad, "Black and White Thinking: Ronald Reagan's Approach to Foreign Policy," *Political Psychology* 4 (1983): 33–76.

3. See, for exmaple, Alexander George, "The 'Operational Code': A Neglected Approach to the Study of Political Leaders and Decision Making," *International Studies Quarterly* 13 (1969): 190–222; and Alexander George, *Presidential Decisionmaking in Foreign Policy: the Effective Use of Information and Advice* (Boulder, Colo.: Westview, 1980).

4. Yaacov V. I. Vertzberger, *The World in Their Minds: Information Processing, Cognition, and Perception in Foreign Policy Decisionmaking* (Stanford: Stanford University Press, 1990).

5. James Gleick, *Chaos: Making a New Science* (New York: Penguin, 1987).

6. George, " 'The Operational Code' "; George, *Presidential Decisionmaking in Foreign Policy;* Stephen Walker and Timothy Murphy, "The Utility of the Operational Code in Political Forecasting," *Political Psychology* 3 (1981–1982): 24–60; and Holsti, "Cognitive Dynamics and Images of the Enemy."

7. General works are Robert Jervis, *Perception and Misperception in International Politics* (Princeton: Princeton University Press, 1976); Richard Ned Lebow, *Between Peace and War* (Baltimore: Johns Hopkins University Press, 1983); Robert Jervis and Jack Snyder, eds., *Dominoes and Bandwagons: Strategic Beliefs and Great Power Competition in the Eurasian Rimland* (Oxford: Oxford University Press, 1990); and Vertzberger, *The World in Their Minds*. On the operational code, see George " 'The Operational Code.' " For examples of a cognitive model based on images, see Richard Cottam, *Foreign Policy Motivation* (Pittsburgh: University of Pittsburgh Press, 1977); Richard Herrmann, *Perception and Behavior in Soviet Foreign Policy* (Pittsburgh: University of Pittsburgh Press, 1985); Martha L. Cottam, *Foreign Policy*

Decision Making: The Influence of Cognition (Boulder, Colo.: Westview, 1986); and Shimko, *Images and Arms Control.*

8. Classic works in this area are Gordon Allport, *The Nature of Prejudice* (Garden City, N.Y.: Doubleday, 1954); Solomon Asch, "Forming Impressions of Personality," *Journal of Abnormal and Social Psychology* 41 (1946): 258–90; Jerome Bruner, "On Perceptual Readiness," in J. M. Anglin and J. S. Bruner, eds., *Beyond the Information Given* (New York: Norton, 1972); and Eleanor Rosch and Barbara Lloyd, eds., *Cognition and Categorization* (Hillsdale, N.J.: Erlbaum, 1978).

9. The psychological reasons supporting this type-of-country categorization are discussed in M. Cottam, *Foreign Policy Decision Making,* chap. 2. For experimental support on the existence and use of these images, see James Voss, Richard Herrmann, Tonya Engstler-Schooler, and Karen VanderPloeg, "On the Existence and Use of Stereotypical Images of Foreign Countries," paper prepared for the 1991 International Studies Association Meeting, Vancouver, British Columbia, March 19–22.

10. See Mark Pavelchak, "Piecemeal and Category-Based Evaluation: An Idiographic Analysis," *Journal of Personality and Social Psychology* 56 (1989): 354–63, for a discussion of psychological studies; and Martha L. Cottam, "Recent Developments in Political Psychology," in Martha Cottam and Chih-yu Shih, eds., *Contending Dramas: A Cognitive Approach to Post Cold War International Organization* (New York: Praeger, 1992), for a fuller discussion of the political implications.

11. Susan Fiske, S. L. Neuberg, A. E. Beattie, and S. J. Miller, "Category-Based and Attitude-Based Reactions to Others: Some Informational Conditions of Stereotyping and Individuating Processes," *Journal of Experimental Social Psychology* 23 (1987): 399–427 (p. 401).

12. R. Cottam, *Foreign Policy Motivation;* Herrmann, *Perception and Behavior in Soviet Foreign Policy;* and M. Cottam, *Foreign Policy Decision Making.*

13. George Miller, "The Magic Number Seven, Plus or Minus Two," *Psychological Review* 63 (1956): 81–97.

14. G. L. Murphy and D. L. Medin argue that a "major respect in which attribute matching may be too limited is that our representations may include information concerning operation, transformations, and (indirectly) relations among attributes. . . . Much of our reasoning about concepts may be based on constraints about operations that are permissible." See "The Role of Theories in Conceptual Coherence," *Psychological Review* 92 (1985): 289–316 (p. 295).

15. R. Cottam, *Foreign Policy Motivation,* pp. 63–68.

16. Susan Folkman, "Personal Control and Stress and Coping Processes: A Theoretical Analysis," *Journal of Personality and Social Psychology* 46 (1984): 839–52 (p. 840).

17. R. Cottam, *Foreign Policy Motivation,* pp. 67–68.

18. Robert Jervis, "Perceiving and Coping with Threat," in Robert Jervis and Richard Ned Lebow, eds., *Perception and Deterrence* (Baltimore: Johns Hopkins University Press, 1985).

19. Dean Pruitt, *Negotiation Behavior* (New York: Academic, 1981); Jeffrey Rubin and Bert Brown, *The Social Psychology of Bargaining and Negotiation* (New York: Academic, 1975); and Dean Tjosvold, "Unequal Power Relationships Within a

Cooperative or Competitive Context," *Journal of Applied Social Psychology* 11 (1981): 137–50.

20. This perceptual tendency is difficult to verify through verbal evidence, particularly in more recent cases, since political decision makers are often reluctant to admit that they use cultural assumptions and generalizations to decide how to approach another country's leaders. The farther back in history one goes, the easier it is to find cultural assessments of other countries in which policy makers gave free rein to their stereotypical judgments. Today, policy makers tend to be careful not to use offensive language, so the analyst must look for patterns in behavior (e.g., contemptuous treatment or a propensity to dictate terms rather than to negotiate) as well as policy makers' predictions of how others will behave, which often allow one to infer their perceptions.

21. M. Cottam, *Foreign Policy Decision Making*, chap. 6.

22. Fiske et al., "Category-Based and Attribute-Based Reactions to Others," pp. 402–03

23. This pattern is strongly criticized by Stephen Walker, "The Impact of Personality Structure and Cognitive Processes Upon American Foreign Policy Decisions," paper prepared for the 1988 American Political Science Association Meeting, Washington, D.C.

24. This debate is reviewed in Susan Fiske and Shelley Taylor, *Social Cognition* (New York: Random House, 1984).

25. Shelley Taylor, *Positive Illusions: Creative Deceptions and the Healthy Mind* (New York: Basic, 1989), p. 68.

26. Fiske et al., "Category-Based and Attribute-Based Reactions to Others," p. 403; M. C. Rush and J. E. A. Russell, "Leader Prototypes and Prototype-Consistent Consensus in Leader Behavior Descriptions," *Journal of Experimental Social Psychology* 24 (1988): 88–104 (pp. 101–102).

27. Fiske et al., "Category-Based and Attribute-Based Reactions to Others," pp. 406, 422.

28. Taylor, *Positive Illusions*, p. 69.

29. Patricia Linville, "Affective Consequences of Complexity Regarding the Self and Others," in M. S. Clarke and S. T. Fiske, eds., *Affect and Cognition: the Seventeenth Annual Carnegie Symposium on Cognition* (Hillsdale, N.J.: Erlbaum, 1982).

30. Jennifer Crocker and Rita Luhatanen, "Collective Self-Esteem and Ingroup Bias," *Journal of Personality and Social Psychology* 58 (1990): 50–67 (p. 51). Eliot R. Smith, "Inferences About Self and Others," *Journal Experimental Social Psychology* 20 (1984): 97–115.

31. E. E. Jones and R. E. Nesbitt, "The Actor and the Observer: Divergent Perceptions of the Causes of Behavior," in E. E. Jones, ed., *Attribution: Perceiving the Causes of Behavior* (Morristown, N.J.: General Learning Press, 1972).

32. E. Smith, "Inferences About Self and Others," p. 111.

33. Richard Cottam and Gerard Gallucci, *The Rehabilitation of Power in International Politics* (Pittsburgh: University of Pittsburgh Press, 1978); and Maurice East, "National Attributes," in Maurice East, Stephen Salmore, and Charles Hermann, eds., *Why Nations Act* (Beverly Hills, Calif.: Sage, 1977).

34. Jerry Burger, "Negative Reactions to Increases in Perceived Personal Control," *Journal of Personality and Social Psychology* 56 (1989): 246–56 (p. 246). Also see Klaus Scherer, "Criteria for Emotion-Antecedent Appraisal: A Review," in Vernon Hamilton, Gordon Bower, and Nico Frijda, eds., *Cognitive Perspectives on Emotion and Motivation* (Boston: Kluwer, 1988), p. 103.

35. Taylor, *Positive Illusions*, p. 132.

36. Albert Bandura, "Self-Referent Thought: A Developmental Analysis of Self-Efficacy," in John Flavell and Lee Ross, eds., *Social Cognitive Development: Frontiers and Possible Futures* (Cambridge: Cambridge University Press, 1981).

37. Gathering empirical evidence about the self-image must be done over a time period far broader than the decision-making under examination in order to avoid mistakenly assuming that the tactics chosen in a particular situation reflect the policy makers' self-image. It is entirely possible that decision makers see their state as weak but act as if they are strong for reasons unrelated to self-image, such as a bluffing ploy, an effort to establish credibility, or the satisfaction of domestic audiences. Verbal and behavioral evidence from contexts other than the immediate situation should be assessed. My thanks to Ole Holsti for pointing this out to me.

38. If this study involved U.S. policy toward Europe as well as to Latin American, it would be necessary to further distinguish between the image of a neutral and the image of a Third World nonaligned country. The prototypical neutral European country is Switzerland, which was hardly nonaligned during the cold war. Americans appear to associate neutrality with positive judgments and nonalignment with negative ones. Moreover, Americans assume that neutral nonaligned countries are pacifist countries, which will only defend themselves and will not engage in offensive actions, again based on perceptions of Switzerland. See M. Cottam, *Foreign Policy Decision Making*, chap. 3.

39. The question arises as to what will happen to this image with the end of the cold war. The term *nonaligned* may be relatively meaningless without the Soviet Union, but the bundle of characteristics that constitute the image are not wholly dependent upon the existence of a cold war. Several crucial attributes—cultural sophistication and nationalism, for example—still make a nonaligned country very different from a dependent country. Therefore, we may expect some modification of the image to suit the post–cold war environment, but as long as it is cognitively useful it will remain a part of the U.S. worldview.

40. This is discussed in R. Cottam, *Foreign Policy Motivation*, pp. 60–68.

41. This definition is from Richard Cottam, "Strategy Working Paper," unpublished paper, 1980.

42. Robert Jervis, *The Logic of Images* (Princeton: Princeton University Press, 1970), chap. 1; see Glenn Snyder and Paul Diesing, *Conflict Among Nations* (Princeton: Princeton University Press, 1977), for a discussion of the sequence of decisions in strategy formation.

43. R. Cottam, *Foreign Policy Motivation*, chap. 5.

44. R. Cottam, "Strategy Working Paper."

45. Folkman, "Personal Control and Stress and Coping Processes," p. 836.

46. R. Cottam and Gallucci, *The Rehabilitation of Power in International Politics*.

47. On the tendency of the powerful parties to use coercion with weaker parties, see Tjosvold, "Unequal Power Relationships within a Cooperative or Competitive Context."

2. INTERVENTION IN GUATEMALA AND CUBA

1. Richard Immerman, *The CIA in Guatemala* (Austin: University of Texas Press, 1982), p. 84.

2. Piero Gleijeses, *Shattered Hope: The Guatemalan Revolution and the United States, 1944–1954* (Princeton: Princeton University Press, 1991), p. 100.

3. Dwight Eisenhower, *The White House Years*, vol. 1, *Mandate for Change 1953–1956* (Garden City, N.Y.: Doubleday, 1963), p. 83.

4. "Text of Address by Dulles in Seattle Redefining Nation's Foreign Policy," *New York Times*, June 11, 1954, p. 2.

5. Quoted in Immerman, *The CIA in Guatemala*, p. 102.

6. U.S. Department of State, *A Case History of Communist Penetration* (Washington, D.C.: U.S. Government Printing Office, 1957), pp. 27, 47.

7. Stephen Schlesinger and Stephen Kinzer, *Bitter Fruit* (Garden City, N.Y.: Anchor, 1982).

8. Gleijeses, *Shattered Hope*, p. 174.

9. Gleijeses notes that the U.S. evaluation of the Guatemalan military was "bizarre." It was at first paid little attention. But when it was analyzed, U.S. analysts "suddenly . . . enter the realm of objectivity." See ibid., pp. 122–23.

10. U.S. Central Intelligence Agency, "National Intelligence Estimate, 1952," in *Foreign Relations of the United States, 1952–1954*, (Washington, D.C.: U.S. Government Printing Office, 1983), 4:1,033.

11. Blasier, *The Hovering Giant*, p. 160

12. Schlesinger and Kinzer, *Bitter Fruit*, p. 103.

13. See Kermit Roosevelt's discussion of his conversation with Dulles, after the success of the plot in Iran, in *Countercoup: The Struggle for the Control of Iran* (New York: McGraw Hill, 1979), p. 102.

14. Schlesinger and Kinzer, *Bitter Fruit*, p. 102.

15. Although no other plans were pursued, the United States did try to use the Organization of American States to isolate Guatemala.

16. "Resistance Force Announces Action," *New York Times*, June 19, 1954, p. 1.

17. U.S. Department of State, *A Case History of Communist Penetration*, pp. 54–55.

18. Carla Robbins, *The Cuban Threat* (Philadelphia: Institute for the Study of Human Issues, 1985).

19. Wayne Smith, *The Closest of Enemies* (New York: Norton, 1987), p. 37.

20. Dwight Eisenhower, *The White House Years*, vol. 2, *Waging Peace, 1956–1961* (Garden City, N.Y.: Doubleday, 1965), p. 521.

21. Richard Nixon, *Six Crises* (Garden City, N.Y.: Doubleday, 1962), pp. 351–52.

22. Eisenhower, *Waging Peace*, p. 523.

23. W. Smith, *The Closest of Enemies*, p. 44.

24. Eisenhower, *Waging Peace*, p. 534.

25. W. Smith, *The Closest of Enemies*, p. 47.

26. U.S. Department of State, *American Foreign Policy, Current Documents, 1958* (Washington, D.C.: U.S. Government Printing Office, 1958), pp. 365, 375.

27. Robbins, *The Cuban Threat*, p. 95.

28. Luis Aguilar, ed., *Operation Zapata: The 'Ultrasensitive' Report and Testimony of the Board of Inquiry on the Bay of Pigs* (Frederick, Md.: Aletheia, 1981), p. 58.

29. Blasier, *The Hovering Giant*, p. 193.

30. Robbins, *The Cuban Threat*, p. 102.

31. *Public Papers of the President, April 18, 1961 (John Fitzgerald Kennedy)* (Washington, D.C.: U.S. Government Printing Office, 1961), p. 131.

32. W. Smith, *The Closest of Enemies*, p. 21.

33. Philip Bonsal, *Cuba, Castro, and the United States* (Pittsburgh: University of Pittsburgh Press, 1971).

34. W. Smith, *The Closest of Enemies*, p. 63.

35. Bonsal, *Cuba, Castro, and the United States*, p. 61.

36. Blasier, *The Hovering Giant*, p. 132.

3. OVERTHROW VERSUS SANCTIONS IN CHILE AND PERU

1. Seymour Hersh, *The Price of Power* (New York: Summit, 1983), p. 263.

2. Henry Kissinger, "Background Briefing at the White House, September 16, 1970," in U.S. Congress, Senate Committee on Foreign Relations, Subcommittee on Multinational Corporations, Hearings, *Multinational Corporations and United States Foreign Policy*, 93d Congress, 1st sess. (Washington, D.C.: U.S. Government Printing Office,, 1973), pp. 542–43.

3. Edward Korry, "U.S. Policies in Chile Under the Allende Government: An Interview to Former Ambassador Edward Korry," in F. Urrego Vicuña, ed., *Chile. The Balanced View* (Santiago: University of Chile Press, 1975), p. 292.

4. U.S. Congress, Senate Select Committee to Study Government Operations with Respect to Intelligence Activities of the United States, Hearings, *Intelligence Activities*, 94th Congress, 1st sess. (Washington, D.C.: U.S. Government Printing Office, 1975), p. 190.

5. Hersh, *The Price of Power*, pp. 270–71.

6. U.S. Congress, *Intelligence Activites*, p. 195.

7. Ibid., p. 171.

8. Hersh, *The Price of Power*, p. 282.

9. "Peruvians and Soviet Sign Their First Trade Accord," *New York Times*, February 18, 1969.

10. Charles Goodsell, *American Corporations and Peruvian Politics* (Cambridge: Harvard University Press, 1974), p. 128; and Richard Goodwin, "Letter from Peru," *New Yorker*, May 17, 1969, p. 60. Goodwin explains that this policy was dropped after it became clear that it contributed to an economic slowdown in Peru and thus to a growing guerrilla movement.

11. U.S. official, quoted in Goodwin, "Letter from Peru," p. 61.

12. "U.S. Tries to Avoid Quarrel on Seizures in Peru,"*New York Times*, January 31, 1969.

13. "Latin America: The 'Gorillas' are on the March," *New York Times*, October, 13, 1968.

14. "U.S. Tries to Avoid Quarrel on Seizures in Peru," *New York Times*, January 31, 1969.

15. Hersh, *The Price of Power*, p. 271.

16. Jessica Einhorn, *Expropriation Politics* (Lexington, Mass.: Lexington Books, 1974), pp. 36–37.

17. Goodsell, *American Corporations and Peruvian Politics*, pp. 130–31.

18. The issue of pressure on the executive branch is an interesting one. Press reports at the time suggest considerable executive concern about congressional reaction to Peru's actions, particularly after the seizure of the fishing boats (see the *New York Times*, February 15 and March 12, 1969). However, Einhorn, *Expropriation Politics*, notes that congressional pressure for sanctions was negligible (p. 54). Further, U.S. firms with investment in Peru argued *against* sanctions.

19. Blasier, *The Hovering Giant*, p. 261.

20. Einhorn, *Expropriation Politics*, p. 59.

21. Ibid. Einhorn also points out that Stedman continued to complain to underlings that Peru should be more severely punished.

4. CRACKS IN THE COLD WAR WORLDVIEW

1. Frank Devine, *El Salvador: Embassy Under Attack* (New York: Vantage, 1981).

2. Schoultz, *National Security and United States Policy Toward Latin America*, p. 49.

3. U.S. Congress, Senate Committee on Foreign Relations, Hearings, *The Situation in El Salvador*, 97th Congress, 1st sess., (Washington, D.C.: U.S. Government Printing Office, 1981), pp. 4, 5.

4. U.S. Congress, *Congressional Record* (Washington, D.C.: U.S. Government Printing Office, 1979), p. 15125.

5. Schoultz, *National Security and United States Policy Toward Latin America*, p. 136.

6. See Ambassador Robert White's testimony in U.S. Congress, *The Situation in El Salvador*.

7. U.S. Department of State, *American Foreign Policy, Basic Documents, 1977–1980* (Washington, D.C.: U.S. Government Printing Office, 1980), p. 10.

8. Jerel Rosati, "The Impact of Beliefs on Behavior: The Foreign Policy of the Carter Administration," in Donald Sylvan and Steve Chan, eds., *Foreign Policy Decision Making: Cognition and Artificial Intelligence* (New York: Praeger, 1984), p. 169.

9. U.S. Department of State, *American Foreign Policy, Basic Documents, 1977–1980*, pp. 47–48.

10. U.S. Congress, *Congressional Record* (Washington, D.C.: U.S. Government Printing Office, 1978), p. 28085.

11. U.S. Congress, *Congressional Record* (Washington, D.C.: U.S. Government Printing Office, 1979), p. 15125.

12. Rosati, "The Impact of Beliefs on Behavior."

13. U.S. Department of State, *American Foreign Policy, Basic Documents, 1977–1980,* p. 6.

14. Schoultz, *National Security and United States Policy Toward Latin America,* p. 138.

15. U.S. Department of State, *American Foreign Policy, Basic Documents, 1977–1980,* p. 8.

16. Jimmy Carter, "State of the Union Address, February, 1980," in U.S. Department of State, *State Department Bulletin,* vol. 80, *Special Supplement M.* (Washington, D.C.: U.S. Government Printing Office, 1980).

17. U.S. Department of State, *American Foreign Policy, Basic Documents, 1977–1980,* p. 1289.

18. Schoultz, *National Security and United States Policy Toward Latin America,* p. 21.

19. U.S. Department of State. *American Foreign Policy, Basic Documents, 1977–1980,* p. 1292.

20. U.S. Congress, *Congressional Record* (1979), p. 10620.

21. U.S. Congress, House Committee on Foreign Affairs, Subcommittee on Inter-American Affairs, Hearings, *United States Policy Towards Nicaragua,* 96th Congress, 1st sess. (Washington, D.C.: U.S. Government Printing Office, 1979), p. 70.

22. Schoultz, *National Security and United States Policy Toward Latin America, p. 291.*

23. Pastor, *Condemned to Repetition,* p. 56.

24. U.S. Congress, *Congressional Record* (1977), p. 39363.

25. Pastor, *Condemned to Repetition,* pp. 58–59.

26. "Human Rights and Nicaragua," September 19, 1978.

27. U.S. Congress, *Congressional Record* (1977), p. 20852.

28. Pastor, *Condemned to Repetitions,* p. 77.

29. Ibid., p. 72; and "Somoza—Near End of Rule," *Christian Science Monitor,* August 28, 1978.

30. Barry Rubin, *Secrets of State* (Oxford: Oxford University Press, 1987), pp. 199–200.

31. Pastor, *Condemned to Repetition,* p. 83.

32. Rubin, *Secrets of State,* pp. 199–200.

33. Pastor, *Condemned to Repetition,* p. 79.

34. "Staying Out of Nicaragua," *Christian Science Monitor,* October 4, 1978.

35. "U.S. Presses Mediation on Bill in Nicaragua," *Christian Science Monitor,* September 28, 1978.

36. "Nicaraguan Conflict Crosses Borders: Somoza's Foes Claim Unity," *Washington Post,* September 15, 1978.

37. Pastor, *Condemned to Repetition,* pp. 97–98.

38. "A U.S. Rebuke for Nicaragua," *Christian Science Monitor,* February 13, 1979.

39. "Nicaraguan Crisis: Was the U.S. Off Guard?" *New York Times*, June 27, 1979.

40. Pastor, *Condemned to Repetition*, p. 135.

41. Speech by Secretary of State Cyrus Vance before the Organization of American States, in U.S. Department of State, *American Foreign Policy, Basic Documents, 1977–1980*, p. 1319.

42. Pastor, *Condemned to Repetition*, p. 142.

43. "U.S. Asks Nicaraguan Rebel Junta to Add Moderates," *New York Times*, July 2, 1979.

44. Pastor, *Condemned to Repetition*, p. 160.

45. Martin Diskin and Kenneth Sharpe, "El Salvador," in Morris Blachman, William LeoGrande, and Kenneth Sharpe, eds., *Confronting Revolution: Security Through Diplomacy in Central America* (New York: Pantheon, 1986), p. 52. 0

46. Enrique Baloyra, *El Salvador in Transition* (Chapel Hill: University of North Carolina Press, 1983), p. 49.

47. U.S. Congress, House Committee on International Relations, Subcommittee on International Organizations and Inter-American Affairs, Hearings, *The Recent Elections in El Salvador: Implications for U.S. Foreign Policy*. 95th Congress, 1st sess. (Washington, D.C.: U.S. Government Printing Office, 1977), p. 15.

48. Michael McClintock, *The American Connection: El Salvador* (London: Zed, 1985), p. 329.

49. Raymond Bonner, *Weakness and Deceit: U.S. Policy and El Salvador* (New York: Times Books, 1984), p. 60.

50. McClintock, *The American Connection*, p. 248.

51. Bonner, *Weakness and Deceit*, p. 151.

52. Baloyra, *El Salvador in Transition*, p. 88.

53. McClintock, *The American Connection*, p. 252.

54. Bonner, *Weakness and Deceit*, p. 164.

55. McClintock, *The American Connection*, p. 261.

56. "U.S. Aid to El Salvador Army: Bid to Bar 'Another Nicaragua,' " *New York Times*, February 23, 1980.

57. The land reform program was presented on March 6 and was divided into three phases (although it began with just two phases in 1980). Phase 1 affected properties of over five hundred hectares (approximately 16 percent of the country's land) and was immediately implemented. Although this phase did redistribute some land, it affected only 9 percent of the coffee-growing properties, the basis of the oligarchy's agricultural power in El Salvador. On March 14, Colonel Gutierrez announced that phase 2 would be canceled. Phase 3, announced at the end of April 1980, was called the Land to the Tiller portion of the program, which was supposed to transfer land from landlords to peasants who were tenant farmers. The purpose of phase 3, according to one AID official, was to create a conservative peasantry loyal to the government. He said, "There is no one more conservative than a small farmer. We're going to be breeding capitalists like rabbits." Phase 3 was only partially implemented. The United States provided an immediate $13 million for the program, in addition to the $5.7 million authorized for military assistance after

the October coup. Peter Shiras, "The False Promise—and Real Violence—of Land Reform in El Salvador," in Marvin Gettleman, Patrick Lacefield, Louis Menashe, David Mermelstein, and Ronald Radosh, eds., *El Salvador: Central America in the New Cold War* (New York: Grove, 1981), p. 166.

58. Bonner, *Weakness and Deceit*, p. 184.

59. Jeff Stein, "The Day of Reckoning Is Coming: An Interview with Robert E. White," in Gettleman, et al., *El Salvador*, p. 354.

60. Richard Feinberg, quoted in Bonner, *Weakness and Deceit*, p. 183.

61. "U.S. Aides Challenge El Salvador Report," *New York Times*, March 7, 1981.

62. Testimony of Robert White, U.S. Congress, *The Situation in El Salvador*, p. 101.

63. U.S. Congress, House Committee on Foreign Affairs, Subcommittee on Inter-American Affairs, Hearings, *U.S. Policy Toward El Salvador*, 97th Congress, 1st sess. (Washington, D.C.: U.S. Government Printing Office, 1981), p. 153.

64. U.S. Congress, *The Situation in El Salvador*, p. 160.

65. McClintock, *The American Connection*, p. 313.

66. Bonner, *Weakness and Deceit*, p. 171.

67. Stein, "An Interview with Robert E. White," p. 256.

68. Testimony before the House Appropriations Committee, February 25, 1981, in U.S. Department of State, *American Foreign Policy, Basic Documents, 1981*, pp. 1240–41.

5. REAGAN AND BUSH IN CENTRAL AMERICA

1. Jeane Kirkpatrick, "U.S. Security and Latin America," in Howard Wiarda, ed., *Rift and Revolution: The Central American Imbroglio* (Washington, D.C.: American Enterprise Institute, 1984), p. 352.

2. See testimony by Walter Stoessel, John Bushnell, and General Ernest Graves, in U.S. Congress, *The Situation in El Salvador*, pp. 4, 5, 54, 91, 24–25.

3. Betsy Conn and Patricia Hynds, "The Manipulation of the Religion Issue," in Thomas Walker, ed., *Reagan Versus the Sandinistas* (Boulder, Colo.: Westview, 1987), p. 105.

4. Alexander Haig, briefing of members of the North Atlantic Treaty Organization, reprinted in Gettleman et al., *El Salvador*, p. 218.

5. U.S. Department of State, "Communist Interference in El Salvador," in Gettleman et al., *El Salvador*, pp. 231, 232.

6. Christopher Dickey, "Central America: From Quagmire to Cauldron?" *Foreign Affairs: America and the World, 1983* 62 (1984): 659–94. This view was also clear in my interviews with U.S. embassy officials in El Salvador, June 20, 1984.

7. Mary Vanderlaan, *Revolution and Foreign Policy in Nicaragua* (Boulder, Colo.: Westview, 1986), p. 136.

8. Philip Taubman, "Latin Policy: U.S. Miscues," *New York Times*, March 17, 1982.

9. Barbara Crossette, "The Two Salvadors," *New York Times*, March 19, 1982.

10. Remarks made at a luncheon in the ambassador's residence, June 18 or 19, 1984.

11. U.S. Congress, House Committee on Foreign Affairs, Subcommittee on Human Rights and International Organizations and on Western Hemisphere Affairs, Hearings, *The Situation in El Salvador,* 98th Congress 2d sess. (Washington, D.C.: U.S. Government Printing Office, 1984), pp. 6–7. In reality, the Christian Democrats were center-right, the left having been eradicated. It is also difficult to argue that ARENA was a political party based upon democratic ideals.

12. Schoultz, *National Security,* pp. 27–29.

13. Lydia Chavez, "The Odds in El Salvador," *New York Times,* June 24, 1983.

14. Interviews, U.S. Embassy, San Salvador, June 20, 1984.

15. Interview, June 21, 1984.

16. Interview, June 23, 1984.

17. Warren Hoge, "Duarte's Party Caught in the Middle in Salvador," *New York Times,* March 22, 1982.

18. U.S. Congress, Senate Committee on Foreign Relations, Subcommittee on Western Hemisphere Affairs, Hearings, *The Prospects for Democracy in Central America and the Caribbean,* 97th Congress, 1st sess. (Washington, D.C.: U.S. Government Printing Office, 1982), p. 85.

19. Martha Cottam and Otwin Marenin, "Predicting the Past: Reagan Administration Assistance to Police Forces in Central America," *Justice Quarterly* 6 (December 1989): 589–618.

20. Ronald Reagan, letter to the presidents of Mexico and Venzuela, October 4, 1981, reprinted in Bruce Bagley, Roberto Alvarez, and Katherine J. Hagedorn, eds., *Contadora and the Central American Peace Process, Selected Documents* (Boulder, Colo.: Westview, 1985), p. 6.

21. National Bipartisan Commission on Central America, *Report to the President, January, 1984* (Washington, D.C.: U.S. Government Printing Office, 1984), p. 29.

22. Roy Gutman, "America's Diplomatic Charade," *Foreign Policy* 56 (Fall 1984): 3–23 (p. 5).

23. Roy Gutman, *Banana Diplomacy* (New York: Simon and Schuster, 1988), p. 73.

24. Transcript of Remarks on Nicaragua, *New York Times,* March 16, 1982.

25. Robert Pastor, "The Bush Administration and Latin America," *Journal of InterAmerican Studies and World Affairs* 33 (Fall 1991): 1–33 (p. 4).

26. "Cristiani as Peace Catalyst," *Washington Post,* January 2, 1992.

27. "Hopes Run High for End to Deadly Salvadoran Civil War," Austin *American-Statesman.* April 22, 1991.

28. "Accord Reached on El Salvador War," *New York Times,* January 1, 1992.

29. U.S. Information Agency, *FBIS: Latin America,* February 4, 1991.

30. Not two weeks after the peace accords went into effect, I was told by a U.S. Army officer and professor at the National War College that Cristiani had won—that all the provisions of the accord were those that he had intended to enact with or without negotiation with the rebels. This statement was made in the face of impressive counterevidence, including the fact that it took nearly two years to

conclude the peace agreement, and is an interesting example of the simplification of the political scene in El Salvador typical of those with dependent images.

31. *New York Times*, July 12, 1990.

6. THE NEW WORLD ORDER

1. John Dinges, *Our Man in Panama* (New York: Random House, 1990), p. 88.

2. Frederick Kempe, *Divorcing the Dictator* (New York: Putnam's, 1990), p. 112.

3. Kevin Buckley, *Panama: The Whole Story* (New York: Simon and Schuster, 1991), p. 51.

4. Alfonso Chardy, "U.S. Wants Friendly Democracy to Inherit Control of the Canal," *Miami Herald*, February 29, 1988.

5. Buckley, *Panama*, p. 51.

6. Demetrio Olaciregui, "New Tactics Used by Panamanian Opposition Against the Government," *Excelsior*, August 31, 1987, reprinted in Central America Resource Center, *Central America Newspack*, August 31–September 13, 1987.

7. "U.S. Weighs Easing Out Panama Chief," *Miami Herald*, June 21, 1987.

8. This applies to the official Washington perception, not to the U.S. embassy's. Contacts between the embassy and the opposition were close, and the embassy's knowledge of the opposition was fairly thorough.

9. Alfonso Chardy, "U.S. Twice Rejected Advice to Break Ties with Noriega," *Miami Herald*, March 3, 1988. The embassy, under Ambassador Everett Briggs, recommended "severing U.S. ties to Noriega to show solidarity with Panama's civilian opposition."

10. Margaret Scranton, *The Noriega Years: U.S.-Panamanian Relations, 1981– 1990* (Boulder, Colo.: Lynne Reinner, 1991), p. 110.

11. Buckley, *Panama*, p. 121.

12. Kempe, *Divorcing the Dictator*, pp. 296–97.

13. "U.S. Weighs Easing Out Panama Chief."

14. Scranton, *The Noriega Years*, pp. 116–17.

15. Kempe, *Divorcing the Dictator*.

16. Scranton, *The Noriega Years*, p. 122.

17. Kempe, *Divorcing the Dictator*, pp. 230–32, for complete details on this.

18. Scranton, *The Noriega Years*, p. 119.

19. Neil Lewis, "U.S. Asking Banks Not to Send Funds to Noriega Regime," *New York Times*, March 3, 1988.

20. Pamela Constable, "Latin Nations Favor Diplomacy in Panama," *Boston Globe*, April 3, 1988.

21. "Two Parties in Panama Break with the Anti-Noriega Alliance," *Los Angeles Times*, April 8, 1988.

22. William Branigan, "U.S. Panama Deal Widens Political Rift," *Washington Post*, May 19, 1988.

23. Kempe, *Divorcing the Dictator*, p. 297.

24. Buckley, *Panama*, p. 141.

25. Kempe, *Divorcing the Dictator*, p. 322.

26. Scranton, *The Noriega Years*, p. 155.

27. Linda Feldman, "Sound and Fury Over U.S. Covert Panama Plan," *Christian Science Monitor*, July 29, 1988.

28. Elaine Sciolino, "As the Election Nears, Talk About Noriega Fades," *New York Times*, October 28, 1988.

29. "Opposition Splits; Noriega Ploy Charged," *Miami Herald*, December 13, 1988.

30. "U.S. Protege Reportedly Vows to Quit," *Washington Post*, December 22, 1988.

31. Scranton, *The Noriega Years*, p. 157.

32. Kempe, *Divorcing the Dictator*, p. 365.

33. Scranton, *The Noriega Years*, p. 166

34. Linda Robinson, *Intervention or Neglect: The United States and Central America Beyond the 1980's* (New York: Council on Foreign Relations Press, 1991), p. 120.

35. Kempe, *Divorcing the Dictator*, p. 367.

36. Robinson, *Intervention or Neglect*, p. 123.

37. "Bloody Attack May Signal Split Within Noriega Ranks," *Miami Herald*, May 11, 1989.

38. Scranton, *The Noriega Years*, p. 167.

39. "OAS Puts Off Efforts to Press Noriega to Allow Democracy," *Miami Herald*, June 7, 1989.

40. "U.S. Is Faulted on Military Maneuvers in Panama," *New York Times*, August 24, 1989.

41. "U.S. Rethinks Plan to Oust Noriega," *Christian Science Monitor*, August 28, 1989.

42. Scranton, *The Noriega Years*, p. 186.

43. "Amateur Hour," *Newsweek*, October 16, 1989.

44. The initial plan was to offer Noriega retirement and exile and, if he refused, to threaten to turn him over to the United States. The Bush administration claimed that the rebels' indecision on what to do with Noriega underlay the U.S. failure to be more helpful. However, Giroldi's widow later stated that the CIA had been informed before the coup of the alternatives that would be given to Noriega. See "Coup Leaders Gave Noriega Two Options," *Los Angeles Times*, October 13, 1989.

45 "Amateur Hour"

46. "U.S. Reportedly Again Trying to Oust Noriega," *Miami Herald*, November 16, 1989.

47. Scranton, *The Noriega Years*, p. 201.

48. Maureen Dowd, "Doing the Inevitable," *New York Times*, December 24, 1989.

49. "It May Prove Difficult to Let Panama Get on with Its Life," *New York Times*, December 31, 1989.

50. U.S. Congress, *Drugs, Law Enforcement, and Foreign Policy*, Senate Report 100-165 (Washington, D.C.: U.S. Government Printing Office, 1989), p. 1.

51. "Shattered Economy Has Guerrillas on Rise in Peru," *New York Times*, June 12, 1989.

52. Martha L. Cottam, "Cognitive Psychology and Bargaining Behavior: Peru Versus the MNCs," *Political Psychology* 10 (September 1989): 445–76.

53. Simon Strong, "Where the Shining Path Leads," *New York Times Magazine*, May 24, 1992, p. 13.

54. Rensselaer, Lee, III, *The White Labyrinth: Cocaine and Political Power* (London: Transaction, 19910, p. 159; chap. 4 discusses the narcotics-guerrilla link.

55. Strong, "Where the Shining Path Leads," p. 16.

56. Lowenthal, *Partners in Conflict*, p. 205.

57. Philip Shenon, "Peru Drug Fund Used in War, Aide Says," *New York Times*, June 21, 1990.

58. James Brooke, "U.S. Will Arm Peru to Fight Leftists in New Drug Push," *New York Times*, April 22, 1990.

59. Shenon, "Peru Drug Fund Used in War."

60. Thomas Friedman, "Bush Backs 'Outside Pressure' to End Peru's Crisis," *New York Times*, April 11, 1992.

61. Thomas Friedman, "U.S. Is Shunning Sanctions Against Peru," *New York Times*, April 14, 1992.

62. Thomas Friedman, "Peru and U.S.: What Course to Take?" *New York Times*, April 15, 1992.

63. See, for example, U.S. Executive Office of the President, Office of National Drug Control Policy, *National Drug Control Strategy, September 1989* (Washington, D.C.: U.S. Government Printing Office, 1989), p. 63; and U.S. Congress, *United States Anti-Narcotics Activities in the Andean Region*, House Report 101-991 (Washington, D.C.: U.S. Government Printing Office, 1991), pp. 8–11.

64. U.S. General Accounting Office, *The Drug War: U.S. Programs in Peru Face Serious Obstacles* (Washington, D.C.: U.S. Government Printing Office, 1991), pp. 2–3.

65. U.S. Congress, *United States Anti-Narcotics Activities in the Andean Region*, p. 10.

66. Washington Office on Latin America, *Clear and Present Dangers: The U.S. Military and the War on Drugs in the Andes* (Washington, D.C.: Washington Office on Latin America, 1991, p. 12.

67. U.S. Congress, *United States Anti-Narcotics Activities in the Andean Region*, p. 15.

68. See "The Newest War," *Newsweek*, January 6, 1992, for one of many stories about the overt and covert activities of U.S. forces in the Andean Initiative.

69. Peter R. Andreas, Eva C. Bertram, Morris J. Blachman, and Kenneth E. Sharpe, "Dead-End Drug Wars," *Foreign Policy* 85 (Winter 1991–1992): 106–28 (p. 112).

70. Washington Office on Latin America, *Clear and Present Dangers*, p. 20.

71. James Smith, "Economic Aid Key to Drug War Victory, Candidate Says," *Los Angeles Times*, May 11, 1990.

72. Washington Office on Latin America, *Clear and Present Dangers*, p. 14.

73. James Smith, "Peruvians Unhappy with Focus of Drug Plan," *Los Angeles Times*, September 7, 1988.

74. Andreas et al., "Dead-End Drug Wars," p. 116.

75. James Smith, "Drug Campaign Put on Back Burner as Peru Battles Rebels," *Los Angeles Times*, January 6, 1990.

76. U.S. Congress, *United States Anti-Narcotics Activities in the Andean Region*, p. 59.

77. U.S. General Accounting Office, *The Drug War.*

78. "The Newest War," *Newsweek*, January 6, 1992.

79. U.S. Congress, *United States Anti-Narcotics Activities in the Andean Region*, pp. 22–25.

80. Douglas Walker, "Risky Business," *Newsweek*, July 16, 1990.

81. Washington Office on Latin America, *Clear and Present Dangers*, p. 32.

CONCLUSION

1. This point was made by an anonymous reviewer of the manuscript of this book.

Bibliography

Aguilar, Luis, ed. *Operation Zapata: The 'Ultrasensitive' Report and Testimony of the Board of Inquiry on the Bay of Pigs*. Frederick, Md.: Aletheia, 1981.

Allport, Gordon. *The Nature of Prejudice*. Garden City, N.Y.: Doubleday, 1954.

Andreas, Peter R., Eva C. Bertram, Morris J. Blachman, and Kenneth E. Sharpe. "Dead-End Drug Wars." *Foreign Policy* 85 (Winter 1991–1992): 106–28.

Asch, Solomon. "Forming Impressions of Personality." *Journal of Abnormal and Social Psychology* 41 (1946): 258–90.

Bagley, Bruce, Robert Alvarez, and Katherine J. Hagedorn, eds. *Contadora and the Central American Peace Process, Selected Documents*. Boulder, Colo.: Westview, 1985.

Bailey, Thomas. *A Diplomatic History of the American People*. 7th ed. New York: Appleton-Century Crofts, 1964.

Baloyra, Enrique. *El Salvador in Transition*. Chapel Hill: University of North Carolina Press, 1983.

Bandura, Albert. "Self-Referent Thought: A Developmental Analysis of Self-Efficacy." In John Flavell and Lee Ross, eds., *Social Cognitive Development: Frontiers and Possible Futures*. Cambridge University Press, 1981.

Blasier, Cole. *The Hovering Giant*. Pittsburgh: University of Pittsburgh Press, 1976.

Bonner, Raymond. *Weakness and Deceit: U.S. Policy and El Salvador*. New York: Times Books, 1984.

Bonsal, Phillip. *Cuba, Castro, and the United States*. Pittsburgh: University of Pittsburgh Press, 1971.

Branigan, William. "U.S. Panama Deal Widens Political Rift." *Washington Post*, May 19, 1988.

Brooke, James. "U.S. Will Arm Peru to Fight Leftists in New Drug Push." *New York Times*, April 22, 1990.

Bruner, Jerome. "On Perceptual Readiness." In J. M. Anglin and J. S. Bruner, eds. *Beyond the Information Given*. New York: Norton, 1972.

Buckley, Kevin. *Panama: The Whole Story*. New York: Simon and Schuster, 1991.

Burger, Jerry. "Negative Reactions to Increase in Perceived Personal Control." *Journal of Personality and Social Psychology* 56 (1989): 246–56.

Chardy, Alfonso. "U.S. Twice Rejected Advice to Break Ties With Noriega." *Miami Herald*, March 3, 1988.

————. "U.S. Wants Friendly Democracy to Inherit Control of the Canal." *Miami Herald*, February 29, 1988.

Chavez, Lydia. "The Odds in El Salvador." *New York Times*, June 24, 1983.

Chilcote, Ronald and Joel Edelstein (eds.), *Latin America: The Struggle With Dependency and Beyond.* New York: Shenkman, 1974.

Coleman, Kenneth. "The Political Mythology of the Monroe Doctrine." In John Martz and Lars Schoultz, eds. *Latin America, the United States, and the Inter-American System.* Boulder, Colo.: Westview, 1980.

Conn, Betsy, and Patricia Hynds. "The Manipulation of the Religion Issue." In Thomas Walker, ed., *Reagan Versus the Sandinistas.* Boulder, Colo.: Westview, 1987.

Constable, Pamela. "Latin Nations Favor Diplomacy in Panama." *Boston Globe*, April 3, 1988.

Cotler, Julio, and Richard Fagen, eds. *Latin America and the United States: The Changing Political Realities.* Stanford: Stanford University Press, 1974.

Cottam, Martha L. "Cognitive Psychology and Bargaining Behavior: Peru Versus the MNCs." *Political Psychology* 10 (September 1989): 445–76.

————. *Foreign Policy Decision Making: The Influence of Cognition.* Boulder, Colo.: Westview, 1986.

————. "Recent Developments in Political Psychology." In Martha Cottam and Chih-yu Shih, eds., *Contending Dramas: A Cognitive Approach to Post Cold War International Organization.* New York: Praeger, 1992.

Cottam, Martha, and Otwin Marenin. "Predicting the Past: Reagan Administration Assistance to Police Forces in Central America." *Justice Quarterly* 6 (December 1989): 589–618.

Cottam, Martha L., and E. Thomas Rowe. "Intervention Decisions: The Interaction of Situational and Psychological Factors." Paper prepared for the 1987 Annual Meeting of the American Political Science Foundation, Chicago,

Cottam, Richard. *Foreign Policy Motivation.* Pittsburgh: University of Pittsburgh Press, 1977.

————. "Strategy Working Paper." Unpublished paper, 1980.

Cottam, Richard, and Gerard Gallucci. *The Rehabilitation of Power in International Politics.* Pittsburgh: University of Pittsburgh Press, 1978.

Crocker, Jennifer, and Rita Luhatanen. "Collective Self-Esteem and Ingroup Bias." *Journal of Personality and Social Psychology* 58 (1990): 50–67.

Crossette, Barbara. "The Two Salvadors." *New York Times*, March 19, 1982.

Devine, Frank. *El Salvador: Embassy Under Attack.* New York: Vantage, 1981.

Dickey, Christopher. "Central America: From Quagmire to Cauldron" *Foreign Affairs: America and the World, 1983* 62 (1984): 659–94.

Dinges, John. *Our Man in Panama.* New York: Random House, 1990.

Diskin, Martin, ed. *Trouble in Our Backyard: Central America and the United States in the Eighties.* New York: Pantheon, 1983.

Diskin, Martin, and Kenneth Sharpe. "El Salvador." In Morris Blachman, William LeoGrande, and Kenneth Sharpe, eds., *Confronting Revolution: Security Through Diplomacy in Central America.* New York: Pantheon, 1986.

dos Santos, Theotonio. "The Structure of Dependence." *American Economic Review* 60 (May 1970): 231–36.

Dowd, Maureen. "Doing the Inevitable." *New York Times,* December 24, 1989.

Dower, John. *War Without Mercy: Race and Power in the Pacific War.* New York: Pantheon, 1986.

Duvall, Raymond. "Dependence and Dependencia Theory." *International Organization* 32 (May 1978): 51–78.

East, Maurice. "National Attributes." In Maurice East, Stephen Salmore, and Charles Hermann, eds., *Why Nations Act.* Beverly Hills, Calif.: Sage, 1977.

Einhorn, Jessica. *Expropriation Politics.* Lexington, Mass.: Lexington Books, 1974.

Eisenhower, Dwight. *The White House Years.* Vol. 1. *Mandate for Change, 1953–1956.* Garden City, N.Y.: Doubleday, 1963.

———. *The White House Years.* Vol. 2. *Waging Peace, 1956–1961.* Garden City, N.Y.: Doubleday, 1965.

Fagen, Richard, and Olga Pellicer, eds. *The Future of Central America.* Stanford, Stanford University Press, 1983.

Feldman, Linda. "Sound and Fury Over U.S. Covert Panama Plan." *Christian Science Monitor,* July 29, 1988.

Fiske, Susan, S. L. Neuberg, A. E. Beattie, and S. J. Miller. "Category-Based and Attribute-Based Reactions to Others: Some Informational Conditions of Stereotyping and Invdividuating Processes." *Journal of Experimental Social Psychology* 23 (1987): 399–427.

Fiske, Susan, and Shelley Taylor. *Social Cognition.* New York: Random House, 1984.

Folkman, Susan. "Personal Control and Stress and Coping Processes: A Theoretical Analysis." *Journal of Personality and Social Psychology* 46 (1984): 839–52.

Friedman, Thomas. "Peru and U.S.: What Course to Take?" *New York Times,* April 15, 1992.

———. "U.S. Is Shunning Sanctions Against Peru." *New York Times,* April 24, 1992.

Gaddis, John Lewis. *Strategies of Containment.* New York: Oxford University Press, 1982.

George, Alexander. "The 'Operational Code': A Neglected Approach to the Study of Political Leaders and Decision Making." *International Studies Quarterly* 13 (1969): 190–222.

———. *Presidential Decisionmaking in Foreign Policy: The Effective Use of Information and Advice.* Boulder, Colo.: Westview, 1980.

George, Alexander, and Juliet George. *Woodrow Wilson and Colonel House: A Personality Study.* New York: J. Day, 1965.

Gitlitz, John, and Henry Landsberger. "The Inter-American Political Economy: How Dependable Is Dependency Theory?" In John Martz and Lars Schoultz, eds., *Latin America, the United States, and the Inter-American System.* Boulder, Colo.: Westview, 1980.

Glad, Betty. "Black and White Thinking: Ronald Reagan's Approach to Foreign Policy." *Political Psychology* 4 (1983): 33–76.

Gleick, James. *Chaos: Making a New Science.* New York: Penguin, 1987.

Gleijeses, Piero. *Shattered Hope: The Guatemalan Revolution and the United States, 1944–1954.* Princeton: Princeton University Press, 1991.

Goodsell, Charles. *American Corporations and Peruvian Politics.* Cambridge: Harvard University Press, 1974.

Goodwin, Richard. "Letter from Peru." *New Yorker,* May 17, 1969.

Gutman, Roy. "America's Diplomatic Charade." *Foreign Policy* 56 (Fall 1984): 3–23.

———. *Banana Diplomacy.* New York: Simon and Schuster, 1988.

Herrmann, Richard. *Perception and Behavior in Soviet Foreign Policy.* Pittsburgh: University of Pittsburgh Press, 1985.

Hersh, Seymour. *The Price of Power.* New York: Summit, 1983.

Hoge, Warren. "Duarte's Party Caught in the Middle in Salvador." *New York Times,* March 22, 1982.

Holsti, Ole. "Cognitive Dynamics and Images of the Enemy: Dulles and Russia." In David Finlay, Ole Holsti, and Richard Fagen, eds., *Enemies in Politics.* Chicago: Rand McNally, 1967.

———. "Public Opinion and Foreign Policy: Challenges to the Almond-Lippman Consensus." *International Studies Quarterly* 36 (1992): 439–66.

Hughes, Steven, and Kenneth Mijeski. "Contemporary Paradigms in the Study of Inter-American Relations." In John Martz and Lars Schoultz, eds., *Latin America, the United States, and the Inter-American System.* Boulder, Colo.: Westview, 1980.

Immerman, Richard. *The CIA in Guatemala.* Austin: University of Texas Press, 1982.

Jervis, Robert, "The Impact of the Korean War on the Cold War." *Journal of Conflict Resolution* 24 (1980): 563–92.

———. *The Logic of Images.* Princeton: Princeton University Press, 1970.

———. "Perceiving and Coping with Threat." In Robert Jervis and Richard Ned Lebow, eds., *Perception and Deterrence.* Baltimore: Johns Hopkins University Press, 1985.

———. *Perception and Misperception in International Politics.* Princeton: Princeton University Press, 1976.

Jervis, Robert, and Jack Snyder, eds. *Dominoes and Bandwagons: Strategic Beliefs and Great Power Competition in the Eurasian Rimland.* Oxford: Oxford University Press, 1990.

Jones, E. E., and R. E. Nesbitt. "The Actor and the Observer: Divergent Perceptions of the Causes of Behavior." In E. E. Jones, ed., *Attribution: Perceiving the Causes of Behavior.* Morristown, N.J.: General Learning Press, 1972.

Kempe, Frederick. *Divorcing the Dictator.* New York: Putnam's, 1990.

Kirkpatrick, Jeane. "Dictatorships and Double Standards." *Commentary* 68 (November 1979): 34–45.

———. "U.S. Security and Latin America." In Howard Wiarda, ed., *Rift and Revolution: The Central American Imbroglio.* Washington, D.C.: American Enterprise Institute, 1984.

Korry, Edward, "U.S. Policies in Chile Under the Allende Government: An Interview to Former Ambassador Edward Korry." In F. Orrego Vicuna, ed., *Chile: The Balance View.* Santiago: University of Chile Press, 1975.

Krasner, Stephen. *Defending the National Interest.* Princeton: Princeton University Press, 1978.

LaFeber, Walter. *Inevitable Revolutions: The United States in Central America.* New York: Norton, 1983.

Lebow, Richard Ned. *Between Peace and War.* Baltimore: Johns Hopkins University Press, 1983.

Lee, Rensselaer, III. *The White Labyrinth: Cocaine and Political Power.* London: Transaction, 1991.

Levinson, Jerome, and Juan de Onis. *The Alliance That Lost Its Way.* Chicago: Quadrangle, 1970.

Lewis, Neil. "U.S. Asking Banks Not to Send Funds to Noriega Regime." *New York Times,* March 3, 1988.

Linville, Patricia. "Affective Consequences of Complexity Regarding the Self and Others." in M. S. Clarke and S. T. Fiske, eds., *Affect and Cognition: the Seventeenth Annual Carnegie Symposium on Cognition.* Hillsdale, N.J.: Erbaum, 1982.

Lowenthal, Abraham. *Partners in Conflict: The United States and Latin American in the 1990's.* Rev. ed. Baltimore: John's Hopkins University Press, 1990.

Luttwak, Edward. "The Nature of the Crisis." In Joseph Cirincone, ed., *Central America and the Western Alliance.* New York: Holmes and Meier, 1985.

McClintock, Michael. *The American Connection: El Salvador.* London: Zed, 1985.

Martz, John. "Democracy and the Imposition of Values." In John Martz and Lars Schoultz, eds., *Latin America, the United States, and the Inter-American System.* Boulder, Colo.: Westview, 1980.

Michel, James. "Defending Democracy." In Joseph Cirincone, ed., *Central America and the Western Alliance.* New York: Holmes and Meier, 1985.

Miller, George. "The Magic Number Seven, Plus or Minus Two." *Psychological Review* 63 (1956): 81–97.

Molineau, Harold. *U.S. Policy Toward Latin America: From Regionalism to Globalism.* 2d ed. Boulder, Colo.: Westview, 1990.

Murphy, G. L., and D. L. Medin. "The Role of Theories in Conceptual Coherence." *Psychological Review* 92 (1985): 289–316.

Nixon, Richard. *Six Crises.* Garden City, N.Y.: Doubleday, 1962.

Olaciregui, Demetrio. "New Tactics Used by Panamanian Opposition Against the Government." *Excelsior,* August 31, 1987. Reprinted in Central America Resource Center, *Central America Newspack,* August 31–September 13, 1987.

Ornstein, Norman and Mark Schmitt. "Post–Cold War Politics." *Foreign Policy* 79 (Summer, 1990): 169–186.

Pastor, Robert. "The Bush Administration and Latin America." *Journal of InterAmerican Studies and World Affairs* 33 (Fall 1991): 1–3.

———. *Condemned to Repetition.* Princeton: Princeton University Press, 1987.

Pastor, Robert. "U.S. Policy Toward the Caribbean: Fixed and Emerging Images." *World Politics* 3 (April 1986): 483–515.

Pavelchak, Mark. "Piecemeal and Category-Based Evaluation: an Idiographic Analysis." *Journal of Personality and Social Psychology* 56 (1989): 354–63.

Poitras, Guy. *The Ordeal of Hegemony.* Boulder, Colo.: Westview, 1990.

216   *Bibliography*

Pruitt, Dean. *Negotiation Behavior.* New York: Academic, 1981.

Robbins, Carla. *The Cuban Threat.* Philadelphia: Institute for the Study of Human Issues, 1985.

Robinson, Linda. *Intervention or Neglect: The United States and Central America Beyond the 1980's.* New York: Council on Foreign Relations Press, 1991.

Roosevelt, Kermit. *Countercoup: The Struggle for the Control of Iran.* New York: Mc-Graw Hill, 1979.

Rosati, Jerel. "The Impact of Beliefs on Behavior: The Foreign Policy of the Carter Administration." In Donald Sylvan and Steve Chan, eds., *Foreign Policy Decision Making: Cognition and Artificial Intelligence.* New York: Praeger, 1984.

Rosch, Eleanor, and Barbara Lloyd, eds. *Cognition and Categorization.* Hillsdale, N.J.: Erlbaum, 1978.

Rothenberg, Morris. "The Soviets and Central America." In Robert Leiken, ed., *Central America: Anatomy of Conflict.* New York: Pergamon, 1984.

Rubin, Barry, *Secrets of State.* Oxford: Oxford University Press, 1987.

Rubin, Jeffrey and Bert Brown. *The Social Psychology of Bargaining and Negotiation.* New York: Academic, 1975.

Rush, M. C., and J. E. A. Russell. "Leader Prototypes and Prototype-Consistent Consensus in Leader Behavior Descriptions." *Journal of Experimental Social Psychology* 24 (1988): 88–104.

Sanjuan, Pedro. "Why We Don't Have a Latin American Policy." *Washington Quarterly* 32 (Autumn 1980): 28–39.

Scherer, Klaus. "Criteria for Emotion-Antecedent Appraisal: A Review." In Vernon Hamilton, Gordon Bower, and Nico Frijda, eds., *Cognitive Perspectives on Emotion and Motivation.* Boston: Kluwer, 1988.

Schlesinger, Stephen, and Stephen Kinzer. *Bitter Fruit.* Garden City, N.Y.: Anchor, 1982.

Schoultz, Lars. *Human Rights and United States Policy Toward Latin America,* Princeton: Princeton University Press, 1981.

———. *National Security and United States Policy Toward Latin America.* Princeton: Princeton University Press, 1987.

Sciolino, Elaine. "As the Election Nears, Talk About Noriega Fades." *New York Times,* October 28, 1988.

Scranton, Margaret. *The Noriega Years: U.S.-Panamanian Relations, 1981–1990.* Boulder, Colo.: Lynne Reinner, 1991.

Shenon, Philip. "Peru Drug Fund Used in War, Aide Says." *New York Times,* June 21, 1990.

Shimko, Keith. *Images and Arms Control: Perceptions of the Soviet Union in the Reagan Administration.* Ann Arbor: University of Michigan Press, 1991.

Shiras, Peter. "The False Promise—and Real Violence—of Land Reform in El Salvador." In Marvin Gettleman, Patrick Lacefield, Louis Menashe, David Mermelstein, and Ronald Radosh, eds., *El Salvador: Central America in the New Cold War.* New York: Grove, 1981.

Smith, Eliot R. "Inferences About Self and Others." *Journal of Experimental Social Psychology* 20 (1984): 97–115.

Smith, James. "Drug Campaign Put on Back Burner as Peru Battles Rebels." *Los Angeles Times*, January 6, 1990.

———. "Economic Aid Key to Drug War Victory, Candidate Says." *Los Angeles Times*, May 11, 1990

———. "Peruvians Unhappy with Focus of Drug Plan." *Los Angeles Times*, September 7, 1988.

Smith, Wayne. *The Closest of Enemies*. New York: Norton, 1987.

Snyder, Glenn, and Paul Diesing. *Conflict Among Nations*. Princeton: Princeton University Press, 1977.

Stanford University Action Network, *Revolution in Central America*. Boulder, Colo.: Westview, 1983.

Stein, Jeff. "The Day of Reckoning Is Coming: An Interview with Robert E. White." In Marvin Gettleman, Patrick Lacefield, Louis Menashe, David Mermelstein, and Ronald Radosh, eds., *El Salvador: Central America in the New Cold War*. New York: Grove, 1981.

Strong, Simon. "Where the Shining Path Leads." *New York Times Magazine*, May 24, 1992.

Sunkel, Osvaldo. "Big Business and 'Dependencia.'" *Foreign Affairs* 50 (April 1972): 517–31.

Taubman, Philip. "Latin Policy: U.S. Miscues." *New York Times*, March 17, 1982.

Taylor, Shelley. *Positive Illusions: Creative Deceptions and the Healthy Mind*. New York: Basic, 1989.

Tjosvold, Dean. "Unequal Power Relationships Within a Cooperative or Competitive Context." *Journal of Applied Social Psychology* 11 (1981): 137–50.

Vanderlaan, Mary. *Revolution and Foreign Policy in Nicaragua*. Boulder, Colo.: Westview, 1986.

Vertzberger, Yaacov V. I. *The World in Their Minds: Information Processing, Cognition, and Perception in Foreign Policy Decisionmaking*. Stanford: Stanford University Press, 1990.

Voss, James, Richard Herrmann, Tonya Engstler-Schooler, and Karen VanderPloeg. "On the Existence and Use of Stereotypical Images of Foreign Countries." Paper prepared for the 1991 International Studies Association Meeting, Vancouver, British Columbia, March 19–22.

Walker, Douglas. "Risky Business." *Newsweek*, July 16, 1990.

Walker, Stephen. "The Impact of Personality Structure and Cognitive Processes Upon American Foreign Policy Decisions." Paper prepared for the 1988 American Political Science Association Meeting, Washington, D.C.

Walker, Stephen, and Timothy Murphy. "The Utility of the Operational Code in Political Forecasting." *Political Psychology* 3 (1981–1982): 24–60.

Washington Office on Latin America, *Clear and Present Dangers: The U.S. Military and the War on Drugs in the Andes*. Washington, D.C.: Washington Office on Latin America, 1991.

Wiarda, Howard. *Finding Our Way? Toward Maturity in U.S.–Latin American Relations*. Washington, D.C.: American Enterprise Institute, 1987.

GOVERNMENT SOURCES

National Bipartisan Commission on Central America. *Report to the President, January 1, 1984*. Washington, D.C.: U.S. Government Printing Office, 1984.

Public Papers of the President, April 18, 1961 (John Fitzgerald Kennedy). Washington, D.C.: U.S. Government Printing Office, 1961.

U.S. Central Intelligence Agency. "National Intelligence Estimate, 1952." In *Foreign Relations of the United States, 1952–1954*. Vol. 4. Washington, D.C.: U.S. Government Printing Office, 1983.

U.S. Congress. *Congressional Record*. Washington, D.C.: U.S. Government Printing Office, 1977, 1978, 1979.

———. House Committee on Foreign Affairs. Subcommittee on Human Rights and International Organizations and on Western Hemisphere Affairs. Hearings. *The Situation in El Salvador*. 98th Congress, 2d sess. Washington, D.C.: U.S. Government Printing Office, 1984.

———. House Committee on Foreign Affairs. Subcommittee on Inter-American Affairs. Hearings. *United States Policy Towards Nicaragua*. 96th Congress, 1st sess. Washington, D.C.: U.S. Government Printing Office, 1979.

———. House Committee of Foreign Affairs. Subcommittee on Inter-American Affairs. Hearings. *U.S. Policy Toward El Salvador*. 97th Congress, 1st sess. Washington, D.C.: U.S. Government Printing Office, 1981.

———. House Committee on International Relations. Subcommittee on International Organizations and Inter-American Affairs. *The Recent Elections in El Salvador: Implications for U.S. Foreign Policy*. Hearings. 95th Congress, 1st sess. Washington, D.C.: U.S. Government Printing Office, 1977.

———. Senate Committee on Foreign Relations. Hearings. *The Situation in El Salvador*. 97th Congress, 1st sess. Wahsington, D.C.: U.S. Government Printing Office, 1981.

———. Senate Committee on Foreign Relations. Subcommittee on Multinational Corporations. Hearings. *Multinational Corporations and United States Foreign Policy*. 93d Congress, 1st sess. Washington, D.C.: U.S. Government Printing Office, 1973.

———. Senate Committee on Foreign Realtions. Subcommittee on Western Hemisphere Affairs. Hearings. *The Prospects for Democracy in Central America and the Caribbean*. 97th Congress, 1st sess. Washington, D.C.: U.S. Government Printing Office, 1982.

———. Senate Select Committee to Study Government Operations with Respect to Intelligence Activities of the United States. Hearings. *Intelligence Activities*. 94th Congress, 1st sess. Washington, D.C.: U.S. Government Printing Office, 1975.

———. *Drugs, Law Enforcement, and Foreign Policy*. Senate Report 100-165 Washington, D.C.: U.S. Government Printing Office, 1989.

———. *United States Anti-Narcotics Activites in the Andean Region*. House Report 101-991. Washington, D.C.: U.S. Government Printing Office, 1991.

U.S. Department of State. *American Foreign Policy, Basic Documents, 1977–1980*. Washington, D.C.: U.S. Government Printing Office, 1980.

————. *American Foreign Policy, Current Documents, 1958*. Washington, D.C.: U.S. Government Printing Office, 1958.

————. *A Case History of Communist Penetration*. Washington, D.C.: U.S. Government Printing Office, 1957.

————. *State Department Bulletin*. Vol. 80. *Special Supplement M*. Washington, D.C.: U.S. Government Printing Office, 1957.

U.S. Executive Office of the President. Office of National Drug Control Policy. *National Drug Control Strategy, September 1989*. Washington, D.C.: U.S. Government Printing Office, 1989.

U.S. General Accounting Office. *The Drug War: U.S. Programs in Peru Face Serious Obstacles*. Washington, D.C.: U.S. Government Printing Office, 1991.

U.S. Information Agency. FBIS (*Foreign Broadcast Information Service*): *Latin America*. February 4, 1991.

Index

PITT LATIN AMERICAN SERIES
James M. Malloy, Editor

ARGENTINA

Argentina Between the Great Powers, 1936–1946
Guido di Tella and D. Cameron Watt, Editors

Argentina in the Twentieth Century
David Rock, Editor

Argentina: Political Culture and Instability
Susan Calvert and Peter Calvert

Argentine Workers: Peronism and Contemporary Class Consciousness
Peter Ranis

Discreet Partners: Argentina and the USSR Since 1917
Aldo César Vacs

The Franco-Perón Alliance: Relations Between Spain and Argentina, 1946–1955
Raanan Rein, translated by Martha Grenzeback

The Life, Music, and Times of Carlos Gardel
Simon Collier

Institutions, Parties, and Coalitions in Argentine Politics
Luigi Manzetti

The Political Economy of Argentina, 1946–1983
Guido di Tella and Rudiger Dornbusch, Editors

BOLIVIA

Unsettling Statecraft: Democracy and Neoliberalism in the Central Andes
Catherine M. Conaghan and James M. Malloy

The State and Capital Accumulation in Latin America. Vol. 1: Brazil, Chile, Mexico. Vol. 2: Argentina, Bolivia, Colombia, Ecuador, Peru, Uruguay, Venezuela
Christian Anglade and Carlos Fortin, Editors

BRAZIL

Capital Markets in the Development Process: The Case of Brazil
John E. Welch

External Constraints on Economic Policy in Brazil, 1899–1930
Winston Fritsch

The Film Industry in Brazil: Culture and the State
Randal Johnson

Kingdoms Come: Religion and Politics in Brazil
Rowan Ireland

The Manipulation of Consent: The State and Working-Class Consciousness in Brazil
Youssef Cohen

The State and Capital Accumulation in Latin America. Vol. 1: Brazil, Chile, Mexico. Vol. 2: Argentina, Bolivia, Colombia, Ecuador, Peru, Uruguay, Venezuela
Christian Anglade and Carlos Fortin, Editors

MEXICO

The Dynamics of Domination: State, Class, and Social Reform in Mexico, 1910–1990
Viviane Brachet-Márquez

The Expulsion of Mexico's Spaniards, 1821–1836
Harold Dana Sims

The Mexican Republic: The First Decade, 1823–1832
Stanley C. Green

Mexico Through Russian Eyes, 1806–1940
William Harrison Richardson

Oil and Mexican Foreign Policy
George W. Grayson

The Politics of Mexican Oil
George W. Grayson

Voices, Visions, and a New Reality: Mexican Fiction Since 1970
J. Ann Duncan

PERU

Domestic and Foreign Finance in Modern Peru, 1850–1950: Financing Visions of Development
Alfonso W. Quiroz

Economic Management and Economic Development in Peru and Colombia
Rosemary Thorp

The Origins of the Peruvian Labor Movement, 1883–1919
Peter Blanchard

Peru and the International Monetary Fund
Thomas Scheetz

Peru Under García: An Opportunity Lost
John Crabtree

Poverty and Peasantry in Peru's Southern Andes
R. F. Watters

Unsettling Statecraft: Democracy and Neoliberalism in the Central Andes
Catherine M. Conaghan and James M. Malloy

CARIBBEAN

The Last Cacique: Leadership and Politics in a Puerto Rican City
Jorge Heine

A Revolution Aborted: The Lessons of Grenada
Jorge Heine, Editor

To Hell with Paradise: A History of the Jamaican Tourist Industry
Frank Fonda Taylor

The Meaning of Freedom: Economics, Politics and Culture After Slavery
Frank McGlynn and Seymour Drescher, Editors

CENTRAL AMERICA

At the Fall of Somoza
Lawrence Pezzullo and Ralph Pezzullo

Black Labor on a White Canal: Panama, 1904–1981
Michael L. Conniff

The Catholic Church and Politics in Nicaragua and Costa Rica
Philip J. Williams

Perspectives on the Agro-Export Economy in Central America
Wim Pelupessy, Editor

OTHER NATIONAL STUDIES

The Overthrow of Allende and the Politics of Chile, 1964–1976
Paul E. Sigmund

Military Rule and Transition in Ecuador: Dancing with the People
Anita Isaacs

Primary Medical Care in Chile: Accessibility Under Military Rule
Joseph L. Scarpaci

Rebirth of the Paraguayan Republic: The First Colorado Era, 1878–1904
Harris G. Warren

Restructuring Domination: Industrialists and the State in Ecuador
Catherine M. Conaghan

U.S. POLICIES

The Hovering Giant: U.S. Responses to Revolutionary Change in Latin America
Cole Blasier

Illusions of Conflict: Anglo-American Diplomacy Toward Latin America
Joseph Smith

Images and Intervention: U.S. Policies in Latin America
Martha L. Cottam

Unequal Giants: Diplomatic Relations Between the United States and Brazil, 1889–1930
Joseph Smith

The United States and Latin America in the 1980s: Contending Perspectives on a Decade of Crisis
Kevin J. Middlebrook and Carlos Rico, Editors

USSR POLICIES

Cuba After the Cold War
Carmelo Mesa-Lago, Editor

Discreet Partners: Argentina and the USSR Since 1917
Aldo César Vacs

The Giant's Rival: The USSR and Latin America
Cole Blasier

Mexico Through Russian Eyes, 1806–1940
William Harrison Richardson

SOCIAL SECURITY

Ascent to Bankruptcy: Financing Social Security in Latin America
Carmelo Mesa-Lago

The Politics of Social Security in Brazil
James M. Malloy

OTHER STUDIES

Adventurers and Proletarians: The Story of Migrants in Latin America
Magnus Mörner, with the collaboration of Harold Sims

Authoritarianism and Corporatism in Latin America
James M. Malloy, Editor